HAMLET

The RSC Shakespeare

Edited by Jonathan Bate and Eric Rasmussen

Chief Associate Editor: Héloïse Sénéchal

Associate Editors: Trey Jansen, Eleanor Lowe, Lucy Munro, Dee Anna Phares, Jan Sewell

Hamlet

Textual editing: Eric Rasmussen

Introduction and "Shakespeare's Career in the Theater": Jonathan Bate

Commentary: Héloïse Sénéchal

Scene-by-Scene Analysis: Esme Miskimmin

In Performance: Karin Brown (RSC stagings), Jan Sewell (overview), Jonathan Bate (captions)

The Director's Cut (interviews by Jonathan Bate and Kevin Wright): Michael Boyd, John Caird, Ron Daniels

The RSC Shakespeare

William Shakespeare

HAMLET

Edited by Jonathan Bate and Eric Rasmussen

Introduction by Jonathan Bate

The Modern Library
New York

2008 Modern Library Paperback Edition

Published in the United States by Modern Library, an imprint of
The Random House Publishing Group, a division of Random House, Inc.,
New York.

MODERN LIBRARY and the TORCHBEARER Design are registered trademarks
of Random House, Inc.

ISBN 978-0-8129-6909-2

Printed in the United States of America

www.modernlibrary.com

2 4 6 8 9 7 5 3 1

CONTENTS

INTRODUCTION

HAMLET'S QUESTIONS

The mood of *Hamlet* is set by its opening exchange: "Who's there?" "Nay, answer me. . . ." The play creates the illusion of asking as many questions of its audience and interpreters as we may ask of it. Shakespeare won't tell us who he is or where he stands. Instead, he makes us—and our culture—reveal ourselves. That is the source of his endurance and one of the reasons why *Hamlet* has long been regarded as his greatest, or at least his most characteristic, play.

The Prince of Denmark himself is the most famously interrogative of all dramatic characters. He is Shakespeare's ultimate man of words. The actor who plays him has to learn over 340 speeches; the role has a higher proportion of its play's words (nearly 40 percent) than any other in Shakespeare. Hamlet's favorite intellectual move is to make an action that he witnesses—a player weeping, a skull tossed from an old grave—into the occasion for speculation: "What's Hecuba to him, or he to Hecuba, / That he should weep for her?," "Where be your gibes now, your gambols, your songs, your flashes of merriment that were wont to set the table on a roar?" In watching or reading the play, we are moved, like Hamlet, to ask the big questions: What should we believe? How should we act? What happens after death? In whose version of the truth should we have faith?

Horatio, the commentator who comes closest to being the voice of the audience, says that he "in part" believes stories about ghosts and portents. His qualifier is a watchword for the whole play. Humankind is *in part* a godlike creature, full of mental and verbal powers, "The beauty of the world, the paragon of animals." But, to take the other part, we are also "quintessence of dust"—the politician, the lawyer, the heroic man of action (Alexander the Great), and the humble clown (Yorick) all end up in the same place.

Like the wood in *A Midsummer Night's Dream*, but with tragic as opposed to comic consequences, Elsinore is a place where "everything seems double." Rosencrantz and Guildenstern are a double act engaged to spy on Hamlet, with the result that he has "at each ear a hearer." Hardly anyone in the play seems able to speak without producing a double epithet: "the sensible and true avouch / Of mine own eyes," "the gross and scope of my opinion," "post-haste and rummage in the land," "the grace and blush of modesty," and so on. Stage props also come in pairs: two contrasting portraits of two brothers, a pair of rapiers (one of which is sharpened and anointed for the kill), two skulls. Entrances seem to repeat themselves: the appearances of the Ghost; Hamlet overheard in meditation, first with a book, later with his reflections on being and not being; the king and Gertrude in their respective private rooms after the trauma of the *Mousetrap* play; Ophelia's two mad scenes.

The story of a son seeking vengeance for his father's death is doubled after Hamlet kills Polonius: "by the image of my cause I see / The portraiture of his," remarks Hamlet of Laertes. The motif is redoubled in the figure of Young Fortinbras out to avenge the defeat of Old Fortinbras. A further commentary is provided by the Player's speech about Pyrrhus, son of Achilles, furiously seeking atonement for his father's loss by slaughtering old King Priam. But this might be construed as a negative example: Priam himself is an "unnervèd father" and his slaughter moves a wife and mother, Hecuba, to distraction. If Hamlet were to become a killing machine like Pyrrhus, he would be diminishing himself to the inhumanity of his adversary, besides emotionally destroying his mother: that is his dilemma "bounded in a nutshell."

Hamlet is a student, a model for the perpetual students and idealists who populate later literature, especially in Germany and Russia. Like Shakespeare's other highly intellectual drama, *Troilus and Cressida*, this is a play that debates the great questions of epistemology, ethics, and metaphysics. "Humanism," the dominant educational theory of the sixteenth century, proposed that wisdom was to be derived from book learning. The student developed the arts of language through his rhetorical training, while collecting the wisdom of the ancients in the form of citations and *sententiae* copied into a commonplace book. Polonius' maxims on how Laertes should behave when away from home, climaxing in the cliché "to thine own self be true," are classic examples. The art of "reason" was refined through the study of "common themes," one of which was "death of fathers." Reason and judgment were supposed to prevail over will and passion. The Stoicism of Seneca provided a model for the use of "philosophy" as protection against the fickleness of fortune and the vicissitudes of court politics.

Hamlet's uncle must once have been a good student. He is a master of balanced rhetoric, the measure and decorum of his verse belying his crime against the order of nature and state:

> . . . as 'twere with a defeated joy,
> With one auspicious and one dropping eye,
> With mirth in funeral and with dirge in marriage,
> In equal scale weighing delight and dole.

He thinks he knows, and that everyone in the court will accept, what is the appropriate length of time to mourn the death of a brother, husband, father.

Hamlet despises such propriety. He is not interested in the "common" way of behaving. He speaks for the "particular," the individual. "Mourning duties," maintained for a set period, are to him mere outward show, the signs of a "seeming" with which he refuses to play along. He has "that within which passeth show": the solitary self is set against social custom. He has returned from university determined to "wipe away" all the customary wisdom of Stoic decorum, all that "discourse of reason" which humanist theorists regarded as the gift that set men above the beasts. He will have nothing to do with "saws of books" or the codes of behavior that "youth and observation" are supposed to copy from their humanist texts. After encountering the ghost, he vows to fill his commonplace book ("my tables") from experience instead of books.

This new way of seeing is initially regarded by his fellow students Horatio and Marcellus as no more than "wild and whirling words," madness brought on by an encounter with an evil spirit. But Hamlet knows what he is doing. He tries on his "antic disposition" as a way of testing the limits of the rational "philosophy" embodied by Horatio. Ophelia tells of how she witnessed Hamlet utter a sigh that seemed to "end his being." That end is also a beginning: the birth of a new man dedicated to the proposition that the opposite of reason is not madness, but true feeling. Later, when Ophelia is mad, she is described as "Divided from herself and her fair judgement, / Without the which we are pictures or mere beasts." When Hamlet feigns madness, by contrast, he speaks with true judgment, as even Polonius half recognizes: "A happiness that often madness hits on, which reason and sanity could not so prosperously be delivered of."

REVENGE

Hamlet is a political drama as well as a play about the journey of an individual self. It begins with portents betokening "some strange eruption to our state." It holds up a mirror to a world of royalty, courtiers, politicians, and ambassadors, but also ordinary people: students, actors, gravediggers, even (on the margins) an underclass of "lawless resolutes" following Fortinbras and a "rabble" who want Laertes to be king.

"Denmark's a prison": Hamlet is cabined, cribbed and confined by his princely birth, by the machinations of statecraft, and by the limitations of the material world. In his melancholy, when he complains that he has lost interest in all gentlemanly pursuits ("custom of exercise"), he points to the "canopy" over the stage. The self-conscious allusion to the architecture of the Globe Theatre hints at how he finds his freedom: in play, first by pretending to be mad, then through theater. It is the arrival of the actors that reinvigorates him. Hamlet loves plays and the players because he recognizes the power of acting to expose the feigning of public life, the fact that courtiership and rhetorical decorum are themselves but performances. He comes to the truth through "a fiction" and "a dream of passion." In this he can only be regarded as an apologist for the art of his creator.

The play was registered in 1602 "as it was lately acted by the Lord Chamberlain his servants" (Shakespeare's theater company), but a book published in 1596 refers to a ghost in a play crying "Hamlet, revenge!," and as early as 1589 Thomas Nashe mentioned "whole *Hamlets*—I should say handfuls—of tragical speeches." Scholars therefore suppose that Shakespeare's play was written in about 1600, but that it was a reworking of an older, now lost play, just as *King Lear* was a reworking of the anonymous *History of King Leir*, which does survive. The old *Hamlet* is sometimes speculatively attributed to Thomas Kyd, whose *Spanish Tragedy* established the late-Elizabethan vogue for blood-and-guts revenge drama. A few scholars suppose that Shakespeare himself wrote the early version and a tiny minority that the poorly printed First Quarto text of 1603 may in some way derive from it. Though there is no firm evidence as to authorship or content, we may safely assume that the old Hamlet play (sometimes known as the *Ur-Hamlet*) was broadly similar to *The Spanish Tragedy* and Shakespeare's early assay in this genre, *Titus Andronicus*, both of which achieved immense popularity with their plotting of revenge by means of feigned madness, their spectacular multiple murders, and the revenger's elaborately rhetorical outbursts of tragic passion. Hamlet's shortest soliloquy, after he has been fired up by the play-within-the-play, is very much in this style: "Now could I drink hot blood / And do such bitter business as the day / Would quake to look on."

Hamlet is as capable of violent action as any other revenger—witness his cruel rejection of Ophelia and his casual lugging of Polonius' guts into the neighboring room. Nor does he delay nearly so much as he tells us he is delaying: he has to establish the authenticity of the Ghost, to ensure that it is not a devil sent to tempt him into evil action, and as soon as he has done this by watching Claudius' reaction to the play he goes off to kill him. He doesn't kill him at prayer because that would be "hire and salary, not revenge," would send him to heaven not to hell. He then thinks that he has killed him in Gertrude's closet, though it turns out that he has killed Polonius instead and as a result he is packed off to England. As soon as he has tricked and dispatched Rosencrantz and Guildenstern, effected his daring escape via the pirate ship and returned to Denmark, he is in a state of "readiness" and the revenge then takes place during the duel. Looked at this way, where is the delay?

But the style of the "hot blood" soliloquy is completely unlike that of the other solo speeches, which are all much longer and more introspective. It is from them that we derive our image of the character of Hamlet. In the first act, he is so disgusted by his mother's hasty remarriage that he wishes he were dead. In the second, he is moved to self-disgust by the way in which the player can work himself into a frenzy for the fictional sorrows of Hecuba, while he himself has not yet done anything about his father's murder. In the third, he meditates on the pros and cons of suicide and in the Quarto text of the fourth, he is still chiding himself when he compares his own inaction with the military activity of Fortinbras and his army ("How all occasions do inform against me / And spur my dull revenge!"). Hamlet's self-analysis has led some commentators to wonder whether his failure to kill the praying usurper might be the result of procrastination, not calculation about whether he would be sending him to heaven or hell. The soliloquies present such a convincing picture of irresolution and inaction that even when it comes to the final scene it may occur to us that the killing of the king seems to be not so much the climax of Hamlet's plans as an incidental consequence of Laertes' quest for revenge for the deaths of his father and sister.

For the Romantics such as Goethe and Coleridge, Hamlet was the archetype of the sensitive man paralyzed into inaction by his sheer capacity for thought—which is to say an image of themselves as poets uneasily inhabiting the public sphere. Debatable as this reading is, there can be little doubt that Shakespeare's innovation in *Hamlet* was to take the figure of the revenger from the old play and turn him into an intellectual, so making revenge into a moral dilemma as opposed to a practical task to be carried out through effective plotting. Hamlet's problem is that his intelligence makes him see both sides of every question, whereas in the drama of revenge there is no place for debate and half measure. The lesson from both the Old Testament and Greek tragedy, which was mediated to Shakespeare via Seneca's Latin plays, was that action requires reactions: a crime in one generation demands the meting out of punishment in the next, an eye for an eye. Requital must be exact and complete. The code of revenge requires Hamlet not to kill the king while he is praying because that would send him straight to heaven, which does not correspond to the fate of Old Hamlet, who was murdered "grossly, full of bread, / With all his crimes broad blown." It is one of the play's many ironies that, immediately on Hamlet's departure, the king acknowledges that his prayer for forgiveness is not working—if Hamlet had struck, he would have damned his enemy.

CONSCIENCE AND RESOLUTION

One of the paradoxes of the play is that the Ghost of Old Hamlet comes from Purgatory, where he is confined in fire "Till the foul crimes done in [his] days of nature / Are burnt and purged away," while Hamlet's speech giving his reasons for not plunging his sword into his praying uncle implies that the act of penitence can instantly purge sin away and allow even a man who has committed the most terrible crime immediate access to heaven on his death. Purgatory is a Roman Catholic doctrine, the leap to grace supposed by Hamlet a Protestant one. At several points, the play engages with the great doctrinal disputes of the Reformation and counter-Reformation. There appear, for instance, to be passing allusions to the nature of the sacrament of Holy Communion, the question of whether the bread and wine at the altar is literally or only symbolically transubstantiated into the body and blood of Christ.

Hamlet longs to be back at Wittenberg, the university of Martin Luther, architect of the Reformation. Wittenberg was the intellectual home of the Protestant revolution, in which the individual's relationship with God matters more than the intercession of priests, saints, and the Church. In Protestantism, authenticity of feeling is paramount and a key term is "conscience." As Hamlet says at the end of "To be, or not to be":

Thus conscience does make cowards of us all:
And thus the native hue of resolution
Is sicklied o'er with the pale cast of thought,
And enterprises of great pith and moment
With this regard their currents turn away,
And lose the name of action. . . .

In Elizabethan English "conscience" meant not only moral scruple but also "consciousness." A polyglot dictionary of the period glossed the word as "witness of one's own mind, knowledge, remorse." It is Hamlet's extreme self-consciousness that sets him apart from the traditional revenger. When alone on stage, reflecting on his own situation, he seems to embody the very nature of human *being*. It is

1. "Rapier and dagger": on-guard position, as illustrated in Vincentio Saviolo's English fencing treatise of 1595. There were strong links between the actors and Saviolo's fencing school in Ludgate.

"conscience" in its multiple senses that forms his self-image, his "character," and in so doing makes it agonizingly difficult for him to perform the action that is demanded of him. Yet when he does come to act, he is decisive and ruthless. He reaches the point of "readiness" when he accepts—never easy for an intellectual—that what will be will be. Thereafter, he considers it "perfect conscience" to kill the king and has no compunction about his treatment of the former schoolfellows who have betrayed not only him but the precious virtue of friendship: Rosencrantz and Guildenstern, he says, "are not near my conscience."

It is sometimes said that chance, not Hamlet, brings the plot to a resolution. Hamlet certainly believes that Providence is operating on his behalf, as witnessed by the good fortune of his having the means to seal Rosencrantz and Guildenstern's fate. But the exchange of rapiers during the fencing match with Laertes is not a matter of chance, as is sometimes suggested. Many modern productions use

2. *They change rapiers:* disarm and exchange by left-hand seizure, as illustrated in Henri de Saint-Didier's French fencing treatise of 1573.

the épée that had not been invented in Shakespeare's time—a flexible foil that may be knocked from the hand, leading to the possibility of an accidental exchange of weapons. But Hamlet and Laertes would originally have dueled with "rapier and dagger," the commonest weapons for such an encounter, as illustrated in Vincentio Saviolo's treatise on fencing skills, *The Art of Practice* (1595).

The grip used for the rapier meant that it was very hard to remove it from the opponent's hand save by an advanced maneuver known as the "left-hand seizure." Hamlet would have dropped his dagger to the ground and grabbed the hilt of Laertes' rapier with his left hand, twisting it out of his grip. Laertes would have responded with the same action, resulting in the switch of weapons.

The move, which is illustrated in continental fencing handbooks of the period, is so skillful that Hamlet's action must have been purposeful. He would not initially have seen that Laertes' rapier was "unbated" (not blunted in the way that was customary to prevent the injury of gentlemen participating in sporting fights), but on receiving a "hit" his skin would have been pierced by the point. Realizing that Laertes is in earnest, not play, he instantly responds with the maneuver that makes the switch. Now he is in deadly earnest himself. Deeds take over from words, revenge is performed without further compunctious visitings of nature, and "the rest is silence."

HOW MANY *HAMLET*S?

Shakespeare couldn't decide what to do with his most famous speech. The earliest surviving text of *Hamlet** is highly inaccurate in many of its particulars, but there is little doubt that its shape reflects that of the play as performed early in its stage history. In that text (known as the "First Quarto"), Hamlet enters "reading on a book" and launches into his soliloquy "To be or not to be there, ay, there's the point." His famous question is asked as if in response to something in the book he is reading. The soliloquy is followed by the "get thee to a nunnery" dialogue with Ophelia and then the "Fishmonger" sequence with her father.

But in the Second Quarto and First Folio texts—published later, but considerably longer and more accurately printed than the First Quarto—Hamlet's entrance with the book leads straight to the "Fishmonger" dialogue (2.2.177–226 in our text). "To be or not to be, that is the question" and the "nunnery" scene are held back until after the arrival of the players (3.1.62–154 in our text). This is only the most striking of the many textual variants between the early versions of *Hamlet*. Is the flesh that Hamlet wishes would melt too "sullied" or too "solid"? Did Old Hamlet smite a leaded or a steeled poleaxe on the ice or did he smite the Polack from a sledge on the ice? So much depends on whether you favor Quarto or Folio.

Scholars traditionally prefer the Second Quarto because it is the fullest text and apparently the one closest to Shakespeare's original manuscript. But it may represent a "reading text" as opposed to a "performance" one. Coming in at around four thousand lines, Second Quarto *Hamlet* could never have been played in full within the

---

*For further discussion of the play's complicated textual history, see "Text," pp. xxxi–xxxii.

160 or so minutes that was the legal maximum for an Elizabethan play (shows began at 2 p.m., there was always a closing comedy and dance routine known as a jig, and then the theater had to be cleared by 5 p.m.). The full flow of Shakespeare's tragic vein must be reined in and cut for performance, and with a play as long as *Hamlet* he must have known that this would be the case.

Every modern production makes its own choice of cuts, of textual variants, and of innovative business. In working on his text for the Royal Shakespeare Company production of 2004, director Michael Boyd* considered not only the three versions that emerged from Shakespeare's own acting company but also the so-called Players' Quarto that was handed down—with cuts marked up—to their Restoration successors, the acting company of Shakespeare's god-son William Davenant. Both the First Quarto and the Players' Quarto offer striking suggestions as to how the play may have been cut in Shakespeare's own time. The cuts are not always the most obvious ones: Reynaldo, whom Polonius commissions to spy on Laertes in Paris, might seem an obvious candidate for the ax, but in the Players' Quarto he remains, probably in order to highlight the way in which the world of Elsinore—like that of Elizabethan England—was one of pervasive spying.

Like most modern directors, Boyd was eclectic in his choices, weighing each textual variant according to its merits, moving freely between the early texts and opting for rigorous pruning rather than reckless lopping. So, for instance, the First Folio cuts the whole of Hamlet's last soliloquy, "How all occasions do inform against me," delivered after witnessing the army of Fortinbras on the march, whereas Boyd retained an abbreviated version of it that makes the key distinction between acting upon "great argument" and finding "quarrel in a straw."

The Reynaldo role was also retained, but the character was merged with Osric. Since one of them only appears near the beginning of the play and the other only near the end, the roles may well have been doubled in the original production. To make them into the

*See further the interview with Michael Boyd about his production in "The Director's Cut."

same character is both an elegant economy and a device to highlight the role of Polonius as spymaster-general. Most boldly, the nunnery scene was placed early, as in the First Quarto, while—as Boyd explains in his interview about the production—a radical new position for "To be or not to be" was seriously considered, but ultimately rejected. The process of thinking through production choices of this sort is what enables directors and actors to defamiliarize and remint the language and action of the best-known play in the history of world drama, and so to keep it alive. The progressive alterations through the early texts are of a piece with the process of remaking in the play's subsequent theatrical life.

TALKING ABOUT HAMLET

Hamlet is not only the pre-eminent talker in Shakespeare. He is also the most talked-about character in western literature. Because he is both poet and philosopher himself, poets and philosophers have been particularly enamored of him. Hamlet-mania reached its zenith with the self-consciously troubled musings on art and life of the nineteenth-century Romantics. One of their favored literary devices was the "imaginary conversation," in which their cultural heroes gathered round a table and talked about a topic of absorbing interest. It was in Samuel Taylor Coleridge's *Table Talk* that he said "I have a smack of Hamlet myself, if I may say so." *Hamlet* is a play that provokes so many opinions, animates so many energetic voices, that the best way to conclude an introduction to it is simply to bring together some of the play's most impassioned readers in an "imaginary conversation."

Let them begin from that key moment when Hamlet decides not to kill King Claudius while he is praying, since that would be to send him to heaven, not hell:

Up, sword, and know thou a more horrid hent:
When he is drunk asleep, or in his rage,
Or in th'incestuous pleasure of his bed,
At gaming, swearing, or about some act
That has no relish of salvation in't,

Then trip him, that his heels may kick at heaven.
And that his soul may be as damned and black
As hell, whereto it goes. . . .

Dr. Samuel Johnson, eighteenth-century Christian of high moral sensitivity: "This speech, in which Hamlet, represented as a virtuous character, is not content with taking blood for blood, but contrives damnation for the man that he would punish, is too horrible to be read or to be uttered."

Samuel Taylor Coleridge, Romantic poet with a smack of Hamlet himself, if he may say so: "Dr. Johnson's mistaking of the marks of reluctance and procrastination for impetuous, horror-striking fiendishness!—Of such importance is it to understand the *germ* of a character."

Johann Wolfgang von Goethe, in the voice of Wilhelm Meister, hero of the archetypal Romantic *Bildungsroman*, the novel in which a young man or woman grows to emotional maturity (a genre for which *Hamlet* itself was a key model): " 'The time is out of joint: O, cursèd spite / That ever I was born to set it right!' In these words, I imagine, will be found the key to Hamlet's whole procedure. To me it is clear that Shakespeare meant, in the present case, to represent the effects of a great action laid upon a soul unfit for the performance of it. In this view the whole piece seems to me to be composed."

August Wilhelm von Schlegel, Romantic critic: "*Hamlet* is singular in its kind: a tragedy of thought inspired by continual and never-satisfied meditation on human destiny and the dark perplexity of the events of this world, and calculated to call forth the very same meditation in the minds of the spectators."

Lord Byron, always glad to play the devil's advocate:

Who can read this wonderful play without the profoundest emotion? And yet what is it but a colossal enigma? We love Hamlet even as we love ourselves. Yet consider his character, and where is either goodness or greatness? He betrays Ophelia's gentlest love; he repulses her in a cruel manner; and when in the most touching way, she speaks to him, and returns his presents, he laughs her off like a man of the town. At her grave, at the new-made grave of Ophelia his first love, whom his unkindness had blasted in the very bud of her beauty, in the morn and liquid dew of youth, what is the behaviour of Hamlet? A blank—worse than a blank; a few ranting lines, instead of true feeling, that prove him perfectly heartless. Then his behaviour in the grave, and his insult to Laertes, why the gentlest verdict one can give is insanity. But he seems by nature, and in his soberest moods, fiend-like in cruelty. His old companions, Rosencrantz and Guildenstern, he murders without the least compunction; he desires them to be put to sudden death, "not shriving-time allowed" . . . Polonius, father of Ophelia, he does actually kill; and for this does he lament or atone for what he has done, by any regret or remorse? "I'll lug the guts into the neighbor room"—"You nose him as you go up the stairs into the lobby!" But suppose him heartless, though he is for ever lamenting, and complaining, and declaiming about the false-heartedness of every one else; Richard III is heartless—Iago—Edmund. The tragic poet of course deals not in your good-boy characters. But neither is he, as Richard is, a hero, a man of mighty strength of mind. He is, according to his own admission, as "unlike Hercules" as possible. He does not, as a great and energetic mind does, exult under the greatness of a grand object. He is weak, so miserably weak as even to complain of his own weakness.

Elaine Showalter, turn-of-the-millennium feminist, as if responding to Byron's remarks about Ophelia:

When Ophelia is mad, Gertrude says that "Her speech is nothing," mere "unshaped use." Ophelia's speech thus represents the horror of having nothing to say in the public terms defined by the court. Deprived of thought, sexuality, language, Ophelia's story becomes the Story of O—the zero, the empty circle or mystery of feminine difference, the cipher of female sexuality . . . we could provide a manual of female insanity by chronicling the illustrations of Ophelia; this is so because the illustrations of Ophelia have played a major role in the theoretical construction of female insanity.

Søren Kierkegaard, melancholy Danish philosopher, himself a Hamlet wracked by sexual guilt, coming perhaps to the heart of the mystery: "Hamlet is deeply tragic because he *suspects* his mother's guilt."

Sigmund Freud, inaugurating the language of psychoanalytic criticism which Showalter has been employing and Kierkegaard subtly anticipating: "In Sophocles' *Oedipus* the child's wishful fantasy that underlies it is brought out into the open and realized as it would be in a dream. In *Hamlet* it remains repressed; and just as in the case of a neurosis, we only learn of its existence from its inhibiting consequences . . . Hamlet is able to do anything—except take vengeance on the man who did away with his father and took that father's place with his mother, the man who shows him the repressed wishes of his childhood realized."

James Joyce, Shakespeare-soaked Irish novelist, in the voice of Stephen Dedalus in *Ulysses*, weaving a somewhat Freudian reading into a biographical fantasy:

The play begins. A player comes on under the shadow, made up in the cast-off mail of a court buck, a well-set man with a bass voice. It is the ghost, the king, a king and no king, and the player is Shakespeare who has studied Hamlet all the years of his life which were not vanity in order to play the part of the spectre. He speaks the words to Burbage, the young player who stands before him beyond the rack of cerecloth, calling him by a name: "Hamlet, I am thy father's spirit," bidding him list. To a son he speaks, the son of his soul, the prince, young Hamlet and to the son of his body, Hamnet Shakespeare, who has died in Stratford that his namesake may live for ever. Is it possible that that player Shakespeare, a ghost by absence, and in the vesture of buried Denmark, a ghost by death, speaking his own words to his own son's name (had Hamnet Shakespeare lived he would have been prince Hamlet's twin), is it possible, I want to know, or probable that he did not draw or foresee the logical conclusion of those premises: you are the dispossessed son: I am the murdered father: your mother is the guilty queen. Ann Shakespeare, born Hathaway?

T. S. Eliot, poet and stern critic, dissatisfied with the Freudian solution, but agreeing that there is a problem: "Shakespeare's *Hamlet*, so far as it is Shakespeare's, is a play dealing with the effect of a mother's guilt upon her son, and . . . Shakespeare was unable to impose this motive successfully upon the 'intractable' material of the old play. . . . So far from being Shakespeare's masterpiece, the play is most certainly an artistic failure."

Jan Kott, Polish critic, writing under tyranny, swinging away from psychology to politics: his Hamlet is not "the moralist, unable to draw a clear-cut line between good and evil" or "the intellectual, unable to find a sufficient reason for action" or "the philosopher, to whom the world's existence is a matter of doubt," but rather "the youth, deeply involved in politics, rid of illusions, sarcastic, passionate and brutal . . . a born conspirator . . . a young rebel who has about him something of the charm of James Dean."

From Wilhelm Meister to Stephen Dedalus to James Dean and beyond, Hamlet is always our contemporary. To be or not to be Hamlet? That is the question for every young aspiring intellectual or actor. Or indeed actress: of all Shakespeare's major male roles, it is the one that has most often and most effectively been played by women. In Renaissance terms, action was the prerogative of the male and feeling of the female, so perhaps Hamlet's intense gift of feeling, and talking about his feelings, makes him a "feminine" character.

For those who do not get to play the part itself, there is the compensation of imagining themselves in a supporting role. Tom Stoppard's razor-sharp existential tragicomedy *Rosencrantz and Guildenstern Are Dead* (1966) rewrites the drama from the point of view of the two men on the margins who are cogs in the wheel, and in the cult film *Withnail & I* (1986), an old actor (Uncle Monty, played by Richard Griffiths) is broken by the realization that he will never "play the Dane" (he has only managed to secure the tiny part of Marcellus the nightwatchman) and a young unemployed actor (Withnail, played by Richard E. Grant) ends up in London Zoo reciting Hamlet's great prose discourse "I have of late—but wherefore I know not—lost all my mirth" (2.2.296–311) to an enclosure of bedraggled wolves. Hardly the "paragon of animals" and yet, because of Hamlet, still he can dream.*

*Further selections from critical commentaries on the play, with linking narrative, are available on the edition website, www.therscshakespeare.com.

ABOUT THE TEXT

Shakespeare endures through history. He illuminates later times as well as his own. He helps us to understand the human condition. But he cannot do this without a good text of the plays. Without editions there would be no Shakespeare. That is why every twenty years or so throughout the last three centuries there has been a major new edition of his complete works. One aspect of editing is the process of keeping the texts up to date—modernizing the spelling, punctuation, and typography (though not, of course, the actual words), providing explanatory notes in the light of changing educational practices (a generation ago, most of Shakespeare's classical and biblical allusions could be assumed to be generally understood, but now they can't).

But because Shakespeare did not personally oversee the publication of his plays, editors also have to make decisions about the relative authority of the early printed editions. Half of the sum of his plays only appeared posthumously, in the elaborately produced First Folio text of 1623, the original "Complete Works" prepared for the press by Shakespeare's fellow actors, the people who knew the plays better than anyone else. The other half had appeared in print in his lifetime, in the more compact and cheaper form of "Quarto" editions, some of which reproduced good quality texts, others of which were to a greater or lesser degree garbled and error-strewn. In the case of *Hamlet*, there are hundreds of differences between each of the three early editions: two Quartos (one short and frequently corrupt, the other very long and generally well printed) and the Folio. As explained above in the discussion of "How Many *Hamlets*?," some of the differences are far from trivial.

Generations of editors have adopted a "pick and mix" approach, moving between Quarto and Folio readings, making choices on either aesthetic or bibliographic grounds, and creating a composite text that Shakespeare never actually wrote. Not until the 1980s did editors follow the logic of what ought to have been obvious to anyone who works in the theater: that the two Quarto and the Folio texts represent three discrete moments in the life of *Hamlet*, that plays change in the course of rehearsal, production, and revival, and that the major variants between the early printed versions almost certainly reflect this process.

If you look at printers' handbooks from the age of Shakespeare, you quickly discover that one of the first rules was that, whenever possible, compositors were recommended to set their type from existing printed books rather than manuscripts. This was the age before mechanical typesetting, where each individual letter had to be picked out by hand from the compositor's case and placed on a stick (upside down and back to front) before being laid on the press. It was an age of murky rush-light and of manuscripts written in a secretary hand which had dozens of different, hard-to-decipher forms. Printers' lives were a lot easier when they were reprinting existing books rather than struggling with handwritten copy. Easily the quickest way to have created the First Folio would have been simply to reprint those eighteen plays that had already appeared in Quarto and only work from manuscript on the other eighteen.

But that is not what happened. Whenever Quartos were used, playhouse "promptbooks" were also consulted and stage directions copied in from them. And in the case of several major plays where a well-printed Quarto was available, *Hamlet* notable among them, the Folio printers were instructed to work from an alternative, playhouse-derived manuscript. This meant that the whole process of producing the first complete Shakespeare took months, even years, longer than it might have done. But for the men overseeing the project, John Hemings and Henry Condell, friends and fellow actors who had been remembered in Shakespeare's will, the additional labor and cost were worth the effort for the sake of producing an edition that was close to the practice of the theater. They wanted all the plays in print so that people could, as they wrote in their prefatory address to the reader, "read him and again and again," but they also wanted "the great variety of readers" to work from texts that were close to the theater-life for which Shakespeare originally intended them. For this reason, the *RSC Shakespeare*, in both *Complete Works* and individual volumes, uses the Folio as base text wherever possible.

Significant Quarto variants are, however, noted in the Textual Notes and Quarto-only passages are appended after the text of *Hamlet*.

The following notes highlight various aspects of the editorial process and indicate conventions used in the text of this edition:

Lists of Parts are supplied in the First Folio for only six plays, not including *Hamlet*, so the list at the beginning of the play is provided by the editors, arranged by groups of characters. Capitals indicate that part of the name which is used for speech headings in the script (thus "HAMLET, Prince of Denmark").

Locations are provided by the Folio for only two plays. Eighteenth-century editors, working in an age of elaborately realistic stage sets, were the first to provide detailed locations. Given that Shakespeare wrote for a bare stage and often an imprecise sense of place, we have relegated locations to the explanatory notes at the foot of the page, where they are given at the beginning of each scene where the imaginary location is different from the one before. We have emphasized broad geographical settings rather than specifics of the kind that suggest anachronistically realistic staging. We have therefore avoided such niceties as "another room in the palace."

Act and Scene Divisions were provided in the Folio in a much more thoroughgoing way than in the Quartos. Sometimes, however, they were erroneous or omitted; corrections and additions supplied by editorial tradition are indicated by square brackets. Five-act division is based on a classical model, and act breaks provided the opportunity to replace the candles in the indoor Blackfriars playhouse which the King's Men used after 1608, but Shakespeare did not necessarily think in terms of a five-part structure of dramatic composition. The Folio convention is that a scene ends when the stage is empty. Nowadays, partly under the influence of film, we tend to consider a scene to be a dramatic unit that ends with either a change of imaginary location or a significant passage of time within the narrative. Shakespeare's fluidity of composition accords well with this convention, so in addition to act and scene numbers we provide a *running scene* count in the right margin at the beginning of each new scene, in the typeface used for editorial directions. Where there is a scene break caused by a momentary bare stage, but the location does not change and extra time does not pass, we use the convention *running scene continues*. There is inevitably a degree of editorial judgment in making such calls, but the system is very valuable in suggesting the pace of the plays.

Speakers' Names are often inconsistent in Folio. We have regularized speech headings, but retained an element of deliberate inconsistency in entry directions, in order to give the flavor of Folio.

Verse is indicated by lines that do not run to the right margin and by capitalization of each line. The Folio printers sometimes set verse as prose, and vice versa (either out of misunderstanding or for reasons of space). We have silently corrected in such cases, although in some instances there is ambiguity, in which case we have leaned toward the preservation of Folio layout. Folio sometimes uses contraction ("turnd" rather than "turned") to indicate whether or not the final "-ed" of a past participle is sounded, an area where there is variation for the sake of the five-beat iambic pentameter rhythm. We use the convention of a grave accent to indicate sounding (thus "turnèd" would be two syllables), but would urge actors not to overstress. In cases where one speaker ends with a verse half line and the next begins with the other half of the pentameter, editors since the late eighteenth century have indented the second line. We have abandoned this convention, since the Folio does not use it, and nor did actors' cues in the Shakespearean theater. An exception is made when the second speaker actively interrupts or completes the first speaker's sentence.

Spelling is modernized, but older forms are occasionally maintained where necessary for rhythm or aural effect.

Punctuation in Shakespeare's time was as much rhetorical as grammatical. "Colon" was originally a term for a unit of thought in an argument. The semicolon was a new unit of punctuation (some of the Quartos lack them altogether). We have modernized punctuation throughout, but have given more weight to Folio punctuation than many editors, since, though not Shakespearean, it reflects the usage of his period. In particular, we have used the colon far more than many editors: it is exceptionally useful as a way of indicating how many Shakespearean speeches unfold clause by clause in a developing argument that gives the illusion of enacting the process of thinking in the moment. We have also kept in mind the origin of punctuation in classical times as a way of assisting the actor and orator: the comma suggests the briefest of pauses for breath, the colon a middling one, and a full stop or period a longer pause. Semicolons, by contrast, belong to an era of punctuation that was only just coming in during Shakespeare's time and that is coming to an end now: we have accordingly used them only where they occur in our copy-texts (and not always then). Dashes are sometimes used for parenthetical interjections where the Folio has brackets. They are also used for interruptions and changes in train of thought. Where a change of addressee occurs within a speech, we have used a dash preceded by a full stop (or occasionally another form of punctuation). Often the identity of the respective addressees is obvious from the context. When it is not, this has been indicated in a marginal stage direction.

Entrances and Exits are fairly thorough in Folio, which has accordingly been followed as faithfully as possible. Where characters are omitted or corrections are necessary, this is indicated by square brackets (e.g. "[*and Attendants*]"). *Exit* is sometimes silently normalized to *Exeunt* and *Manet* anglicized to "remains." We trust Folio positioning of entrances and exits to a greater degree than most editors.

Editorial Stage Directions such as stage business, asides, indications of addressee and of characters' position on the gallery stage are used only sparingly in Folio. Other editions mingle directions of this kind with original Folio and Quarto directions, sometimes marking them by means of square brackets. We have sought to distinguish what could be described as *directorial* interventions of this kind from Folio-style directions (either original or supplied) by placing them in the right margin in a different typeface. There is a degree of subjectivity about which directions are of which kind, but the procedure is intended as a reminder to the reader and the actor that Shakespearean stage directions are often dependent upon editorial inference alone and are not set in stone. We also depart from editorial tradition in sometimes admitting uncertainty and thus printing permissive stage directions, such as an *Aside?* (often a line may be equally effective as an aside or a direct address—it is for each production or reading to make its own decision) or a *may exit* or a piece of business placed between arrows to indicate that it may occur at various different moments within a scene.

Line Numbers in the left margin are editorial, for reference and to key the explanatory and textual notes.

Explanatory Notes at the foot of each page explain allusions and gloss obsolete and difficult words, confusing phraseology, occasional major textual cruxes, and so on. Particular attention is given to nonstandard usage, bawdy innuendo, and technical terms (e.g. legal and military language). Where more than one sense is given, commas indicate shades of related meaning, slashes alternative or double meanings.

Textual Notes at the end of the play indicate major departures from the Folio. They take the following form: the reading of our text is given in bold and its source given after an equals sign, with "Q" indicating that it derives from the principal Quarto (Q2 in the case of *Hamlet*, though we also record some significant Q1 readings) and "Ed" that it derives from the editorial tradition. The rejected Folio ("F") reading is then given. A selection of Quarto variants and plausible unadopted editorial readings are also included. Thus, for example, "**3.4.181 bloat** = Ed. F = blunt. Q = blowt," indicates that we have adopted the editorial reading "bloat" where Folio has "blunt" and Quarto "blowt."

KEY FACTS

MAJOR PARTS: (*with percentage of lines/number of speeches/scenes on stage*) Hamlet (37%/341/12), King (14%/100/11), Polonius (9%/86/8), Horatio (7%/105/9), Laertes (5%/60/6), Ophelia (4%/58/5), Gertrude (4%/70/10), Rosencrantz (2%/44/6), First Player (2%/8/2), Ghost (2%/15/2), First Clown (2%/34/1), Marcellus (2%/34/4), Guildenstern (1%/29/5), Osric (1%/19/1).

LINGUISTIC MEDIUM: 75% verse, 25% prose.

DATE: 1600? Not mentioned by Meres in 1598; registered for publication in summer 1602. Allusions to *Julius Caesar* (1599) in the dialogue suggest that it was performed after that play; a reference to Shakespeare's *Hamlet* by the Cambridge academic Gabriel Harvey seems to date from before February 1601. The exchange concerning boy actors alludes to rivalries in the London theaters during 1600 and 1601, but it may have been inserted in the play sometime after its original composition (the passage is absent from the Second Quarto text). An old *Hamlet* play, of unknown authorship and now lost, was extant in the late 1580s to mid-1590s; it is not known whether Shakespeare had any direct involvement with it.

SOURCES: Given the frequency with which Shakespeare reworked old plays, it may be assumed that the old *Hamlet* play was his chief source. The Danish prince Amleth is a revenger in the twelfth-century *Historiae Danicae* of Saxo Grammaticus, familiar to Elizabethan readers via a retelling in François de Belleforest's *Histoires tragiques* (1570). In Belleforest, the Gertrude figure definitely begins her affair with her husband's brother before the murder, in which she is suspected of complicity. The Player's speech on the fall of Troy is influenced by the language of Christopher Marlowe's

Dido Queen of Carthage; Hamlet's philosophizing sometimes resembles the tone of Michel de Montaigne's *Essais*, but a direct link has not been proved.

TEXT: The First Quarto was published in 1603 under the title *The Tragicall Historie of HAMLET Prince of Denmarke by William Shakespeare. As it hath beene diuerse times acted by his Highnesse seruants in the Cittie of London: as also in the two Vniuersities of Cambridge and Oxford, and else-where.* Much shorter than the later texts, and with many garbled lines, it seems to be a reconstruction of an acting version. There are some notable differences from the later texts (e.g. Polonius called Corambis, "To be or not to be" and the "nunnery" dialogue positioned with the "fishmonger" exchange, not after the arrival of the players), but some of the stage directions are valuable (e.g. *"Enter Ofelia playing on a Lute, and her haire downe singing"* for the mad scene). The Second Quarto, published in 1604/05, was clearly an "authorized" text, intended to displace the First Quarto, as may be seen from its title-page claim, "Newly imprinted and enlarged to almost as much againe as it was, according to the true and perfect Coppie." Most scholars believe that the text derives from Shakespeare's manuscript; over 4,000 lines long, it is unlikely to have been staged in full. The text in the 1623 Folio seems to have been set from the theater promptbook or a transcript of it. It has much fuller stage directions than the Second Quarto, and considerable textual variations: about 70 new lines are present, while about 230 Quarto lines are absent, including the whole of Hamlet's last major soliloquy, "How all occasions do inform against me"—in Folio, he is not there to witness Fortinbras' army. Hundreds of individual readings differ, strongly suggesting that the Second Quarto and Folio represent different stages in the play's life. Some scholars regard the revision as systematic (e.g. making subtle changes to Hamlet's relationship with Rosencrantz and Guildenstern), but it may have been more incremental and haphazard. Given the major differences, the editorial practice of conflation, which began with Nicholas Rowe's insertion of the Second Quarto's final soliloquy in his Folio-based text of 1709, has recently fallen into disrepute. We edit the Folio text, but include the Quarto-only passages (edited and annotated) independently at the end. Though Folio seems to have been set from a theatrical manuscript, it was also influenced by the Quarto tradition; so too, a modern edition of Folio can benefit from Quarto readings when the Folio text is manifestly erroneous, as it is on numerous occasions.

THE TRAGEDY
OF HAMLET,
PRINCE OF DENMARK

LIST OF PARTS

HAMLET, Prince of Denmark

KING of Denmark, Hamlet's uncle

GHOST of old Hamlet, former King of Denmark, Hamlet's father

GERTRUDE, queen of Denmark, Hamlet's mother

POLONIUS, councillor to the state of Denmark

LAERTES, Polonius' son

OPHELIA, Polonius' daughter

REYNALDO, Polonius' servant

HORATIO, Hamlet's friend and fellow student

ROSENCRANTZ and GUILDENSTERN } two courtiers, former schoolfellows of Hamlet

VOLTEMAND and CORNELIUS } ambassadors to Norway

MARCELLUS BARNARDO } sentinels of the king's guard, seemingly also friends and fellow students of Hamlet and Horatio

FRANCISCO, another sentinel of the king's guard

OSRIC, a courtier

PLAYERS, who take the roles of PROLOGUE, PLAYER KING, BAPTISTA and LUCIANUS

FORTINBRAS, Prince of Norway

A CAPTAIN in his army

Two CLOWNS, a gravedigger and his companion

TWO MESSENGERS

A SAILOR

A PRIEST

AMBASSADOR from England

Lords, Soldiers, Attendants, Servants, Followers of Laertes

List of parts KING called Claudius in his first entry direction, but never named in the dialogue, so a theater audience would not know what he is called

Act 1 Scene 1

Enter Barnardo and Francisco, two sentinels   *Meeting*

	BARNARDO	Who's there?
	FRANCISCO	Nay, answer me: stand and unfold yourself.
	BARNARDO	Long live the king!
	FRANCISCO	Barnardo?
5	BARNARDO	He.
	FRANCISCO	You come most carefully upon your hour.
	BARNARDO	'Tis now struck twelve: get thee to bed, Francisco.
	FRANCISCO	For this relief much thanks: 'tis bitter cold,

And I am sick at heart.

	BARNARDO	Have you had quiet guard?
10	BARNARDO	Have you had quiet guard?
	FRANCISCO	Not a mouse stirring.
	BARNARDO	Well, goodnight.

If you do meet Horatio and Marcellus,
The rivals of my watch, bid them make haste.

Enter Horatio and Marcellus

	FRANCISCO	I think I hear them.— Stand! Who's there?
15	FRANCISCO	I think I hear them.— Stand! Who's there?
	HORATIO	Friends to this ground.
	MARCELLUS	And liegemen to the Dane.
	FRANCISCO	Give you goodnight.
	MARCELLUS	O, farewell, honest soldier. Who hath relieved you?
20	FRANCISCO	Barnardo has my place. Give you goodnight.

Exit Francisco

	MARCELLUS	Holla! Barnardo!
	BARNARDO	Say, what, is Horatio there?
	HORATIO	A piece of him.
	BARNARDO	Welcome, Horatio: welcome, good Marcellus.
25	MARCELLUS	What, has this thing appeared again tonight?
	BARNARDO	I have seen nothing.

1.1 *Location: the gun terrace of the royal castle at Elsinore, Denmark*   **2 me** Francisco asserts that, as the sentry on guard, he is the one who should be making the challenge **unfold** reveal/identify   **6 carefully . . . hour** responsibly at your appointed time   **14 rivals** partners   **16 ground** country   **17 liegemen . . . Dane** sworn servants of the Danish king **18 Give** God give

MARCELLUS Horatio says 'tis but our fantasy,
And will not let belief take hold of him
Touching this dreaded sight twice seen of us:
30 Therefore I have entreated him along
With us to watch the minutes of this night,
That if again this apparition come,
He may approve our eyes and speak to it.

HORATIO Tush, tush, 'twill not appear.

35 BARNARDO Sit down awhile,
And let us once again assail your ears,
That are so fortified against our story,
What we two nights have seen.

HORATIO Well, sit we down,
40 And let us hear Barnardo speak of this.

BARNARDO Last night of all,
When yond same star that's westward from the pole
Had made his course t'illume that part of heaven
Where now it burns, Marcellus and myself,
45 The bell then beating one—

MARCELLUS Peace, break thee off.

Enter the Ghost

                                          Look where it comes again.

BARNARDO In the same figure like the king that's dead.

MARCELLUS Thou art a scholar; speak to it, Horatio.

BARNARDO Looks it not like the king? Mark it, Horatio.

50 HORATIO Most like: it harrows me with fear and wonder.

BARNARDO It would be spoke to.

MARCELLUS Question it, Horatio.

HORATIO What art thou that usurp'st this time of night,
Together with that fair and warlike form

---

27 fantasy imagination   **29 Touching** concerning   **of** by   **30 along** to come along
31 watch remain awake during/keep guard through   **33 approve** corroborate the
reliability of   **36 assail** attack   **41 Last . . . all** this very night past   **42 yond** yonder, that
pole Pole Star (i.e. North Star)   **43 t'illume** to illuminate   **47 figure** appearance/likeness
48 scholar i.e. one knowledgeable enough to know how to address a ghost; a ghost was
thought to be unable to speak until spoken to   **49 Mark it** observe it closely   **50 harrows**
wounds/distresses   **51 would** wants to   **53 usurp'st** wrongfully occupies (both the night
and the form of the dead king)

55   In which the majesty of buried Denmark
            Did sometimes march? By heaven I charge thee speak!

MARCELLUS   It is offended.

BARNARDO   See, it stalks away.

HORATIO   Stay! Speak, speak! I charge thee, speak!   *Exit the Ghost*

60   MARCELLUS   'Tis gone and will not answer.

BARNARDO   How now, Horatio? You tremble and look pale.
            Is not this something more than fantasy?
            What think you on't?

HORATIO   Before my God, I might not this believe

65   Without the sensible and true avouch
            Of mine own eyes.

MARCELLUS   Is it not like the king?

HORATIO   As thou art to thyself.
            Such was the very armour he had on

70   When he th'ambitious Norway combated:
            So frowned he once when, in an angry parle,
            He smote the steelèd pole-axe on the ice.
            'Tis strange.

MARCELLUS   Thus twice before, and just at this dead hour,

75   With martial stalk hath he gone by our watch.

HORATIO   In what particular thought to work I know not,
            But in the gross and scope of my opinion,
            This bodes some strange eruption to our state.

MARCELLUS   Good now, sit down and tell me, he that knows,

80   Why this same strict and most observant watch
            So nightly toils the subject of the land,
            And why such daily cast of brazen cannon
            And foreign mart for implements of war:
            Why such impress of shipwrights, whose sore task

---

55 **Denmark** the King of Denmark   56 **sometimes** formerly   **charge** order   63 **on't** of it
65 **sensible** perceptible to the senses   **avouch** assurance   70 **Norway** King of Norway
71 **parle** negotiation   72 **steelèd pole-axe** halberd or similar long-handled weapon (tempered
with steel) carried by the bodyguard of a king   76 **In . . . not** i.e. I don't know exactly what to
think   **work** occupy myself, engage   77 **gross and scope** general drift   78 **eruption**
disturbance, turmoil   79 **Good now** a polite entreaty for attention   81 **toils** causes to toil
subject subjects   82 **cast** casting, manufacturing   **brazen** brass   83 **mart** trading
84 **impress** conscription

85 Does not divide the Sunday from the week:
What might be toward, that this sweaty haste
Doth make the night joint-labourer with the day:
Who is't that can inform me?

HORATIO   That can I,

90 At least, the whisper goes so: our last king,
Whose image even but now appeared to us,
Was, as you know, by Fortinbras of Norway,
Thereto pricked on by a most emulate pride,
Dared to the combat, in which our valiant Hamlet —

95 For so this side of our known world esteemed him —
Did slay this Fortinbras, who by a sealed compact,
Well ratified by law and heraldry,
Did forfeit, with his life, all those his lands
Which he stood seized on to the conqueror:

100 Against the which, a moiety competent
Was gagèd by our king, which had returned
To the inheritance of Fortinbras,
Had he been vanquisher, as, by the same cov'nant,
And carriage of the article designed,

105 His fell to Hamlet. Now, sir, young Fortinbras,
Of unimprovèd mettle hot and full,
Hath in the skirts of Norway here and there
Sharked up a list of landless resolutes
For food and diet to some enterprise

110 That hath a stomach in't, which is no other —
And it doth well appear unto our state —

---

85 Does . . . week i.e. they work seven days a week including Sundays   **86 toward**
impending/afoot   **90 whisper** rumor   **93 Thereto . . . pride** refers to Fortinbras, not
Hamlet, the Danish king   **pricked** spurred   **emulate** ambitious, rivalrous   **96 sealed
compact** formally certified agreement   **99 seized on** legally possessed of   **100 moiety
competent** sufficient portion   **101 gagèd** pledged   **had returned** would have gone
103 cov'nant i.e. the sealed compact   **104 carriage . . . designed** carrying out of the clause
that had been drawn up in it   **106 unimprovèd** untested/undisciplined/uncensured
mettle temperament, spirit   **107 skirts** outlying parts   **108 sharked up** gathered up
indiscriminately, as a shark does fish/seized upon like a predator   **list** troop   **resolutes**
resolved people/desperadoes   **109 For . . . enterprise** i.e. men who will serve in return for
food/men who will serve to feed the enterprise   **110 a stomach** courage/an appetite
111 state governing powers

But to recover of us, by strong hand
And terms compulsative, those foresaid lands
So by his father lost: and this, I take it,
115   Is the main motive of our preparations,
The source of this our watch and the chief head
Of this post-haste and rummage in the land.

Enter Ghost again

But soft, behold! Lo, where it comes again!
I'll cross it, though it blast me. Stay, illusion!
120   If thou hast any sound or use of voice,
Speak to me:
If there be any good thing to be done
That may to thee do ease and grace to me,
Speak to me:
125   If thou art privy to thy country's fate —
Which, haply, foreknowing may avoid — O, speak!
Or if thou hast uphoarded in thy life
Extorted treasure in the womb of earth —   ↓*A cock crows*↓
For which, they say, you spirits oft walk in death —
130   Speak of it: stay and speak!— Stop it, Marcellus.

MARCELLUS   Shall I strike at it with my partisan?

HORATIO   Do, if it will not stand.   *They attempt to strike it*

BARNARDO   'Tis here!

HORATIO   'Tis here!

135   MARCELLUS   'Tis gone!   *Exit Ghost*

We do it wrong, being so majestical,
To offer it the show of violence,
For it is as the air invulnerable,
And our vain blows malicious mockery.
140   BARNARDO   It was about to speak when the cock crew.

HORATIO   And then it started like a guilty thing
Upon a fearful summons. I have heard

---

113 compulsative compulsory   **116 head** origin   **117 post-haste** great speed   **rummage**
turmoil, bustle   **118 soft** wait a moment   **Lo** look   **119 cross it** challenge it/make the sign
of the cross at it/cross its path (believed to expose one to evil influence)   **blast** wither/destroy
126 haply perhaps   **127 uphoarded** hoarded up   **128 Extorted** wrongfully obtained
131 partisan long-handled spear   **132 stand** stop, remain

The cock, that is the trumpet to the day,
Doth with his lofty and shrill-sounding throat
145 Awake the god of day, and at his warning,
Whether in sea or fire, in earth or air,
Th'extravagant and erring spirit hies
To his confine: and of the truth herein
This present object made probation.

150 MARCELLUS   It faded on the crowing of the cock.
Some say that ever gainst that season comes
Wherein our Saviour's birth is celebrated,
The bird of dawning singeth all night long,
And then, they say, no spirit can walk abroad:
155 The nights are wholesome, then no planets strike,
No fairy talks, nor witch hath power to charm,
So hallowed and so gracious is the time.

HORATIO   So have I heard and do in part believe it.
But, look, the morn in russet mantle clad,
160 Walks o'er the dew of yon high eastern hill.
Break we our watch up, and by my advice,
Let us impart what we have seen tonight
Unto young Hamlet, for upon my life,
This spirit, dumb to us, will speak to him.
165 Do you consent we shall acquaint him with it,
As needful in our loves, fitting our duty?

MARCELLUS   Let's do't, I pray, and I this morning know
Where we shall find him most conveniently.   *Exeunt*

---

147 **Th'extravagant and erring** the wandering and straying (out of bounds)   **hies** hastens
148 **confine** specific region/place of confinement   149 **probation** proof   151 **gainst** in
anticipation of/just before   152 **our Saviour** i.e. Jesus Christ   153 **bird of dawning** i.e. the
cock   155 **wholesome** healthy (damp night air was usually viewed as noxious)   **strike**
destroy with evil influence   156 **talks** whispers spells (some editors prefer Quarto's "takes,"
enchants/steals)   **charm** cast spells   157 **hallowed** holy   **gracious** full of divine grace
159 **russet** reddish brown (from the coarse cloth of that color)

Act 1 Scene 2   *running scene 2*

Enter Claudius King of Denmark, Gertrude the Queen, Hamlet,
Polonius, Laertes and his sister Ophelia, Lords Attendant

KING   Though yet of Hamlet our dear brother's death
    The memory be green, and that it us befitted
    To bear our hearts in grief and our whole kingdom
    To be contracted in one brow of woe,
5   Yet so far hath discretion fought with nature
    That we with wisest sorrow think on him
    Together with remembrance of ourselves.
    Therefore our sometime sister, now our queen,
    Th'imperial jointress of this warlike state,
10   Have we, as 'twere with a defeated joy,
    With one auspicious and one dropping eye,
    With mirth in funeral and with dirge in marriage,
    In equal scale weighing delight and dole,
    Taken to wife; nor have we herein barred
15   Your better wisdoms, which have freely gone
    With this affair along. For all, our thanks.
    Now follows that you know young Fortinbras,
    Holding a weak supposal of our worth,
    Or thinking by our late dear brother's death
20   Our state to be disjoint and out of frame,
    Colleaguèd with the dream of his advantage,
    He hath not failed to pester us with message
    Importing the surrender of those lands
    Lost by his father, with all bonds of law,
25   To our most valiant brother. So much for him.
    Enter Voltemand and Cornelius

1.2 Location: the royal castle at Elsinore   **2 green** fresh   **4 contracted** knit together
5 discretion good judgment, reason   **8 sometime** former   **9 jointress** widow with rights to
property that she formerly owned with her husband   **11 one . . . eye** one eye looking
cheerfully to the future and the other downcast and tearful   **13 dole** sorrow   **14 barred**
ignored/excluded   **17 that you know** what you should know, that/what you already know
18 supposal estimate   **21 Colleaguèd** joined, allied   **dream . . . advantage** illusion of his
superior position/dream of what he might gain   **23 Importing** concerning

Now for ourself and for this time of meeting,
Thus much the business is: we have here writ
To Norway, uncle of young Fortinbras —
Who, impotent and bedrid, scarcely hears
30   Of this his nephew's purpose — to suppress
His further gait herein, in that the levies,
The lists and full proportions, are all made
Out of his subject. And we here dispatch
You, good Cornelius, and you, Voltemand,
35   For bearing of this greeting to old Norway,
Giving to you no further personal power
To business with the king, more than the scope
Of these dilated articles allow.   *Gives a paper*
Farewell, and let your haste commend your duty.
40 VOLTEMAND   In that, and all things, will we show our duty.
    KING   We doubt it nothing: heartily farewell.—

Exeunt Voltemand and Cornelius

And now, Laertes, what's the news with you?
You told us of some suit: what is't, Laertes?
You cannot speak of reason to the Dane
45   And lose your voice: what wouldst thou beg, Laertes,
That shall not be my offer, not thy asking?
The head is not more native to the heart,
The hand more instrumental to the mouth,
Than is the throne of Denmark to thy father.
50   What wouldst thou have, Laertes?
    LAERTES   Dread my lord,
Your leave and favour to return to France,
From whence though willingly I came to Denmark
To show my duty in your coronation,

---

29 **impotent** powerless, frail   **bedrid** bedridden   31 **His** i.e. Fortinbras'   **gait** proceeding
in . . . subject since the full number of troops mustered is drawn from his (the king's) subjects
37 **To** for   38 **dilated articles** detailed, fully expressed terms   39 **haste . . . duty** speedy
departure, rather than words, convey your dutifulness   41 **nothing** not at all   43 **suit** formal
request   44 **Dane** Danish king   45 **lose your voice** waste your words   46 **That . . . asking**
that I shall not give you rather than have you ask for it   47 **native** closely related
48 **instrumental** serviceable   51 **Dread my lord** my revered lord   52 **leave and favour**
kind permission

55   Yet now I must confess, that duty done,
        My thoughts and wishes bend again towards France
        And bow them to your gracious leave and pardon.

KING   Have you your father's leave? What says Polonius?

POLONIUS   He hath, my lord:

60   I do beseech you, give him leave to go.

KING   Take thy fair hour, Laertes: time be thine,
        And thy best graces spend it at thy will.—
        But now, my cousin Hamlet, and my son—

HAMLET   A little more than kin and less than kind.

65 KING   How is it that the clouds still hang on you?

HAMLET   Not so, my lord:— I am too much i'th'sun.   *Aside?*

GERTRUDE   Good Hamlet, cast thy nightly colour off,
        And let thine eye look like a friend on Denmark.
        Do not forever with thy veilèd lids

70   Seek for thy noble father in the dust:
        Thou know'st 'tis common, all that lives must die,
        Passing through nature to eternity.

HAMLET   Ay, madam, it is common.

GERTRUDE   If it be,

75   Why seems it so particular with thee?

HAMLET   'Seems', madam? Nay it is: I know not 'seems'.
        'Tis not alone my inky cloak, good mother,
        Nor customary suits of solemn black,
        Nor windy suspiration of forced breath,

80   No, nor the fruitful river in the eye,
        Nor the dejected 'haviour of the visage,
        Together with all forms, moods, shows of grief,
        That can denote me truly: these indeed seem,

---

57 bow them submit themselves   **leave and pardon** indulgent permission   **62 graces**
qualities/virtues   **63 cousin** a general term for a relative   **64 A . . . kind** i.e. after his
marriage to Gertrude, Claudius has become more closely (too closely) related to Hamlet, but
the relationship is lacking in natural feeling   **kind** natural/familial/affectionate   **67 nightly
colour** dark mourning clothes/gloomy demeanor   **69 veilèd lids** lowered eyes
71 common universal; in his reply, Hamlet engineers a dig at Gertrude by playing on the senses
of "vulgar/whorish"   **75 particular** specific, personal   **78 customary** habitual to me/socially
conventional   **79 suspiration** sighing   **81 'haviour . . . visage** facial expression   **82 moods**
outward expressions of mood   **83 denote** depict

For they are actions that a man might play,
85 But I have that within which passeth show;
These but the trappings and the suits of woe.
KING   'Tis sweet and commendable in your nature, Hamlet,
To give these mourning duties to your father:
But you must know your father lost a father,
90 That father lost, lost his, and the survivor bound
In filial obligation for some term
To do obsequious sorrow. But to persever
In obstinate condolement is a course
Of impious stubbornness: 'tis unmanly grief:
95 It shows a will most incorrect to heaven,
A heart unfortified, a mind impatient,
An understanding simple and unschooled.
For what we know must be and is as common
As any the most vulgar thing to sense,
100 Why should we in our peevish opposition
Take it to heart? Fie, 'tis a fault to heaven,
A fault against the dead, a fault to nature,
To reason most absurd, whose common theme
Is death of fathers, and who still hath cried,
105 From the first corpse till he that died today,
'This must be so.' We pray you throw to earth
This unprevailing woe, and think of us
As of a father; for let the world take note,
You are the most immediate to our throne,
110 And with no less nobility of love
Than that which dearest father bears his son,
Do I impart towards you. For your intent
In going back to school in Wittenberg,
It is most retrograde to our desire,

---

85 passeth surpasses, exceeds   **92 obsequious** relating to obsequies (commemorative rites for the dead)   **persever** persevere   **93 condolement** grieving   **95 incorrect** disobedient **96 impatient** unwilling to endure (suffering)   **99 any . . . sense** the most ordinary thing we may experience   **100 peevish** stubborn, willful   **101 Fie** expression of disgust or indignation **104 still** always   **107 unprevailing** unavailing, pointless   **109 most immediate** i.e. heir **112 For** as for   **113 Wittenberg** city in Germany, home to a well-known Protestant university **114 retrograde** contrary

115   And we beseech you bend you to remain
    Here in the cheer and comfort of our eye,
    Our chiefest courtier, cousin, and our son.

GERTRUDE   Let not thy mother lose her prayers, Hamlet:
    I prithee stay with us, go not to Wittenberg.

120 HAMLET   I shall in all my best obey you, madam.

KING   Why, 'tis a loving and a fair reply.
    Be as ourself in Denmark.— Madam, come:
    This gentle and unforced accord of Hamlet
    Sits smiling to my heart, in grace whereof,

125   No jocund health that Denmark drinks today
    But the great cannon to the clouds shall tell,
    And the king's rouse the heavens shall bruit again,
    Re-speaking earthly thunder. Come away.

Exeunt. Hamlet remains

HAMLET   O, that this too too solid flesh would melt,

130   Thaw and resolve itself into a dew!
    Or that the Everlasting had not fixed
    His canon gainst self-slaughter! O God, O God!
    How weary, stale, flat and unprofitable
    Seem to me all the uses of this world!

135   Fie on't! O, fie, fie! 'Tis an unweeded garden
    That grows to seed: things rank and gross in nature
    Possess it merely. That it should come to this!
    But two months dead: nay, not so much, not two.
    So excellent a king, that was to this

140   Hyperion to a satyr, so loving to my mother
    That he might not beteem the winds of heaven
    Visit her face too roughly. Heaven and earth,
    Must I remember? Why, she would hang on him

---

115 bend you incline yourself   **123 gentle** kind/noble   **accord** consent   **124 grace whereof** thanksgiving for which   **125 jocund health** merry toast   **Denmark** i.e. himself, king of Denmark   **126 tell** report/count out (i.e. a celebratory cannon shot will be fired for each toast)   **127 rouse** (drinking of a) full draught of liquor   **bruit** proclaim/celebrate   **128 Re-speaking** echoing, repeating   **130 resolve** dissolve   **131 Everlasting** i.e. God   **132 canon** law, decree   **134 uses** habits, customary practices   **136 rank and gross** coarsely profuse in growth   **137 merely** completely   **139 to** compared to   **140 Hyperion** Greek god of the sun, and one of the Titans   **satyr** mythological creature, part man and part goat (often associated with lechery)   **141 beteem** permit

As if increase of appetite had grown
145   By what it fed on, and yet within a month —
Let me not think on't: frailty, thy name is woman! —
A little month, or ere those shoes were old
With which she followed my poor father's body,
Like Niobe, all tears: why she, even she —
150   O, heaven! A beast that wants discourse of reason
Would have mourned longer — married with mine uncle,
My father's brother but no more like my father
Than I to Hercules. Within a month?
Ere yet the salt of most unrighteous tears
155   Had left the flushing of her gallèd eyes,
She married. O, most wicked speed, to post
With such dexterity to incestuous sheets!
It is not nor it cannot come to good:
But break my heart, for I must hold my tongue.

Enter Horatio, Barnardo and Marcellus

160   **HORATIO**   Hail to your lordship!

HAMLET   I am glad to see you well:
Horatio — or I do forget myself.   *Recognizes him*

HORATIO   The same, my lord, and your poor servant ever.

HAMLET   Sir, my good friend, I'll change that name with you.
165   And what make you from Wittenberg, Horatio?—
Marcellus.

MARCELLUS   My good lord.

HAMLET   I am very glad to see you.— Good even, sir.—

To Barnardo

But what in faith make you from Wittenberg?   *To Horatio*

HORATIO   A truant disposition, good my lord.

---

147 or ere before   **149 Niobe** for boasting that she had more children than the goddess Leto,
Niobe's offspring were killed; she grieved until she was turned into a stone, from which tears
continued to stream   **150 wants . . . reason** lacks the faculty of reason   **153 Hercules**
famously strong Greek hero who completed twelve arduous labors   **154 unrighteous**
wicked/insincere   **155 flushing** redness   **gallèd** sore, irritated   **156 post** rush (literally, ride
swiftly)   **164 change . . . you** exchange the name of **servant** for that of **friend**/exchange the
name of servant with you (and become yours)/mutually exchange the name of friend with
you   **165 make you from** are you doing away from   **167 even** evening (also used in the
afternoon)   **169 truant** lazy, negligent

170 HAMLET   I would not have your enemy say so,
            Nor shall you do mine ear that violence,
            To make it truster of your own report
            Against yourself: I know you are no truant.
            But what is your affair in Elsinore?
175   We'll teach you to drink deep ere you depart.

    HORATIO   My lord, I came to see your father's funeral.

    HAMLET   I pray thee do not mock me, fellow student:
            I think it was to see my mother's wedding.

    HORATIO   Indeed, my lord, it followed hard upon.

180 HAMLET   Thrift, thrift, Horatio! The funeral baked meats
            Did coldly furnish forth the marriage tables.
            Would I had met my dearest foe in heaven
            Ere I had ever seen that day, Horatio.
            My father, methinks I see my father.

185 HORATIO   O, where, my lord?

    HAMLET   In my mind's eye, Horatio.

    HORATIO   I saw him once; he was a goodly king.

    HAMLET   He was a man, take him for all in all:
            I shall not look upon his like again.

190 HORATIO   My lord, I think I saw him yesternight.

    HAMLET   Saw who?

    HORATIO   My lord, the king your father.

    HAMLET   The king my father?

    HORATIO   Season your admiration for a while
195   With an attent ear till I may deliver,
            Upon the witness of these gentlemen,
            This marvel to you.

    HAMLET   For heaven's love, let me hear.

    HORATIO   Two nights together had these gentlemen,
200   Marcellus and Barnardo, on their watch,
            In the dead waste and middle of the night,
            Been thus encountered. A figure like your father,

---

175 ere before   **179 hard** close   **180 Thrift** economy   **baked meats** meat pies, pastries
182 dearest closest, greatest   **190 yesternight** last night   **194 Season your admiration**
control your astonishment   **195 attent** attentive   **deliver** report   **201 waste** desolate
expanse (puns on "waist")

Armed at all points exactly, cap-à-pie,
Appears before them, and with solemn march
205 Goes slow and stately: by them thrice he walked,
By their oppressed and fear-surprisèd eyes
Within his truncheon's length, whilst they, distilled
Almost to jelly with the act of fear
Stand dumb and speak not to him. This to me
210 In dreadful secrecy impart they did,
And I with them the third night kept the watch,
Where, as they had delivered, both in time,
Form of the thing, each word made true and good,
The apparition comes. I knew your father:
215 These hands are not more like.

HAMLET   But where was this?

MARCELLUS   My lord, upon the platform where we watched.

HAMLET   Did you not speak to it?

HORATIO   My lord, I did;
220 But answer made it none. Yet once methought
It lifted up its head and did address
Itself to motion, like as it would speak:
But even then the morning cock crew loud,
And at the sound it shrunk in haste away
225 And vanished from our sight.

HAMLET   'Tis very strange.

HORATIO   As I do live, my honoured lord, 'tis true;
And we did think it writ down in our duty
To let you know of it.

230 **HAMLET**   Indeed, indeed, sirs; but this troubles me.
Hold you the watch tonight?

MARCELLUS *AND* **BARNARDO**   We do, my lord.

HAMLET   Armed, say you?

---

203 at all points in every respect   **cap-à-pie** from head to foot   **205 Goes** walks/passes
along   **206 oppressed and fear-surprisèd** overcome and taken prisoner by fear
207 truncheon staff carried as a symbol of military authority   **distilled** dissolved   **208 act**
action/influence   **210 dreadful** full of dread and fear   **215 These . . . like** my two hands are
not more alike than the ghost was like your father   **217 platform** terrace on which guns were
mounted   **221 address . . . speak** prepare itself for action as if it were about to speak

MARCELLUS *AND* BARNARDO   Armed, my lord.

235   HAMLET   From top to toe?

MARCELLUS *AND* BARNARDO   My lord, from head to foot.

HAMLET   Then saw you not his face?

HORATIO   O, yes, my lord, he wore his beaver up.

HAMLET   What, looked he frowningly?

240   HORATIO   A countenance more in sorrow than in anger.

HAMLET   Pale or red?

HORATIO   Nay, very pale.

HAMLET   And fixed his eyes upon you?

HORATIO   Most constantly.

245   HAMLET   I would I had been there.

HORATIO   It would have much amazed you.

HAMLET   Very like, very like. Stayed it long?

HORATIO   While one with moderate haste might tell a
hundred.

MARCELLUS *AND* BARNARDO   Longer, longer.

250   HORATIO   Not when I saw't.

HAMLET   His beard was grizzly, no?

HORATIO   It was, as I have seen it in his life,
A sable silvered.

HAMLET   I'll watch tonight; perchance 'twill walk again.

255   HORATIO   I warrant you it will.

HAMLET   If it assume my noble father's person,
I'll speak to it though hell itself should gape
And bid me hold my peace. I pray you all,
If you have hitherto concealed this sight,

260   Let it be tenable in your silence still,
And whatsoever else shall hap tonight,
Give it an understanding but no tongue.
I will requite your loves. So, fare ye well:
Upon the platform 'twixt eleven and twelve

265   I'll visit you.

---

238 beaver visor of a helmet   **240 countenance** facial expression   **248 tell** count
251 grizzly gray   **253 sable silvered** black mixed with silver hairs   **255 warrant** assure
260 tenable capable of being held   **still** plays on the sense of "silent"   **263 requite** reward

ALL   Our duty to your honour.   *Exeunt [all but Hamlet]*

HAMLET   Your love, as mine to you: farewell.—

My father's spirit in arms? All is not well:

I doubt some foul play. Would the night were come.

270   Till then, sit still my soul: foul deeds will rise,

Though all the earth o'erwhelm them, to men's eyes.   *Exit*

Act 1 Scene 3   *running scene 3*

Enter Laertes and Ophelia

LAERTES   My necessaries are embarked, farewell:

And, sister, as the winds give benefit

And convoy is assistant, do not sleep

But let me hear from you.

5   OPHELIA   Do you doubt that?

LAERTES   For Hamlet and the trifling of his favours,

Hold it a fashion and a toy in blood,

A violet in the youth of primy nature,

Froward, not permanent, sweet, not lasting,

10   The suppliance of a minute, no more.

OPHELIA   No more but so?

LAERTES   Think it no more,

For nature crescent does not grow alone

In thews and bulk, but as his temple waxes,

15   The inward service of the mind and soul

Grows wide withal. Perhaps he loves you now,

And now no soil nor cautel doth besmirch

The virtue of his will: but you must fear,

His greatness weighed, his will is not his own;

20   For he himself is subject to his birth:

---

269 **doubt** suspect/fear   **1.3** *Location: within the castle*   2 **as** whenever   3 **convoy is assistant** transport (for letters) is available   7 **toy in blood** amorous whim   8 **primy** in its prime/early/wonderful/sexually excited   9 **Froward** perverse/obstinate/willful/ungovernable   10 **suppliance** fulfillment/pastime   11 **but so** than that   13 **crescent** growing   14 **thews** bodily proportions, muscles   **temple** i.e. body (the temple of the soul)   16 **withal** with it   17 **soil nor cautel** stain nor deceit   18 **will** intent/(sexual) desire   19 **weighed** being considered

He may not, as unvalued persons do,
Carve for himself, for on his choice depends
The sanctity and health of the whole state,
And therefore must his choice be circumscribed
25 Unto the voice and yielding of that body
Whereof he is the head. Then if he says he loves you,
It fits your wisdom so far to believe it
As he in his peculiar sect and force
May give his saying deed, which is no further
30 Than the main voice of Denmark goes withal.
Then weigh what loss your honour may sustain
If with too credent ear you list his songs,
Or lose your heart, or your chaste treasure open
To his unmastered importunity.
35 Fear it, Ophelia, fear it, my dear sister,
And keep within the rear of your affection,
Out of the shot and danger of desire.
The chariest maid is prodigal enough
If she unmask her beauty to the moon:
40 Virtue itself scapes not calumnious strokes:
The canker galls the infants of the spring
Too oft before the buttons be disclosed,
And in the morn and liquid dew of youth
Contagious blastments are most imminent.
45 Be wary then: best safety lies in fear.
Youth to itself rebels, though none else near.

---

21 unvalued i.e. without rank   **22 Carve** choose (from the image of serving oneself meat;
with sexual connotations)   **23 sanctity** inviolability/worthiness of religious respect
25 yielding consent   **28 peculiar . . . force** particular circumstances of rank and power
30 main voice general agreement   **withal** along with   **32 credent** credulous, trusting   **list**
listen to   **33 chaste treasure** i.e. virginity (**treasure** was slang for "vagina")   **34 unmastered**
importunity unrestrained persistence   **36 keep . . . affection** i.e. do not advance headlong into
the dangerous territory your affection might lead you into   **rear** back portion of an army,
which moves last   **37 shot** maintains the military image, with suggestions of phallic attack
38 chariest most modest/cautious/frugal   **39 If she** i.e. if she does no more than   **moon**
symbol of chastity   **40 scapes** escapes   **calumnious strokes** slanderous blows   **41 canker**
canker-worm, a grub that destroys plants   **galls** wounds, destroys   **infants . . . spring** i.e.
young plants   **42 buttons be disclosed** buds be open   **44 blastments** blights/withering
46 to against

OPHELIA   I shall th'effect of this good lesson keep
As watchman to my heart. But, good my brother,
Do not, as some ungracious pastors do,
50   Show me the steep and thorny way to heaven,
Whilst, like a puffed and reckless libertine
Himself the primrose path of dalliance treads,
And recks not his own rede.

LAERTES   O, fear me not.

Enter Polonius

55   I stay too long. But here my father comes.
A double blessing is a double grace;
Occasion smiles upon a second leave.

POLONIUS   Yet here, Laertes? Aboard, aboard, for shame!
The wind sits in the shoulder of your sail,
60   And you are stayed for there. My blessing with you!
And these few precepts in thy memory
See thou character. Give thy thoughts no tongue,
Nor any unproportioned thought his act.
Be thou familiar, but by no means vulgar.
65   The friends thou hast, and their adoption tried,
Grapple them to thy soul with hoops of steel,
But do not dull thy palm with entertainment
Of each new-hatched, unfledged comrade: beware
Of entrance to a quarrel, but being in,
70   Bear't that th'opposèd may beware of thee.
Give every man thine ear, but few thy voice:
Take each man's censure, but reserve thy judgement:
Costly thy habit as thy purse can buy,
But not expressed in fancy; rich, not gaudy:

---

49 ungracious ungodly   **51 puffed** swollen with pride and vanity   **53 recks** heeds
rede advice   **54 fear me not** do not worry about me   **55 stay** delay   **56 double blessing** i.e.
a second chance to say goodbye to and receive the blessing of Polonius
57 Occasion opportunity   **leave** leave-taking, farewell   **60 stayed** waited   **62 See thou**
character make sure that you inscribe   **63 unproportioned** immoderate/unruly
his its   **64 familiar** friendly, sociable   **65 adoption tried** worthiness to be adopted as friends
having been tested   **66 Grapple** fasten firmly   **67 dull thy palm** i.e. by shaking hands too
often   **68 unfledged** still unfeathered (i.e. new, untried)   **70 Bear't that th'opposèd** manage
it so that your opponent   **72 censure** judgment/opinion   **73 habit** clothing   **74 fancy**
elaborate, fanciful style

75   For the apparel oft proclaims the man,
       And they in France of the best rank and station
       Are of a most select and generous chief in that.
       Neither a borrower nor a lender be,
       For loan oft loses both itself and friend,
80   And borrowing dulls the edge of husbandry.
       This above all: to thine own self be true,
       And it must follow, as the night the day,
       Thou canst not then be false to any man.
       Farewell: my blessing season this in thee!

85 LAERTES   Most humbly do I take my leave, my lord.
    POLONIUS   The time invites you. Go, your servants tend.
    LAERTES   Farewell, Ophelia, and remember well
       What I have said to you.
    OPHELIA   'Tis in my memory locked,
90   And you yourself shall keep the key of it.
    LAERTES   Farewell.   *Exit Laertes*
    POLONIUS   What is't, Ophelia, he hath said to you?
    OPHELIA   So please you, something touching the lord Hamlet.
    POLONIUS   Marry, well bethought.
95   'Tis told me, he hath very oft of late
       Given private time to you; and you yourself
       Have of your audience been most free and bounteous:
       If it be so, as so 'tis put on me,
       And that in way of caution, I must tell you
100   You do not understand yourself so clearly
       As it behoves my daughter and your honour.
       What is between you? Give me up the truth.
    OPHELIA   He hath, my lord, of late made many tenders
       Of his affection to me.

---

77 **Are . . . that** are of a most distinguished and noble pre-eminence in their choice garments
80 **husbandry** economy   83 **false** dishonest, disloyal   84 **season** ripen   **this** i.e. his advice
86 **tend** await   93 **touching** concerning   94 **Marry** by the Virgin Mary   **bethought** thought
of   97 **audience** hearing, reception   98 **put on** conveyed to/impressed upon   101 **behoves**
befits, is appropriate for   103 **tenders** offers (Polonius subsequently shifts the sense to "offers
of money")

HORATIO   Is it a custom?

15   HAMLET   Ay, marry, is't:
And to my mind, though I am native here
And to the manner born, it is a custom
More honoured in the breach than the observance.

Enter Ghost

HORATIO   Look, my lord, it comes!

20   HAMLET   Angels and ministers of grace defend us!
Be thou a spirit of health or goblin damned,
Bring with thee airs from heaven or blasts from hell,
Be thy intents wicked or charitable,
Thou com'st in such a questionable shape

25   That I will speak to thee: I'll call thee Hamlet,
King, father, royal Dane. O, O, answer me!
Let me not burst in ignorance, but tell
Why thy canonized bones, hearsèd in death,
Have burst their cerements, why the sepulchre

30   Wherein we saw thee quietly inurned,
Hath oped his ponderous and marble jaws
To cast thee up again. What may this mean,
That thou, dead corpse, again in complete steel
Revisits thus the glimpses of the moon,

35   Making night hideous, and we fools of nature
So horridly to shake our disposition
With thoughts beyond the reaches of our souls?
Say, why is this? Wherefore? What should we do?

Ghost beckons Hamlet

HORATIO   It beckons you to go away with it,

---

17 manner custom   **18 More . . . observance** better being broken than observed
20 ministers of grace God's messengers, angels   **21 Be thou** whether you are   **health**
benevolence/salvation   **goblin** demon   **24 questionable shape** form that invites question
28 canonized consecrated, buried according to Christian rite (three syllables, stress on second)
hearsèd entombed   **29 cerements** grave clothes   **sepulchre** tomb   **30 inurned**
enclosed/buried   **31 ponderous** weighty   **32 cast** vomit   **33 complete steel** full armor
34 glimpses . . . moon earth by moonlight, literally "flashes of moonlight"   **35 hideous**
frightening, full of horror   **fools of nature** ignorant mortals/playthings of nature
36 horridly dreadfully/with horror   **disposition** ordinary temperaments/mental composure
38 Wherefore? Why?

40   As if it some impartment did desire
        To you alone.

MARCELLUS Look, with what courteous action
        It wafts you to a more removèd ground:
        But do not go with it.

45 HORATIO   No, by no means.

HAMLET   It will not speak; then will I follow it.

HORATIO   Do not, my lord.

HAMLET   Why, what should be the fear?
        I do not set my life at a pin's fee;

50   And for my soul, what can it do to that,
        Being a thing immortal as itself?
        It waves me forth again: I'll follow it.

HORATIO   What if it tempt you toward the flood, my lord,
        Or to the dreadful summit of the cliff

55   That beetles o'er his base into the sea,
        And there assumes some other horrible form
        Which might deprive your sovereignty of reason
        And draw you into madness? Think of it.

HAMLET   It wafts me still.— Go on, I'll follow thee.

60 MARCELLUS You shall not go, my lord.   *Holds him back*

HAMLET   Hold off your hand.

HORATIO   Be ruled: you shall not go.

HAMLET   My fate cries out,
        And makes each petty artery in this body

65   As hardy as the Nemean lion's nerve.—
        Still am I called?— Unhand me, gentlemen.
        By heav'n, I'll make a ghost of him that lets me!
        I say, away!— Go on, I'll follow thee.   *Exeunt Ghost and Hamlet*

HORATIO   He waxes desperate with imagination.

70 MARCELLUS Let's follow; 'tis not fit thus to obey him.

---

40 impartment communication   **43 wafts** waves, beckons   **49 a pin's fee** the (tiny) worth of a pin   **53 flood** sea   **55 beetles o'er** overhangs (like frowning eyebrows)   **57 deprive . . . reason** remove your reason from its position of control   **64 artery** thought not to convey blood, but the ethereal fluid known as "vital spirits"   **65 Nemean lion** supposedly invincible beast strangled by Hercules as one of his twelve labors   **nerve** sinew, tendon   **67 lets** hinders   **69 waxes** grows

HORATIO	Have after. To what issue will this come?
MARCELLUS	Something is rotten in the state of Denmark.
HORATIO	Heaven will direct it.
MARCELLUS	Nay, let's follow him.	*Exeunt*

[Act 1 Scene 5]   *running scene 4 continues*

Enter Ghost and Hamlet

	HAMLET	Where wilt thou lead me? Speak; I'll go no further.
	GHOST	Mark me.
	HAMLET	I will.
	GHOST	My hour is almost come,
5		When I to sulphurous and tormenting flames
		Must render up myself.
	HAMLET	Alas, poor ghost!
	GHOST	Pity me not, but lend thy serious hearing
		To what I shall unfold.
10	HAMLET	Speak: I am bound to hear.
	GHOST	So art thou to revenge, when thou shalt hear.
	HAMLET	What?
	GHOST	I am thy father's spirit,
		Doomed for a certain term to walk the night,
15		And for the day confined to fast in fires,
		Till the foul crimes done in my days of nature
		Are burnt and purged away. But that I am forbid
		To tell the secrets of my prison-house,
		I could a tale unfold whose lightest word
20		Would harrow up thy soul, freeze thy young blood,
		Make thy two eyes like stars start from their spheres,
		Thy knotty and combinèd locks to part
		And each particular hair to stand on end

71 Have after let's follow   **issue** outcome   **73 it** i.e. the **issue**   **1.5   2 Mark** listen, pay
attention to   **9 unfold** reveal   **10 bound** ready/under obligation   **17 But** were it not
20 harrow up distress/tear up   **21 like . . . spheres** individual stars and planets were thought
to be contained within concentric hollow spheres that revolved around the earth
22 knotty . . . locks neat and carefully styled hair

Like quills upon the fretful porpentine.
25   But this eternal blazon must not be
To ears of flesh and blood. List, Hamlet, O, list!
If thou didst ever thy dear father love—

HAMLET   O heaven!

GHOST   Revenge his foul and most unnatural murder.

30   HAMLET   Murder?

GHOST   Murder most foul, as in the best it is,
But this most foul, strange and unnatural.

HAMLET   Haste, haste me to know it, that I with wings as swift
As meditation or the thoughts of love
35   May sweep to my revenge.

GHOST   I find thee apt,
And duller shouldst thou be than the fat weed
That roots itself in ease on Lethe wharf,
Wouldst thou not stir in this. Now, Hamlet, hear:
40   It's given out that, sleeping in mine orchard,
A serpent stung me, so the whole ear of Denmark
Is by a forgèd process of my death
Rankly abused. But know thou, noble youth,
The serpent that did sting thy father's life
45   Now wears his crown.

HAMLET   O, my prophetic soul! Mine uncle!

GHOST   Ay, that incestuous, that adulterate beast,
With witchcraft of his wit, with traitorous gifts —
O, wicked wit and gifts, that have the power
50   So to seduce! — won to his shameful lust
The will of my most seeming-virtuous queen.
O Hamlet, what a falling-off was there!
From me, whose love was of that dignity

24 **porpentine** porcupine   25 **eternal blazon** revelation of the secrets of the eternal world
26 **List** listen   31 **in the best** even at best   34 **meditation** thought   35 **sweep** swoop in
sudden attack   36 **apt** fit/ready/responsive   37 **duller . . . be** you would be more sluggish
38 **Lethe wharf** the banks of the Lethe, the river of forgetfulness in the classical underworld
40 **orchard** garden   42 **forgèd process** fabricated account   43 **Rankly** excessively/foully
47 **adulterate** adulterous   48 **gifts** natural talents/presents   51 **will** sexual desire
53 **dignity** worth, excellence

That it went hand in hand even with the vow
55   I made to her in marriage, and to decline
Upon a wretch whose natural gifts were poor
To those of mine!
But virtue, as it never will be moved,
Though lewdness court it in a shape of heaven,
60   So lust, though to a radiant angel linked,
Will sate itself in a celestial bed,
And prey on garbage.
But, soft, methinks I scent the morning's air;
Brief let me be. Sleeping within mine orchard,
65   My custom always in the afternoon,
Upon my secure hour thy uncle stole,
With juice of cursèd hebenon in a vial,
And in the porches of mine ears did pour
The leperous distilment, whose effect
70   Holds such an enmity with blood of man
That swift as quicksilver it courses through
The natural gates and alleys of the body,
And with a sudden vigour it doth posset
And curd, like eager droppings into milk,
75   The thin and wholesome blood: so did it mine,
And a most instant tetter barked about,
Most lazar-like, with vile and loathsome crust,
All my smooth body.
Thus was I, sleeping, by a brother's hand
80   Of life, of crown and queen, at once dispatched:
Cut off even in the blossoms of my sin,
Unhouseled, disappointed, unaneled,

---

55 decline Upon sink to   **58 virtue, as it** as virtue   **61 sate itself** become satiated/grow
weary   **62 garbage** filth/animal entrails   **66 secure** carefree, unsuspecting
67 hebenon a poisonous substance—possibly "henbane" or "yew" (*hebenus*)   **69 leperous
distilment** distillation causing leprosy-like symptoms (i.e. corrosion of the skin)
71 quicksilver liquid mercury   **73 posset And curd** clot, curdle   **74 eager** sour/acid
76 tetter eruption of the skin   **barked about** covered with a bark-like crust   **77 lazar-like**
leperlike   **80 dispatched** deprived through death   **82 Unhouseled, disappointed, unaneled**
without having received Holy Communion (the "housel"), unprepared, and without having
received extreme unction (being anointed with holy oil before death)

No reckoning made, but sent to my account
With all my imperfections on my head.

85   O horrible, O horrible, most horrible!
If thou hast nature in thee, bear it not;
Let not the royal bed of Denmark be
A couch for luxury and damnèd incest.
But, howsoever thou pursuest this act,

90   Taint not thy mind nor let thy soul contrive
Against thy mother aught; leave her to heaven
And to those thorns that in her bosom lodge,
To prick and sting her. Fare thee well at once;
The glow-worm shows the matin to be near,

95   And 'gins to pale his uneffectual fire.
Adieu, adieu, Hamlet: remember me.   *Exit*

HAMLET   O all you host of heaven! O earth! What else?
And shall I couple hell? O, fie! Hold, my heart;
And you, my sinews, grow not instant old,

100   But bear me stiffly up. Remember thee?
Ay, thou poor ghost, while memory holds a seat
In this distracted globe. Remember thee?
Yea, from the table of my memory
I'll wipe away all trivial fond records,

105   All saws of books, all forms, all pressures past
That youth and observation copied there;
And thy commandment all alone shall live
Within the book and volume of my brain,
Unmixed with baser matter: yes, yes, by heaven!

110   O most pernicious woman!
O villain, villain, smiling, damnèd villain!
My tables,
My tables: meet it is I set it down

---

83 reckoning settling of debts   **account** i.e. judgment   **86 nature** natural feeling
88 luxury lust   **90 Taint** pollute   **91 aught** anything   **94 matin** morning   **95 'gins** begins
uneffectual i.e. no longer providing light   **97 host** angels   **98 couple** add (to **heaven** and
earth)   **102 distracted** distressed, agitated   **globe** world/head (plays on the name of the
Globe Theatre)   **103 table** writing tablet, slate   **104 fond** foolish   **records** memories/written
accounts   **105 saws** sayings, maxims   **pressures** impressions, stamps   **110 pernicious**
destructive/wicked   **113 meet** fitting

That one may smile and smile and be a villain;

115 At least I'm sure it may be so in Denmark.   *Writes*

So, uncle, there you are. Now to my word:

It is 'Adieu, adieu, remember me.'

I have sworn't.

HORATIO *AND* MARCELLUS   My lord, my lord!   *Within*

Enter Horatio and Marcellus

120 MARCELLUS   Lord Hamlet!

HORATIO   Heaven secure him.

HAMLET   So be it.

HORATIO   Hillo, ho, ho, my lord!

HAMLET   Hillo, ho, ho, boy! Come, bird, come.

125 MARCELLUS   How is't, my noble lord?

HORATIO   What news, my lord?

HAMLET   O, wonderful!

HORATIO   Good my lord, tell it.

HAMLET   No, you'll reveal it.

130 HORATIO   Not I, my lord, by heaven.

MARCELLUS   Nor I, my lord.

HAMLET   How say you, then, would heart of man once think it?

But you'll be secret?

BOTH   Ay, by heaven, my lord.

135 HAMLET   There's ne'er a villain dwelling in all Denmark

But he's an arrant knave.

HORATIO   There needs no ghost, my lord, come from the grave

To tell us this.

HAMLET   Why, right, you are i'th'right;

140 And so, without more circumstance at all,

I hold it fit that we shake hands and part:

You, as your business and desires shall point you,

For every man has business and desire,

---

116 word watchword/motto   **124 Hillo . . . come** Hamlet mockingly responds as if Horatio's call were that of a falconer summoning his bird to return   **125 How is't** how is it with you, how are you   **127 wonderful** astonishing, extraordinary   **132 once** ever   **136 arrant** downright/notorious   **140 circumstance** roundabout talk/details   **142 as** i.e. in the direction that

Such as it is: and for mine own poor part,
145 Look you, I'll go pray.

HORATIO   These are but wild and whirling words, my lord.

HAMLET   I'm sorry they offend you, heartily:
Yes, faith, heartily.

HORATIO   There's no offence, my lord.

150 HAMLET   Yes, by Saint Patrick, but there is, Horatio,
And much offence too. Touching this vision here,
It is an honest ghost, that let me tell you:
For your desire to know what is between us,
O'ermaster't as you may. And now, good friends,
155 As you are friends, scholars and soldiers,
Give me one poor request.

HORATIO   What is't, my lord? We will.

HAMLET   Never make known what you have seen tonight.

BOTH   My lord, we will not.

160 HAMLET   Nay, but swear't.

HORATIO   In faith, my lord, not I.

MARCELLUS   Nor I, my lord, in faith.

HAMLET   Upon my sword.   *Holds out his sword*

MARCELLUS   We have sworn, my lord, already.

165 HAMLET   Indeed, upon my sword, indeed.

GHOST   Swear.   *Ghost cries under the stage*

HAMLET   Ah ha, boy, say'st thou so? Art thou there,
truepenny?—
Come on, you hear this fellow in the cellarage:
170 Consent to swear.

HORATIO   Propose the oath, my lord.

HAMLET   Never to speak of this that you have seen,
Swear by my sword.

GHOST   Swear.   *They swear*

175 HAMLET   *Hic et ubique?* Then we'll shift our ground.   *Moves*

---

150 Saint Patrick the keeper of Purgatory   **152 honest** genuine (i.e. not an evil spirit)
154 O'ermaster't repress it   **161 not I** i.e. I will not tell (not "I will not swear")   **163 sword**
i.e. the hilt of the sword (the shape of a cross)   **166 *under the stage*** accessed through the
trapdoor, this region was often associated with hell   **167 truepenny** honest fellow
169 cellarage cellars   **175 *Hic et ubique?*** "Here and everywhere?" (Latin)

Come hither, gentlemen,
And lay your hands again upon my sword:
Never to speak of this that you have heard,
Swear by my sword.

180 GHOST   Swear.   *They swear*

HAMLET   Well said, old mole. Canst work i'th'ground so fast?
A worthy pioneer! Once more remove, good friends.

HORATIO   O, day and night, but this is wondrous strange!

HAMLET   And therefore as a stranger give it welcome.

185 There are more things in heaven and earth, Horatio,

Aside to Horatio?

Than are dreamt of in our philosophy.— But come,
Here, as before, never, so help you mercy,
How strange or odd soe'er I bear myself —
As I perchance hereafter shall think meet
190 To put an antic disposition on —
That you, at such time seeing me, never shall,
With arms encumbered thus, or thus headshake,
Or by pronouncing of some doubtful phrase,
As 'Well, we know' or 'We could, an if we would'
195 Or 'If we list to speak' or 'There be, an if they might'
Or such ambiguous giving out, to note
That you know aught of me: this not to do,
So grace and mercy at your most need help you. Swear.

GHOST   Swear.   *They swear*

200 HAMLET   Rest, rest, perturbèd spirit!— So, gentlemen,
With all my love I do commend me to you:
And what so poor a man as Hamlet is
May do t'express his love and friending to you,
God willing, shall not lack. Let us go in together:
205 And still your fingers on your lips, I pray.

---

182 pioneer soldier whose responsibility it was to dig trenches   **remove** move   **184 stranger** i.e. one in need of hospitality   **187 never . . . mercy** never, as you hope for God's mercy (Hamlet begins the oath)   **188 How . . . soe'er** however strangely or oddly   **190 antic** grotesque/fantastic/bizarre   **192 encumbered** entangled (i.e. folded)   **headshake** shaking the head   **193 doubtful** ambiguous   **194 an if** if   **195 list** wished   **'There . . . might'** there are those who might tell, if they could   **196 giving out** utterance/suggestion   **note** indicate   **201 commend me** entrust myself   **202 what** whatever   **203 friending** friendship   **205 still** always

The time is out of joint: O, cursèd spite
That ever I was born to set it right!
Nay, come, let's go together.

Exeunt

Act 2 Scene 1

Enter Polonius and Reynaldo

POLONIUS   Give him this money and these notes, Reynaldo.

Gives money and papers

REYNALDO   I will, my lord.

POLONIUS   You shall do marvellous wisely, good Reynaldo,
Before you visit him, you make inquiry
5   Of his behaviour.

REYNALDO   My lord, I did intend it.

POLONIUS   Marry, well said; very well said. Look you, sir,
Inquire me first what Danskers are in Paris,
And how, and who, what means and where they keep,
10   What company, at what expense, and finding
By this encompassment and drift of question
That they do know my son, come you more nearer
Than your particular demands will touch it:
Take you, as 'twere, some distant knowledge of him,
15   As thus, 'I know his father and his friends
And in part him.' Do you mark this, Reynaldo?

REYNALDO   Ay, very well, my lord.

POLONIUS   'And in part him, but', you may say, 'not well,
But if't be he I mean, he's very wild;
20   Addicted so and so', and there put on him
What forgeries you please: marry, none so rank
As may dishonour him — take heed of that —

---

206 **The time** things generally, the age   **out of joint** dislocated, disordered   **2.1 *Location:*** *within the royal castle at Elsinore; this remains the location for all scenes until Act 4 scene 3*   3 **marvellous** marvelously, extremely   4 **you** i.e. if you   8 **Inquire me** inquire (**me** is emphatic)   **Danskers** Danes   9 **keep** lodge   11 **encompassment** roundabout manner of talking   **drift** general aim   12 **come . . . it** you will come closer to the truth than you would were you to ask specific, pointed questions   14 **Take you** assume, affect   20 **Addicted** devoted or inclined to   21 **forgeries** fabrications   **rank** excessive/coarse

But, sir, such wanton, wild and usual slips
As are companions noted and most known
25   To youth and liberty.

REYNALDO   As gaming, my lord.

POLONIUS   Ay, or drinking, fencing, swearing, quarrelling,
Drabbing: you may go so far.

REYNALDO   My lord, that would dishonour him.

30 POLONIUS   Faith, no, as you may season it in the charge.
You must not put another scandal on him,
That he is open to incontinency;
That's not my meaning: but breathe his faults so quaintly
That they may seem the taints of liberty,
35   The flash and outbreak of a fiery mind,
A savageness in unreclaimèd blood,
Of general assault.

REYNALDO   But, my good lord—

POLONIUS   Wherefore should you do this?

40 REYNALDO   Ay, my lord, I would know that.

POLONIUS   Marry, sir, here's my drift,
And I believe, it is a fetch of warrant:
You laying these slight sullies on my son,
As 'twere a thing a little soiled i'th'working,
45   Mark you, your party in converse, him you would sound,
Having ever seen in the prenominate crimes
The youth you breathe of guilty, be assured
He closes with you in this consequence:
'Good sir' or so, or 'friend' or 'gentleman',
50   According to the phrase and the addition
Of man and country.

---

23 wanton boisterous/wild/lustful   **slips** flaws, foibles   **26 gaming** gambling   **28 Drabbing** using prostitutes   **30 season . . . charge** moderate the accusation   **32 incontinency** excessive sexual license   **33 quaintly** artfully, skillfully   **34 taints of liberty** faults resulting from too much freedom   **36 savageness** wildness   **unreclaimèd** untamed   **37 Of general assault** by which all men are affected   **41 drift** intention/plan   **42 fetch of warrant** legitimate stratagem   **44 As 'twere** as if he were   **i'th'working** in the handling, the manufacture   **45 party in converse** the person with whom you are conversing   **sound** question, probe   **46 Having ever** if he has ever   **prenominate** aforementioned   **47 breathe of** speak about (i.e. Laertes)   **48 closes . . . consequence** agrees with you in the following way   **50 addition** form of address

REYNALDO   Very good, my lord.

POLONIUS   And then, sir, does he this — he does — what
was I about to say? I was about to say something:
55   where did I leave?

REYNALDO   At 'closes in the consequence' at 'friend or so'
and 'gentleman'.

POLONIUS   At 'closes in the consequence', ay, marry.
He closes with you thus: 'I know the gentleman,
60   I saw him yesterday, or t'other day',
Or then, or then, with such and such; and, as you say,
There was he gaming, there o'ertook in's rouse,
There falling out at tennis, or perchance,
'I saw him enter such a house of sale',
65   Videlicet, a brothel, or so forth.
See you now;
Your bait of falsehood takes this carp of truth:
And thus do we of wisdom and of reach,
With windlasses and with assays of bias,
70   By indirections find directions out:
So by my former lecture and advice,
Shall you my son. You have me, have you not?

REYNALDO   My lord, I have.

POLONIUS   God buy you; fare you well.

75   REYNALDO   Good my lord.

POLONIUS   Observe his inclination in yourself.

REYNALDO   I shall, my lord.

POLONIUS   And let him ply his music.

REYNALDO   Well, my lord.   *Exit*

Enter Ophelia

80   POLONIUS   Farewell.— How now, Ophelia, what's the
matter?

---

58 ay, marry yes, by the Virgin Mary, i.e. yes, of course   **62 o'ertook in's rouse** overcome in his carousals (i.e. drunk)   **65 Videlicet** "that is to say" (Latin)   **67 carp** type of fish
68 we . . . reach we who are wise and widely perceptive   **69 windlasses** roundabout routes
assays of bias indirect ventures   **70 directions** the way things are really going   **71 lecture**
lesson   **72 have** understand   **74 buy** i.e. be with   **76 Observe . . . yourself** observe his
behavior in person/go along with his inclinations   **78 ply his music** (literally) practice his
musical skills/(metaphorically) go his own way   **79 Well** very well

OPHELIA   Alas, my lord, I have been so affrighted!

POLONIUS   With what, in the name of heaven?

OPHELIA   My lord, as I was sewing in my chamber,

85   Lord Hamlet, with his doublet all unbraced,

No hat upon his head, his stockings fouled,

Ungartered, and down-gyvèd to his ankle,

Pale as his shirt, his knees knocking each other,

And with a look so piteous in purport

90   As if he had been loosèd out of hell

To speak of horrors — he comes before me.

POLONIUS   Mad for thy love?

OPHELIA   My lord, I do not know, but truly I do fear it.

POLONIUS   What said he?

95   OPHELIA   He took me by the wrist and held me hard;

Then goes he to the length of all his arm,

And with his other hand thus o'er his brow

He falls to such perusal of my face

As he would draw it. Long stayed he so.

100   At last, a little shaking of mine arm

And thrice his head thus waving up and down,

He raised a sigh so piteous and profound

That it did seem to shatter all his bulk

And end his being: that done, he lets me go,

105   And, with his head over his shoulders turned,

He seemed to find his way without his eyes,

For out o'doors he went without their help,

And to the last, bended their light on me.

POLONIUS   Go with me: I will go seek the king.

110   This is the very ecstasy of love,

Whose violent property fordoes itself

And leads the will to desperate undertakings

---

85 doublet close-fitting jacket with buttons down the front   **unbraced** undone   **86 No hat** Elizabethans usually wore hats indoors when in company   **87 Ungartered** falling down, untied (garters were bands that held the stockings in place)   **down-gyvèd** fallen down and resembling fetters (gyves)   **89 purport** meaning   **96 goes . . . arm** he backs away until he stands at arm's length   **99 As** as if   **108 bended their light** i.e. directed their gaze   **110 ecstasy** frenzy, madness   **111 Whose . . . itself** the violent nature of which causes self-destruction

As oft as any passion under heaven
That does afflict our natures. I am sorry.
115 What, have you given him any hard words of late?

OPHELIA   No, my good lord, but as you did command,
I did repel his letters and denied
His access to me.

POLONIUS   That hath made him mad.
120 I am sorry that with better speed and judgement
I had not quoted him: I feared he did but trifle,
And meant to wreck thee. But beshrew my jealousy!
It seems it is as proper to our age
To cast beyond ourselves in our opinions
125 As it is common for the younger sort
To lack discretion. Come, go we to the king:
This must be known, which, being kept close, might move
More grief to hide than hate to utter love.   *Exeunt*

Act 2 Scene 2   *running scene 6*

Enter King, Queen, Rosencrantz and Guildenstern, with others

KING   Welcome, dear Rosencrantz and Guildenstern.
Moreover that we much did long to see you,
The need we have to use you did provoke
Our hasty sending. Something have you heard
5 Of Hamlet's transformation, so I call it,
Since not th'exterior nor the inward man
Resembles that it was. What it should be,
More than his father's death, that thus hath put him
So much from th'understanding of himself,
10 I cannot deem of. I entreat you both,
That, being of so young days brought up with him,

---

120 **speed** profit/promptness   121 **quoted** observed   122 **wreck** dishonor, ruin sexually
beshrew my jealousy curse my suspicion   123 **proper . . . age** i.e. typical of old men
124 **cast beyond ourselves** miscalculate/miss the mark (another angling metaphor)
127 **close** secret   **move . . . love** cause more unhappiness by concealment than
unpleasantness by coming forward   **2.2**   2 **Moreover that** in addition to the fact that
10 **deem** think, discern/judge

And since so neighboured to his youth and humour,
That you vouchsafe your rest here in our court
Some little time, so by your companies
15 To draw him on to pleasures, and to gather
So much as from occasions you may glean,
Whether aught, to us unknown, afflicts him thus,
That, opened, lies within our remedy.

GERTRUDE   Good gentlemen, he hath much talked of you,
20 And sure I am two men there are not living
To whom he more adheres. If it will please you
To show us so much gentry and good will
As to expend your time with us awhile,
For the supply and profit of our hope,
25 Your visitation shall receive such thanks
As fits a king's remembrance.

ROSENCRANTZ   Both your majesties
Might, by the sovereign power you have of us,
Put your dread pleasures more into command
30 Than to entreaty.

GUILDENSTERN   We both obey,
And here give up ourselves in the full bent
To lay our services freely at your feet,
To be commanded.

35 KING   Thanks, Rosencrantz and gentle Guildenstern.

GERTRUDE   Thanks, Guildenstern and gentle Rosencrantz.
And I beseech you instantly to visit
My too much changèd son.— Go, some of ye,
And bring the gentlemen where Hamlet is.

40 GUILDENSTERN   Heavens make our presence and our practices
Pleasant and helpful to him.

Exeunt [Ros. and Guild. with some Attendants]

---

12 **neighboured to** familiar with   **humour** temperament   13 **vouchsafe your rest** consent to
stay   16 **occasions** opportunities   18 **opened** revealed   21 **more adheres** is more attached
22 **gentry** courtesy   24 **supply and profit** fulfillment and advancement   28 **of** over
29 **dread pleasures** revered wishes   32 **in . . . bent** to the utmost   40 **practices** actions
(perhaps playing on the sense of "schemes")

GERTRUDE   Amen.

Enter Polonius

POLONIUS   Th'ambassadors from Norway, my good lord,
Are joyfully returned.

45 KING   Thou still hast been the father of good news.

POLONIUS   Have I, my lord? I assure you, my good liege,
I hold my duty, as I hold my soul,
Both to my God and to my gracious king:
And I do think, or else this brain of mine
50 Hunts not the trail of policy so sure
As I have used to do, that I have found
The very cause of Hamlet's lunacy.

KING   O, speak of that: that I do long to hear.

POLONIUS   Give first admittance to th'ambassadors:
55 My news shall be the fruit to that great feast.

KING   Thyself do grace to them and bring them in.—

[*Exit Polonius*]

He tells me, my sweet queen, that he hath found
The head and source of all your son's distemper.

GERTRUDE   I doubt it is no other but the main:
60 His father's death and our o'erhasty marriage.

Enter Polonius, Voltemand and Cornelius

KING   Well, we shall sift him.— Welcome, good friends.
Say, Voltemand, what from our brother Norway?

VOLTEMAND   Most fair return of greetings and desires.
Upon our first, he sent out to suppress
65 His nephew's levies, which to him appeared
To be a preparation gainst the Polack,
But, better looked into, he truly found
It was against your highness: whereat grieved
That so his sickness, age and impotence

---

45 **still** always   47 **hold** regard/uphold   50 **policy** shrewdness/statecraft   55 **fruit** i.e. dessert
56 **grace** honor (plays on sense of "prayer before a meal")   58 **distemper** illness,
derangement   59 **doubt** suspect   **main** chief concern   61 **sift him** question him (Polonius)
closely   63 **desires** good wishes   64 **Upon our first** as soon as we raised the matter
66 **Polack** Polish/King of Poland   69 **impotence** frailty, helplessness

70   Was falsely borne in hand, sends out arrests
     On Fortinbras, which he, in brief, obeys,
     Receives rebuke from Norway, and in fine
     Makes vow before his uncle never more
     To give th'assay of arms against your majesty.
75   Whereon old Norway, overcome with joy,
     Gives him three thousand crowns in annual fee
     And his commission to employ those soldiers,
     So levied as before, against the Polack,
     With an entreaty, herein further shown,   *Gives a paper*
80   That it might please you to give quiet pass
     Through your dominions for his enterprise
     On such regards of safety and allowance
     As therein are set down.
     KING   It likes us well,
85   And at our more considered time we'll read,
     Answer and think upon this business.
     Meantime we thank you for your well-took labour.
     Go to your rest: at night we'll feast together.
     Most welcome home!   *Exeunt Ambassadors*
90   POLONIUS   This business is very well ended.
     My liege, and madam, to expostulate
     What majesty should be, what duty is,
     Why day is day, night night, and time is time,
     Were nothing but to waste night, day and time.
95   Therefore, since brevity is the soul of wit,
     And tediousness the limbs and outward flourishes,
     I will be brief: your noble son is mad:
     Mad call I it, for, to define true madness,

---

70 borne in hand deluded, taken advantage of   **arrests** orders to cease military activity
72 fine conclusion   **74 give . . . arms** attempt to use force   **76 crowns** gold coins (of
varying values according to the countries they were used in)   **77 commission** authority
80 quiet pass safe passage   **82 On . . . allowance** i.e. according to conditions regarding the
safety of Denmark and your permission for such an enterprise   **84 likes** pleases   **85 at . . .
time** when we have the time for proper consideration   **91 expostulate** discuss/ask   **95 wit**
intellect/good sense   **98 for . . . mad** Polonius means that it would be mad to attempt to
define madness, but ends up implying, rather nonsensically, that the definition of madness is
"being mad"

What is't but to be nothing else but mad?

100   But let that go—

GERTRUDE   More matter, with less art.

POLONIUS   Madam, I swear I use no art at all.

That he is mad, 'tis true: 'tis true 'tis pity,

And pity it is true: a foolish figure,

105   But farewell it, for I will use no art.

Mad let us grant him, then, and now remains

That we find out the cause of this effect,

Or rather say, the cause of this defect,

For this effect defective comes by cause.

110   Thus it remains, and the remainder thus. Perpend:

I have a daughter — have whilst she is mine —

Who, in her duty and obedience, mark,

Hath given me this: now gather, and surmise.   *Shows a letter*

The letter   *Reads*

'To the celestial and my soul's idol, the most beautified

115   Ophelia'— That's an ill phrase, a vile phrase:

'beautified' is a vile phrase. But you shall hear these, 'in her

excellent white bosom', these—

GERTRUDE   Came this from Hamlet to her?

POLONIUS   Good madam, stay awhile: I will be faithful.

120   'Doubt thou the stars are fire,   *Reads*

Doubt that the sun doth move,

Doubt truth to be a liar,

But never doubt I love.

O dear Ophelia, I am ill at these numbers: I have not art to

125   reckon my groans; but that I love thee best, O, most best,

believe it. Adieu. Thine evermore, most dear lady, whilst this

machine is to him, Hamlet.'

---

104 figure figure of speech   109 this . . . cause this defective behavior (Hamlet's madness)
has a cause   110 Thus . . . thus this is the current state of affairs, and now for the rest
Perpend consider   113 gather, and surmise collect your thoughts, draw your conclusions (or
gather may be a request to Claudius and Gertrude to draw closer and look at the letter)
117 these i.e. this letter/these phrases   119 faithful i.e. to the letter/in reading the letter fully
122 Doubt in this third line the sense shifts to "suspect"   124 ill . . . numbers poor at writing
verse   125 reckon my groans count my groans/make my groans scan poetically
127 machine is to bodily structure belongs to

This in obedience hath my daughter showed me,
And more above, hath his solicitings,
130 As they fell out by time, by means and place,
All given to mine ear.

KING   But how hath she received his love?

POLONIUS   What do you think of me?

KING   As of a man faithful and honourable.

135 **POLONIUS**   I would fain prove so. But what might you think,
When I had seen this hot love on the wing —
As I perceived it, I must tell you that,
Before my daughter told me — what might you,
Or my dear majesty your queen here, think,
140 If I had played the desk or table-book,
Or given my heart a winking, mute and dumb,
Or looked upon this love with idle sight?
What might you think? No, I went round to work,
And my young mistress thus I did bespeak:
145 'Lord Hamlet is a prince, out of thy star:
This must not be.' And then I precepts gave her
That she should lock herself from his resort,
Admit no messengers, receive no tokens:
Which done, she took the fruits of my advice,
150 And he, repulsèd — a short tale to make —
Fell into a sadness, then into a fast,
Thence to a watch, thence into a weakness,
Thence to a lightness, and, by this declension
Into the madness whereon now he raves,
155 And all we wail for.

KING   Do you think 'tis this?   *To Gertrude*

GERTRUDE   It may be, very likely.

---

129 more above moreover   **130 fell out** occurred   **135 fain** willingly   **140 played . . . table-book** remained silent and withheld the information/assisted in conveying messages between them   **141 given . . . winking** closed the eyes of my heart   **142 with idle sight** complacently/without recognizing its significance   **143 round** roundly, in a forthright manner   **144 bespeak** address/speak angrily to   **145 out . . . star** beyond your reach/outside your destiny   **146 precepts** instructions   **147 resort** visits   **152 a watch** sleeplessness   **153 lightness** light-headedness   **declension** decline (plays on the grammatical sense)

POLONIUS   Hath there been such a time — I'd fain know that —
That I have positively said ''Tis so'
160   When it proved otherwise?

KING   Not that I know.

POLONIUS   Take this from this, if this be otherwise:

Points to his head and shoulders?

If circumstances lead me, I will find
Where truth is hid, though it were hid indeed
165   Within the centre.

KING   How may we try it further?

POLONIUS   You know sometimes he walks four hours together
Here in the lobby.

GERTRUDE   So he does indeed.

170   POLONIUS   At such a time I'll loose my daughter to him:
Be you and I behind an arras then: *To the King*
Mark the encounter: if he love her not
And be not from his reason fall'n thereon,
Let me be no assistant for a state,
175   But keep a farm and carters.

KING   We will try it.

Enter Hamlet reading on a book

GERTRUDE   But look where sadly the poor wretch comes
reading.

POLONIUS   Away, I do beseech you both away:
180   I'll board him presently. O, give me leave.—

Exeunt King and Queen

How does my good lord Hamlet?

HAMLET   Well, God-a-mercy.

POLONIUS   Do you know me, my lord?

HAMLET   Excellent, excellent well: you're a fishmonger.

185   POLONIUS   Not I, my lord.

---

163 circumstances circumstantial evidence   **165 centre** i.e. of the earth   **166 try** test   **170 loose** set loose (often used of an animal; sometimes with the sense of releasing the female to the male for sex, which would lend sexual connotations to **encounter**)   **171 arras** large tapestry wall-hanging   **173 thereon** on that account   **174 assistant . . . state** policy adviser   **175 carters** cart drivers   **177 sadly** solemnly   **180 board** accost   **presently** immediately   **give me leave** a polite way of asking to be left alone   **182 God-a-mercy** God have mercy (i.e. thank you)   **184 fishmonger** plays on slang senses of "lecher" and "pimp"

HAMLET	Then I would you were so honest a man.
POLONIUS	Honest, my lord?
HAMLET	Ay, sir: to be honest, as this world goes, is to be one man picked out of two thousand.
190	POLONIUS	That's very true, my lord.
HAMLET	For if the sun breed maggots in a dead dog, being a good kissing carrion— Have you a daughter?
POLONIUS	I have, my lord.
HAMLET	Let her not walk i'th'sun: conception is a blessing,
195		but not as your daughter may conceive. Friend, look to't.
POLONIUS	How say you by that? Still harping on my *Aside*
	daughter: yet he knew me not at first; he said I was a fishmonger. He is far gone, far gone: and truly in my youth I suffered much extremity for love, very near this. I'll speak to
200		him again.— What do you read, my lord?
HAMLET	Words, words, words.
POLONIUS	What is the matter, my lord?
HAMLET	Between who?
POLONIUS	I mean, the matter that you read, my lord.
205	HAMLET	Slanders, sir, for the satirical slave says here that old men have grey beards, that their faces are wrinkled, their eyes purging thick amber or plum-tree gum and that they have a plentiful lack of wit, together with weak hams: all which, sir, though I most powerfully and potently believe, yet
210		I hold it not honesty to have it thus set down, for you yourself, sir, should be old as I am, if like a crab you could go backward.
POLONIUS	Though this be madness, yet there is *Aside*
	method in't.— Will you walk out of the air, my lord?
215	HAMLET	Into my grave?
POLONIUS	Indeed, that is out o'th'air.— *Aside*

---

192 **good kissing carrion** good piece of rotting flesh to kiss (**carrion** also suggests "whore")
194 **i'th'sun** in public/in the sun (or "son") that causes breeding   **conception** understanding/
becoming pregnant   202 **matter** content (Hamlet plays on sense of "cause of a dispute")
207 **purging** discharging   **amber . . . gum** tree resin   208 **hams** legs   210 **honesty**
decent/honorable   211 **old** as old

How pregnant sometimes his replies are! A happiness that often madness hits on, which reason and sanity could not so prosperously be delivered of. I will leave him and suddenly contrive the means of meeting between him and my daughter.— My honourable lord, I will most humbly take my leave of you.

HAMLET   You cannot, sir, take from me anything that I will more willingly part withal: except my life, my life.

POLONIUS   Fare you well, my lord.

HAMLET   These tedious old fools.

Enter Rosencrantz and Guildenstern

POLONIUS   You go to seek my lord Hamlet; there he is.

ROSENCRANTZ   God save you, sir!   *To Polonius*

GUILDENSTERN   Mine honoured lord!   *[Exit Polonius]*

ROSENCRANTZ   My most dear lord!

HAMLET   My excellent good friends! How dost thou, Guildenstern? O, Rosencrantz! Good lads, how do ye both?

ROSENCRANTZ   As the indifferent children of the earth.

GUILDENSTERN   Happy, in that we are not over-happy: On fortune's cap we are not the very button.

HAMLET   Nor the soles of her shoe?

ROSENCRANTZ   Neither, my lord.

HAMLET   Then you live about her waist, or in the middle of her favours?

GUILDENSTERN   Faith, her privates we.

HAMLET   In the secret parts of fortune? O, most true: she is a strumpet. What's the news?

ROSENCRANTZ   None, my lord, but that the world's grown honest.

HAMLET   Then is doomsday near. But your news is not true. Let me question more in particular: what have you, my good friends, deserved at the hands of fortune that she sends you to prison hither?

---

217 **pregnant** meaningful/quick-witted (with childbearing connotations, continued in **delivered of**)   **happiness** fortuitousness   219 **suddenly** immediately   224 **withal** with   233 **indifferent** ordinary, average   234 **Happy** fortunate   235 **button** i.e. point at the very top of the cap   239 **favours** sexual favors (**middle** has vaginal connotations)   240 **privates** ordinary citizens/genitals   242 **strumpet** prostitute   245 **particular** detail

GUILDENSTERN   Prison, my lord?

HAMLET   Denmark's a prison.

250 ROSENCRANTZ   Then is the world one.

HAMLET   A goodly one, in which there are many confines,
wards and dungeons, Denmark being one o'th'worst.

ROSENCRANTZ   We think not so, my lord.

HAMLET   Why, then, 'tis none to you; for there is nothing
255   either good or bad but thinking makes it so: to me it is a
prison.

ROSENCRANTZ   Why then, your ambition makes it one: 'tis too
narrow for your mind.

HAMLET   O God, I could be bounded in a nutshell and count
260   myself a king of infinite space, were it not that I have bad
dreams.

GUILDENSTERN   Which dreams indeed are ambition, for the very
substance of the ambitious is merely the shadow of a dream.

HAMLET   A dream itself is but a shadow.

265 ROSENCRANTZ   Truly, and I hold ambition of so airy and light a
quality that it is but a shadow's shadow.

HAMLET   Then are our beggars bodies, and our monarchs
and outstretched heroes the beggars' shadows. Shall we to
th'court? For, by my fay, I cannot reason.

270 BOTH   We'll wait upon you.

HAMLET   No such matter: I will not sort you with the rest of
my servants, for, to speak to you like an honest man, I am
most dreadfully attended. But, in the beaten way of
friendship, what make you at Elsinore?

275 ROSENCRANTZ   To visit you, my lord, no other occasion.

---

251 confines places of confinement   **252 wards** prison cells   **263 substance . . . ambitious**
material that fuels ambition/stuff ambitious men are made of   **267 Then . . . shadows** i.e. if
ambition is nothing but shadow, then only unambitious beggars have bodily substance; their
shadows must then be made up of ambitious people such as **monarchs** and **heroes**
outstretched reaching out ambitiously/elongated like shadows   **269 fay** faith   **270 wait**
upon accompany (Hamlet emphasizes the sense of "serve")   **271 No such matter** i.e. I'll have
no such thing   **sort** class   **273 dreadfully attended** poorly waited upon (with possible play
on sense of "haunted by dire visions")   **beaten way** well-trodden path

HAMLET   Beggar that I am, I am even poor in thanks; but I thank you, and sure, dear friends, my thanks are too dear a halfpenny. Were you not sent for? Is it your own inclining? Is it a free visitation? Come, deal justly with me: come, come;
280   nay, speak.

GUILDENSTERN   What should we say, my lord?

HAMLET   Why, anything, but to the purpose. You were sent for, and there is a kind of confession in your looks which your modesties have not craft enough to colour: I know the
285   good king and queen have sent for you.

ROSENCRANTZ   To what end, my lord?

HAMLET   That you must teach me. But let me conjure you, by the rights of our fellowship, by the consonancy of our youth, by the obligation of our ever-preserved love, and by what
290   more dear a better proposer could charge you withal, be even and direct with me whether you were sent for or no?

ROSENCRANTZ   What say you?   *Aside to Guildenstern?*

HAMLET   Nay, then, I have an eye of you.—   *Aside?*
If you love me, hold not off.

295   GUILDENSTERN   My lord, we were sent for.

HAMLET   I will tell you why; so shall my anticipation prevent your discovery, and your secrecy to the king and queen moult no feather. I have of late — but wherefore I know not — lost all my mirth, forgone all custom of exercise; and
300   indeed it goes so heavily with my disposition that this goodly frame, the earth, seems to me a sterile promontory, this most excellent canopy, the air, look you, this brave o'erhanging

---

277 **too . . . halfpenny** too expensive at a halfpenny (i.e. worthless)/too expensive by a halfpenny (if the visitors are not being honest about the reason for their visit)
282 **anything . . . purpose** anything irrelevant, any lie you wish   284 **modesties** decency/sense of shame   **colour** disguise, excuse   287 **conjure** entreat, appeal to
288 **consonancy** harmony, friendship   289 **what more dear** whatever more precious thing
290 **proposer** questioner   **charge** urge, entreat   291 **even** level/honest   293 **of** on
296 **my . . . discovery** my saying it first mean that you are not forced to reveal anything
298 **moult no feather** remain undiminished   299 **custom of exercise** usual pursuits/gentlemanly activities   300 **heavily** dejectedly   301 **frame** framework, structure (like **canopy**, may also evoke the physical structure of the theater building)   **sterile promontory** barren point of land jutting out into the sea   302 **brave** splendid

firmament, this majestical roof fretted with golden fire, why,
it appears no other thing to me than a foul and pestilent
305   congregation of vapours. What a piece of work is a man!
How noble in reason, how infinite in faculty, in form and
moving how express and admirable, in action how like an
angel, in apprehension how like a god! The beauty of the
world, the paragon of animals — and yet, to me, what is this
310   quintessence of dust? Man delights not me — no, nor
woman neither, though by your smiling you seem to say so.

ROSENCRANTZ   My lord, there was no such stuff in my thoughts.

HAMLET   Why did you laugh when I said 'Man delights not
me'?

315   ROSENCRANTZ   To think, my lord, if you delight not in man,
what Lenten entertainment the players shall receive from
you: we coted them on the way, and hither are they coming
to offer you service.

HAMLET   He that plays the king shall be welcome; his majesty
320   shall have tribute of me: the adventurous knight shall use
his foil and target: the lover shall not sigh *gratis*: the
humorous man shall end his part in peace: the clown shall
make those laugh whose lungs are tickled o'th'sear: and the
lady shall say her mind freely, or the blank verse shall halt
325   for't. What players are they?

ROSENCRANTZ   Even those you were wont to take delight in, the
tragedians of the city.

HAMLET   How chances it they travel? Their residence, both in
reputation and profit, was better both ways.

---

303 firmament sky   fretted adorned   307 express well-designed/expressive/exact
308 apprehension understanding   310 quintessence essence/purest form (literally the "fifth
essence," of which heavenly bodies were composed and supposedly present in all matter)
316 Lenten entertainment poor reception/meager employment, i.e. appropriate to Lent
317 coted overtook   320 tribute homage/payment   321 foil and target sword and shield
gratis for nothing (Latin)   322 humorous moody or ill-tempered (with an imbalance of the
four bodily "humours," fluids thought to control mood)   323 tickled o'th'sear easily triggered
(to laughter)   sear part of the mechanism involved in firing a gun   324 halt limp (if the
actor playing the lady is interrupted by heckling from the audience the rhythm of his speech
will be lost)   326 wont accustomed   328 residence remaining in their usual home

330   ROSENCRANTZ   I think their inhibition comes by the means of the late innovation.

HAMLET   Do they hold the same estimation they did when I was in the city? Are they so followed?

ROSENCRANTZ   No, indeed, they are not.

335   HAMLET   How comes it? Do they grow rusty?

ROSENCRANTZ   Nay, their endeavour keeps in the wonted pace. But there is, sir, an eyrie of children, little eyases, that cry out on the top of question and are most tyrannically clapped for't: these are now the fashion, and so berattle the common

340   stages — so they call them — that many wearing rapiers are afraid of goose-quills and dare scarce come thither.

HAMLET   What, are they children? Who maintains 'em? How are they escoted? Will they pursue the quality no longer than they can sing? Will they not say afterwards, if they should

345   grow themselves to common players — as it is most like, if their means are no better — their writers do them wrong, to make them exclaim against their own succession?

ROSENCRANTZ   Faith, there has been much to-do on both sides, and the nation holds it no sin to tar them to controversy.

350   There was for a while no money bid for argument unless the poet and the player went to cuffs in the question.

HAMLET   Is't possible?

GUILDENSTERN   O, there has been much throwing about of brains.

355   HAMLET   Do the boys carry it away?

---

330 **inhibition** (city) ban on performing plays   331 **late innovation** recent political insurrection/new fashion for boy actors   332 **estimation** reputation   337 **eyrie** nest/brood **eyases** young hawks   **cry . . . question** shrilly dominate the debate (i.e. the rivalry between child and adult acting companies)   338 **tyrannically** outrageously/vehemently 339 **berattle . . . stages** clamor against the public theaters (where the adult acting companies perform)   340 **many . . . thither** many fashionable young men hardly dare attend the public theaters as they are so afraid of being mocked by the playwrights working for the boy actors 343 **escoted** supported   **quality** (acting) profession   **no . . . sing** i.e. only until their voices break   345 **common** i.e. adult   **like** likely   346 **means** financial resources 347 **succession** future professions   349 **tar** incite   350 **no . . . question** the acting companies paid for the plots of no new plays unless they featured the quarrel between the children's dramatists and the adult actors (or "without the playwright and the adult acting company coming to blows over the controversy")   355 **carry it away** win the day

ROSENCRANTZ   Ay, that they do, my lord: Hercules and his load
too.

HAMLET   It is not strange, for mine uncle is King of Denmark,
and those that would make mows at him while my father
360   lived, give twenty, forty, an hundred ducats a-piece for his
picture in little. There is something in this more than
natural, if philosophy could find it out.

Flourish for the Players

GUILDENSTERN   There are the players.

HAMLET   Gentlemen, you are welcome to Elsinore. Your hands,
365   come: the appurtenance of welcome is fashion and ceremony:
let me comply with you in the garb, lest my extent to the
players — which, I tell you, must show fairly outward —
should more appear like entertainment than yours. You are
welcome: but my uncle-father and aunt-mother are deceived.

370   GUILDENSTERN   In what, my dear lord?

HAMLET   I am but mad north-north-west: when the wind is
southerly I know a hawk from a handsaw.

Enter Polonius

POLONIUS   Well be with you, gentlemen.

HAMLET   Hark you, Guildenstern, and you too — at each ear
375   a hearer: that great baby you see there is not yet out of his
swathing-clouts.

ROSENCRANTZ   Happily he's the second time come to them, for
they say an old man is twice a child.

HAMLET   I will prophesy: he comes to tell me of the players,
380   mark it.— You say right, sir: for a Monday morning, 'twas so
indeed.

---

356 his load i.e. the world, carried on Hercules' shoulders (possibly a reference to the emblem
of the Globe Theatre)   **359 mows** mouths, grimaces   **360 ducats** gold coins   **361 picture in
little** miniature portrait   **more than natural** i.e. unnatural   **362 philosophy** science
Flourish trumpet fanfare   **365 appurtenance** appropriate accompaniment   **366 comply**
observe proper courtesies   **garb** appropriate manner   **my extent** the behavior I extend
367 fairly courteously   **368 entertainment** welcome   **371 but mad north-north-west** only
mad when the wind is in the north-northwest/only slightly mad (like a faulty compass that
points north-northwest rather than north)   **372 handsaw** handheld saw (some editors
emend to "hernshaw," a type of heron)   **376 swathing-clouts** swaddling-clothes in which a
newborn **baby** was wrapped   **377 Happily** perhaps   **380 You . . . indeed** Hamlet pretends to
Polonius that he is mid-conversation with his friends

POLONIUS   My lord, I have news to tell you.

HAMLET   My lord, I have news to tell you.
            When Roscius, an actor in Rome—

385   POLONIUS   The actors are come hither, my lord.

HAMLET   Buzz, buzz!

POLONIUS   Upon mine honour—

HAMLET   Then came each actor on his ass—

POLONIUS   The best actors in the world, either for tragedy,
390   comedy, history, pastoral, pastorical-comical, historical-
pastoral, tragical-historical, tragical-comical-historical-
pastoral, scene individable, or poem unlimited. Seneca
cannot be too heavy, nor Plautus too light. For the law of
writ and the liberty, these are the only men.

395   HAMLET   O Jephthah, judge of Israel, what a treasure hadst
thou!

POLONIUS   What a treasure had he, my lord?

HAMLET   Why,
            'One fair daughter and no more,
400   The which he loved passing well.'

POLONIUS   Still on my daughter.   *Aside*

HAMLET   Am I not i'th'right, old Jephthah?

POLONIUS   If you call me Jephthah, my lord, I have a daughter
that I love passing well.

405   HAMLET   Nay, that follows not.

POLONIUS   What follows, then, my lord?

HAMLET   Why,
            'As by lot, God wot',

---

384 Roscius a famous Roman actor   **386 Buzz, buzz!** dismissive exclamation made in
response to idle gossip or old news   **388 ass** may pun on "arse"   **392 scene individable** a
play observing the unities of time, place and action/a play whose genre is unclassifiable
poem unlimited dramatic verse (a play) that does not observe the unities of time, place and
action/a play whose genre is all-inclusive/a play that explores a general rather than a specific
question (a rhetorical application of **unlimited**)   **392 Seneca** Roman writer of tragedies
393 heavy sorrowful/weighty   **Plautus** Roman writer of comedies   **For . . . liberty** for plays
written according to the rules and for those that disregard all prescriptions   **395 O . . . thou!**
In the Bible, Jephthah vowed to God that if he was successful in war he would sacrifice the first
creature he met on his return home; he encountered his daughter but kept his word
399 "One . . . well." lines from a well-known ballad   **400 passing** surpassingly, exceedingly
405 follows not is not logical/is not the next line   **408 lot** chance   **wot** knows

and then, you know,

410   'It came to pass, as most like it was' —
       the first row of the pious chanson will show you more,
       for look where my abridgements come.—

Enter four or five Players

You're welcome, masters, welcome all.— I am glad to see
thee well.— Welcome, good friends.— O, my old friend! Thy
415   face is valanced since I saw thee last: com'st thou to beard
me in Denmark?— What, my young lady and mistress! By'r
lady, your ladyship is nearer heaven than when I saw you
last, by the altitude of a chopine. Pray God your voice, like a
piece of uncurrent gold, be not cracked within the ring.
420   Masters, you are all welcome. We'll e'en to't like French
falconers, fly at anything we see. We'll have a speech
straight: come, give us a taste of your quality: come, a
passionate speech.

FIRST PLAYER What speech, my lord?

425   HAMLET   I heard thee speak me a speech once, but it was
never acted, or if it was, not above once, for the play, I
remember, pleased not the million: 'twas caviar to the
general. But it was — as I received it, and others, whose
judgement in such matters cried in the top of mine — an
430   excellent play, well digested in the scenes, set down with as
much modesty as cunning. I remember one said there was
no sallets in the lines to make the matter savoury, nor no
matter in the phrase that might indict the author of

---

410 like likely   **411 row** line   **chanson** song   **412 my abridgements** things that cut me
short/entertainment (in either case, the arrival of the players)   **415 valanced** fringed (with a
beard)   **beard** defy, affront (plays on the usual sense)   **416 By'r lady** by Our Lady (the Virgin
Mary)   **417 your ladyship** addressed to a teenage apprentice actor who plays women's parts
418 chopine high woman's shoe with a very thick platform sole   **419 uncurrent** not legal
tender   **cracked . . . ring** i.e. broken, and therefore unfit for women's roles, with play on the
sense of "deflowered" (coins featured the monarch's head within a ring; if the coin was
damaged within the ring it was no longer valid)   **420 e'en to't** go straight to it   **422 straight**
straightaway   **quality** skill   **427 caviar . . . general** i.e. wasted on the unappreciative
multitude   **429 cried . . . of** was superior to   **430 digested** arranged   **431 modesty**
restraint/propriety   **cunning** skill, artistry   **432 sallets** salads or their components (i.e. spicy
parts, vulgar phrases)   **savoury** highly flavored   **433 indict** accuse

affectation, but called it an honest method, as wholesome as
435   sweet, and by very much more handsome than fine. One
speech in it I chiefly loved: 'twas Aeneas' tale to Dido, and
thereabout of it especially where he speaks of Priam's
slaughter: if it live in your memory, begin at this line — let
me see, let me see —

440   'The rugged Pyrrhus, like th'Hyrcanian beast'—
It is not so: it begins with Pyrrhus:

'The rugged Pyrrhus, he whose sable arms,
Black as his purpose, did the night resemble
When he lay couchèd in the ominous horse,
445   Hath now this dread and black complexion smeared
With heraldry more dismal: head to foot
Now is he total gules, horridly tricked
With blood of fathers, mothers, daughters, sons,
Baked and impasted with the parching streets
450   That lend a tyrannous and damnèd light
To their vile murders: roasted in wrath and fire,
And thus o'er-sizèd with coagulate gore,
With eyes like carbuncles, the hellish Pyrrhus
Old grandsire Priam seeks.'

455   So, proceed you.

POLONIUS   Fore God, my lord, well spoken, with good accent
and good discretion.

---

434 as . . . fine this line is missing from the Folio text, probably due to printer's error (the same goes for the short line at the end of Hamlet's speech)   **435 handsome than fine** seemly and graceful rather than showy   **436 Aeneas' . . . Dido** after the Trojan war Aeneas landed at Carthage, where Dido was queen; he told of his experiences and she fell in love with him   **437 Priam** king of Troy, killed by **Pyrrhus** during the attack on his city   **440 rugged** harsh, severe   **Pyrrhus** Achilles' son; after the death of his father in the Trojan war, he took part in the conflict and was noted for his vengeful savagery   **th'Hyrcanian beast** the tiger of Hyrcania (land bordering the Caspian Sea), known for its ferocity   **442 sable** black   **444 couchèd** hidden   **ominous horse** fateful wooden horse by which the Greeks gained access to Troy   **446 heraldry more dismal** i.e. blood, imaged as heraldic markings   **dismal** ominous, fatal   **447 total gules** entirely red (**gules** is a heraldic term)   **tricked** adorned/delineated (heraldic term for the sketching of a coat of arms)   **449 impasted** dried into a crust   **parching** scorching (because burning)   **450 tyrannous** harsh   **452 o'er-sizèd** covered, as if with size (a sticky substance used to treat paper)/rendered larger (through a thick covering of blood)   **coagulate** coagulated, congealed   **453 carbuncles** red gems supposed to emit light in the dark   **454 grandsire** grandfather (Priam had fifty sons and numerous grandchildren)   **457 discretion** judgment

FIRST PLAYER 'Anon he finds him
　　　　　　Striking too short at Greeks: his antique sword,
460　　　　Rebellious to his arm, lies where it falls,
　　　　　　Repugnant to command. Unequal matched,
　　　　　　Pyrrhus at Priam drives, in rage strikes wide,
　　　　　　But with the whiff and wind of his fell sword
　　　　　　Th'unnervèd father falls. Then senseless Ilium,
465　　　　Seeming to feel this blow, with flaming top
　　　　　　Stoops to his base, and with a hideous crash
　　　　　　Takes prisoner Pyrrhus' ear, for, lo, his sword,
　　　　　　Which was declining on the milky head
　　　　　　Of reverend Priam, seemed i'th'air to stick:
470　　　　So as a painted tyrant Pyrrhus stood,
　　　　　　And, like a neutral to his will and matter,
　　　　　　Did nothing.
　　　　　　But as we often see against some storm
　　　　　　A silence in the heavens, the rack stand still,
475　　　　The bold winds speechless and the orb below
　　　　　　As hush as death, anon the dreadful thunder
　　　　　　Doth rend the region, so, after Pyrrhus' pause,
　　　　　　Arousèd vengeance sets him new a-work,
　　　　　　And never did the Cyclops' hammers fall
480　　　　On Mars his armours forged for proof eterne
　　　　　　With less remorse than Pyrrhus' bleeding sword
　　　　　　Now falls on Priam.
　　　　　　Out, out, thou strumpet Fortune! All you gods
　　　　　　In general synod take away her power,
485　　　　Break all the spokes and fellies from her wheel,

---

458 Anon shortly   459 too short inadequately (presumably because of his old age)   antique
old   461 Repugnant resistant   463 whiff and wind i.e. mere slicing through the air   fell
fierce   464 Th'unnervèd the weakened   senseless incapable of feeling   Ilium Troy/the
royal palace at Troy   467 Takes . . . ear i.e. the noise arrests him in mid-action
468 declining descending   milky white with age   470 painted motionless as if in a
painting/blood-covered   471 like . . . matter suspended between his will and its effect
473 against in anticipation of/before   474 rack clouds   475 orb i.e. earth   477 region sky
479 Cyclops one-eyed giants who worked for the blacksmith god Vulcan making armor for the
gods   480 Mars his Mars' (Roman god of war)   proof eterne eternal impenetrability
481 remorse pity   484 synod assembly   485 fellies pieces of wood that form the rim of a
wheel   wheel the wheel of Fortune, according to the turns of which men rose or fell

And bowl the round nave down the hill of heaven,
As low as to the fiends!'

POLONIUS   This is too long.

HAMLET   It shall to th'barber's, with your beard.— Prithee,
490   say on: he's for a jig or a tale of bawdry, or he sleeps: say on;
come to Hecuba.

FIRST PLAYER 'But who, O, who had seen the mobled queen—'

HAMLET   'The mobled queen.'

POLONIUS   That's good: 'mobled queen' is good.

495 FIRST PLAYER 'Run barefoot up and down, threat'ning the flame
With bisson rheum, a clout about that head
Where late the diadem stood, and for a robe,
About her lank and all o'er-teemèd loins
A blanket, in th'alarm of fear caught up.
500   Who this had seen, with tongue in venom steeped,
Gainst Fortune's state would treason have pronounced:
But if the gods themselves did see her then
When she saw Pyrrhus make malicious sport
In mincing with his sword her husband's limbs,
505   The instant burst of clamour that she made —
Unless things mortal move them not at all —
Would have made milch the burning eyes of heaven,
And passion in the gods.'

POLONIUS   Look, whe'er he has not turned his colour and has
510   tears in's eyes. Pray you no more.

HAMLET   'Tis well: I'll have thee speak out the rest soon.—
Good my lord, will you see the players well bestowed? Do ye
hear, let them be well used, for they are the abstracts and
brief chronicles of the time: after your death you were better
515   have a bad epitaph than their ill report while you lived.

---

486 nave central part of the wheel, the hub   490 jig a light, often bawdy, entertainment that
took place after the main play and involved singing and dancing   491 Hecuba wife of King
Priam   492 who whoever   mobled muffled/veiled   496 bisson rheum blinding tears
clout cloth   497 late recently   diadem crown   498 lank shrunken, empty   o'er-teemèd
exhausted with childbearing   500 Who . . . seen whoever had seen this   501 state rule,
government   pronounced spoken   507 milch milk-producing, i.e. tearful   508 passion
(produced) grief   509 whe'er whether   512 bestowed lodged   513 used treated
abstracts summaries, epitomes

POLONIUS   My lord, I will use them according to their desert.

HAMLET   God's bodikins, man, better: use every man after his
desert, and who should scape whipping? Use them after your
own honour and dignity: the less they deserve, the more
520   merit is in your bounty. Take them in.

POLONIUS   Come, sirs.   *Exit Polonius*

HAMLET   Follow him, friends: we'll hear a play tomorrow.—
Dost thou hear me, old friend? Can you play   *To a Player*
The Murder of Gonzago?

A PLAYER   Ay, my lord.

525   HAMLET   We'll ha't tomorrow night. You could, for a need,
study a speech of some dozen or sixteen lines which I would
set down and insert in't, could ye not?

A PLAYER   Ay, my lord.

HAMLET   Very well. Follow that lord, and look you mock him
530   not.—   [*Exeunt Players*]
My good friends, I'll leave you till night. You are welcome to
Elsinore.

ROSENCRANTZ   Good my lord.

Exeunt [Rosencrantz and Guildenstern]. Hamlet remains

HAMLET   Ay, so, God buy ye.— Now I am alone.
535   O, what a rogue and peasant slave am I!
Is it not monstrous that this player here,
But in a fiction, in a dream of passion,
Could force his soul so to his whole conceit
That from her working all his visage wanned,
540   Tears in his eyes, distraction in's aspect,
A broken voice, and his whole function suiting
With forms to his conceit? And all for nothing!
For Hecuba!

516 **desert** merit, worth   517 **God's bodikins** by God's little body   **after** according to
520 **bounty** generosity   525 **ha't** have it   **for a need** if necessary   526 **study** memorize
537 **But** merely   538 **conceit** imagination   539 **her** i.e. conceit's, imagination's   **wanned**
paled   540 **distraction** distress, agitation   **aspect** expression/glance   541 **his . . . conceit**
all of his natural powers furnishing actions to match his imaginings

What's Hecuba to him, or he to Hecuba,
545   That he should weep for her? What would he do
Had he the motive and the cue for passion
That I have? He would drown the stage with tears
And cleave the general ear with horrid speech,
Make mad the guilty and appal the free,
550   Confound the ignorant and amaze indeed
The very faculty of eyes and ears. Yet I,
A dull and muddy-mettled rascal, peak
Like John-a-dreams, unpregnant of my cause,
And can say nothing: no, not for a king
555   Upon whose property and most dear life
A damned defeat was made. Am I a coward?
Who calls me villain? Breaks my pate across?
Plucks off my beard and blows it in my face?
Tweaks me by th'nose? Gives me the lie i'th'throat,
560   As deep as to the lungs? Who does me this?
Ha!
Why, I should take it, for it cannot be
But I am pigeon-livered and lack gall
To make oppression bitter, or ere this
565   I should have fatted all the region kites
With this slave's offal: bloody, bawdy villain!
Remorseless, treacherous, lecherous, kindless villain!
O, vengeance!
Why, what an ass am I! Ay, sure, this is most brave,
570   That I, the son of the dear murderèd,
Prompted to my revenge by heaven and hell,

---

546 **motive** provocation (modern sense of "motivation" of a dramatic character did not yet exist, though **cue** is clearly an actor's term)   548 **horrid** terrifying, horrifying   549 **appal** make pale/shock   **free** innocent   550 **Confound** stun/confuse   **the ignorant** those who know nothing of the crime   **amaze** bewilder/terrify/stun   552 **muddy-mettled** dull-spirited **peak** mope, languish   553 **John-a-dreams** general name for a dreamy person   **unpregnant of** sluggish toward, not prompted by   555 **property** regal identity/kingdom   556 **defeat** destruction   557 **pate** head   558 **Plucks off** pulls a tuft from   559 **Gives . . . lungs?** Calls me an outrageous liar?   560 **me this** this to me   563 **pigeon-livered** pigeons were proverbially gentle birds, supposed to lack **gall** (bitterness/anger)   565 **region kites** sky's birds of prey 566 **offal** intestines/remains   567 **Remorseless** pitiless   **kindless** unnatural   569 **brave** fine/bold

Must like a whore unpack my heart with words
And fall a-cursing, like a very drab, a scullion!
Fie upon't, foh! About, my brain! I have heard
575   That guilty creatures sitting at a play
Have by the very cunning of the scene
Been struck so to the soul that presently
They have proclaimed their malefactions:
For murder, though it have no tongue, will speak
580   With most miraculous organ. I'll have these players
Play something like the murder of my father
Before mine uncle: I'll observe his looks,
I'll tent him to the quick: if he but blench,
I know my course. The spirit that I have seen
585   May be the devil, and the devil hath power
T'assume a pleasing shape, yea, and perhaps,
Out of my weakness and my melancholy,
As he is very potent with such spirits,
Abuses me to damn me. I'll have grounds
590   More relative than this: the play's the thing
Wherein I'll catch the conscience of the king.   *Exit*

[Act 3 Scene 1]

running scene 7

*Enter King, Queen, Polonius, Ophelia, Rosencrantz, Guildenstern
and Lords*

KING   And can you by no drift of circumstance
Get from him why he puts on this confusion,
Grating so harshly all his days of quiet
With turbulent and dangerous lunacy?
5   ROSENCRANTZ   He does confess he feels himself distracted,
But from what cause he will by no means speak.

---

573 **drab** prostitute/slut   **scullion** lowest domestic servant   574 **About** about it, to work
576 **cunning** skill   577 **presently** immediately   578 **malefactions** wrongdoings, crimes
583 **tent** probe (as one would a wound)   **blench** flinch/turn pale   588 **spirits** i.e. **melancholy**
590 **relative** relevant/cogent/substantial   **3.1**   1 **drift of circumstance** course of roundabout
talk   3 **Grating** fretting/harping, dwelling querulously upon/wearing away

GUILDENSTERN   Nor do we find him forward to be sounded,
But with a crafty madness keeps aloof
When we would bring him on to some confession
10   Of his true state.

GERTRUDE   Did he receive you well?

ROSENCRANTZ   Most like a gentleman.

GUILDENSTERN   But with much forcing of his disposition.

ROSENCRANTZ   Niggard of question, but of our demands
15   Most free in his reply.

GERTRUDE   Did you assay him to any pastime?

ROSENCRANTZ   Madam, it so fell out that certain players
We o'erraught on the way: of these we told him,
And there did seem in him a kind of joy
20   To hear of it: they are about the court,
And, as I think, they have already order
This night to play before him.

POLONIUS   'Tis most true:
And he beseeched me to entreat your majesties
25   To hear and see the matter.

KING   With all my heart, and it doth much content me
To hear him so inclined.
Good gentlemen, give him a further edge
And drive his purpose on to these delights.

30   ROSENCRANTZ   We shall, my lord.

Exeunt [Rosencrantz and Guildenstern]

KING   Sweet Gertrude, leave us too.   ↓*Exit Lords*↓
For we have closely sent for Hamlet hither,
That he, as 'twere by accident, may here
Affront Ophelia:
35   Her father and myself, lawful espials,
Will so bestow ourselves that, seeing unseen,
We may of their encounter frankly judge,

---

7 forward ready, inclined   **sounded** questioned, probed   **13 disposition** inclination
14 Niggard of question sparing in his questions/reluctant to initiate conversation   **demands**
questions   **16 assay** try to tempt   **18 o'erraught** overtook   **28 edge** sharpness of
inclination/incitement   **32 closely** secretly/privately   **34 Affront** come face-to-face with
35 espials spies

And gather by him, as he is behaved,
If't be th'affliction of his love or no

40   That thus he suffers for.

GERTRUDE   I shall obey you.—
And for your part, Ophelia, I do wish
That your good beauties be the happy cause
Of Hamlet's wildness: so shall I hope your virtues

45   Will bring him to his wonted way again,
To both your honours.

OPHELIA   Madam, I wish it may.   *[Exit Gertrude]*

POLONIUS   Ophelia, walk you here.— Gracious, so please you,
We will bestow ourselves.— Read on this book,   *To Ophelia*

50   That show of such an exercise may colour   *Gives a book*
Your loneliness. We are oft to blame in this —
'Tis too much proved — that with devotion's visage
And pious action we do sugar o'er
The devil himself.

55   **KING**   O, 'tis true!   *Aside*
How smart a lash that speech doth give my conscience!
The harlot's cheek, beautied with plast'ring art,
Is not more ugly to the thing that helps it
Than is my deed to my most painted word.

60   O, heavy burden!

POLONIUS   I hear him coming: let's withdraw, my lord.

Exeunt [King and Polonius]

To a place from where they eavesdrop, while Ophelia pretends to read

Enter Hamlet

HAMLET   To be, or not to be, that is the question:
Whether 'tis nobler in the mind to suffer
The slings and arrows of outrageous fortune,

65   Or to take arms against a sea of troubles,
And by opposing end them? To die, to sleep —

---

48 Gracious your grace (addressed to the king)   **50 exercise** devout practice (the book is presumably of a religious nature)   **colour Your loneliness** account for the fact that you are alone   **52 visage** face, appearance   **57 plast'ring art** i.e. cosmetics   **58 to . . . it** compared to the cosmetics that improve it   **64 slings** catapults, ballista, cannons or the missiles hurled by them   **outrageous** excessively wicked/violent, cruel

No more — and by a sleep to say we end
The heartache and the thousand natural shocks
That flesh is heir to: 'tis a consummation
70   Devoutly to be wished. To die, to sleep:
To sleep, perchance to dream: ay, there's the rub,
For in that sleep of death what dreams may come
When we have shuffled off this mortal coil,
Must give us pause: there's the respect
75   That makes calamity of so long life,
For who would bear the whips and scorns of time,
The oppressor's wrong, the proud man's contumely,
The pangs of disprized love, the law's delay,
The insolence of office and the spurns
80   That patient merit of the unworthy takes,
When he himself might his quietus make
With a bare bodkin? Who would these fardels bear,
To grunt and sweat under a weary life,
But that the dread of something after death,
85   The undiscovered country from whose bourn
No traveller returns, puzzles the will,
And makes us rather bear those ills we have
Than fly to others that we know not of?
Thus conscience does make cowards of us all:
90   And thus the native hue of resolution
Is sicklied o'er with the pale cast of thought,
And enterprises of great pith and moment
With this regard their currents turn away,
And lose the name of action. Soft you now,

---

68 **shocks** violent blows/clashes with the enemy   69 **consummation** ending   71 **rub**
obstacle (a bowling term)   73 **shuffled off** cast off/evaded/got rid of in a perfunctory or
unsatisfactory manner   **mortal coil** bustle or turmoil of this mortal life   74 **respect**
consideration   75 **of . . . life** continue for so long   76 **scorns** insults, mockeries
77 **contumely** insolence, contempt, insulting language or behavior   78 **disprized**
undervalued/dishonored   79 **office** office-holders   **spurns** kicks   80 **of . . . takes** receives
from those who are unworthy   81 **quietus** discharge of debts (i.e. death)   82 **bare**
mere/unsheathed   **bodkin** dagger/awl/pointed instrument   **fardels** burdens   85 **bourn**
boundary   86 **puzzles** bewilders, confounds   89 **conscience** consciousness/introspection/
awareness of right and wrong   90 **native hue** natural color   91 **cast** tinge, shade   92 **pith**
and moment substance and importance   94 **Soft you** wait a moment

95   The fair Ophelia.— Nymph, in thy orisons
        Be all my sins remembered.

OPHELIA   Good my lord,
        How does your honour for this many a day?

HAMLET   I humbly thank you: well, well, well.

100 OPHELIA   My lord, I have remembrances of yours,
        That I have longèd long to re-deliver:
        I pray you now receive them.   *Offers love tokens*

HAMLET   No, no: I never gave you aught.

OPHELIA   My honoured lord, I know right well you did,
105   And with them words of so sweet breath composed
        As made the things more rich: their perfume lost,
        Take these again, for to the noble mind
        Rich gifts wax poor when givers prove unkind.
        There, my lord.   *Tries to hand over tokens*

110 HAMLET   Ha, ha! Are you honest?

OPHELIA   My lord?

HAMLET   Are you fair?

OPHELIA   What means your lordship?

HAMLET   That if you be honest and fair, your honesty should
115 admit no discourse to your beauty.

OPHELIA   Could beauty, my lord, have better commerce than
with honesty?

HAMLET   Ay, truly, for the power of beauty will sooner
transform honesty from what it is to a bawd than the force of
120 honesty can translate beauty into his likeness: this was
sometime a paradox, but now the time gives it proof. I did
love you once.

OPHELIA   Indeed, my lord, you made me believe so.

HAMLET   You should not have believed me, for virtue cannot so
125 inoculate our old stock but we shall relish of it: I loved you not.

---

95 orisons prayers   **100 remembrances** keepsakes, love tokens   **110 honest** chaste
112 fair beautiful   **114 your . . . beauty** your chastity should hold no dealings with your
beauty/your chastity should not permit anyone to converse with your beauty
116 commerce interaction (Hamlet picks up on the sense of "sexual dealings")   **120 his** its
(i.e. honesty's)   **121 sometime** once   **paradox** seemingly absurd statement/observation that
contradicts commonly held beliefs   **124 virtue . . . it** virtue cannot be so successfully grafted
onto an old sinful tree without some flavor of sin being retained

OPHELIA   I was the more deceived.

HAMLET   Get thee to a nunnery. Why wouldst thou be a breeder of sinners? I am myself indifferent honest, but yet I could accuse me of such things that it were better my mother
130   had not borne me: I am very proud, revengeful, ambitious, with more offences at my beck than I have thoughts to put them in, imagination to give them shape, or time to act them in. What should such fellows as I do crawling between heaven and earth? We are arrant knaves all: believe none of
135   us. Go thy ways to a nunnery. Where's your father?

OPHELIA   At home, my lord.

HAMLET   Let the doors be shut upon him, that he may play the fool nowhere but in's own house. Farewell.

OPHELIA   O, help him, you sweet heavens!

140   HAMLET   If thou dost marry, I'll give thee this plague for thy dowry: be thou as chaste as ice, as pure as snow, thou shalt not escape calumny. Get thee to a nunnery: go, farewell. Or, if thou wilt needs marry, marry a fool, for wise men know well enough what monsters you make of them. To a
145   nunnery, go, and quickly too. Farewell.

OPHELIA   O heavenly powers, restore him!

HAMLET   I have heard of your paintings too, well enough. God has given you one face and you make yourself another: you jig, you amble and you lisp, and nickname God's
150   creatures, and make your wantonness your ignorance. Go to, I'll no more on't: it hath made me mad. I say we will have no more marriages: those that are married already, all but one shall live: the rest shall keep as they are. To a nunnery, go.   *Exit Hamlet*

155   OPHELIA   O, what a noble mind is here o'erthrown!
The courtier's, soldier's, scholar's, eye, tongue, sword,

---

127 nunnery convent, playing on slang sense of "brothel"   **128 indifferent honest** moderately virtuous   **131 beck** command   **142 calumny** slander   **144 monsters** men with unfaithful wives were traditionally supposed to grow horns   **147 paintings** use of cosmetics
149 amble walk with an easy (or an exaggerated) motion   **lisp** speak in an affected manner
150 make . . . ignorance use innocence as an excuse for behavior that is willful/affected/promiscuous   **151 on't** of it

Th'expectancy and rose of the fair state,
The glass of fashion and the mould of form,
Th'observed of all observers, quite, quite down!
160 And I, of ladies most deject and wretched,
That sucked the honey of his music vows,
Now see that noble and most sovereign reason
Like sweet bells jangled out of tune and harsh,
That unmatched form and feature of blown youth
165 Blasted with ecstasy. O, woe is me,
T'have seen what I have seen, see what I see!

Enter King and Polonius   *From their hiding place*

KING   Love? His affections do not that way tend,
Nor what he spake, though it lacked form a little,
Was not like madness. There's something in his soul
170 O'er which his melancholy sits on brood,
And I do doubt the hatch and the disclose
Will be some danger, which to prevent,
I have in quick determination
Thus set it down: he shall with speed to England
175 For the demand of our neglected tribute.
Haply the seas and countries different
With variable objects shall expel
This something-settled matter in his heart,
Whereon his brains still beating puts him thus
180 From fashion of himself. What think you on't?

POLONIUS   It shall do well. But yet do I believe
The origin and commencement of this grief
Sprung from neglected love.— How now, Ophelia?
You need not tell us what Lord Hamlet said:
185 We heard it all. My lord, do as you please,

---

157 expectancy hope   **158 glass of fashion** mirror on whose image men model themselves
form etiquette/ideal pattern   **164 blown** blooming   **165 Blasted with ecstasy** destroyed by
madness   **167 affections** emotions   **170 on brood** brooding, like a bird sitting on eggs
171 doubt fear   **disclose** disclosure/hatching   **174 set it down** decided   **175 tribute**
regular amount paid by one state to another, usually in return for peace   **176 Haply**
perhaps/with luck   **177 objects** sights   **178 something-settled matter** somewhat fixed
preoccupation (perhaps with medical sense "festering pus" or, sinisterly, "stagnant blood")
180 fashion of himself his usual behavior, his old self

ld it fit, after the play

            nother all alone entreat him

        fs: let her be round with him,

      :d, so please you, in the ear

    .ir conference. If she find him not,

.v England send him, or confine him where

Your wisdom best shall think.

KING   It shall be so:

Madness in great ones must not unwatched go.   *Exeunt*

[Act 3 Scene 2]

Enter Hamlet and two or three of the Players

HAMLET   Speak the speech, I pray you, as I pronounced it to
you, trippingly on the tongue: but if you mouth it, as many
of your players do, I had as lief the town-crier had spoke my
lines. Nor do not saw the air too much with your hand, thus,

5   but use all gently; for in the very torrent, tempest, and, as I
may say, the whirlwind of passion, you must acquire and
beget a temperance that may give it smoothness. O, it offends
me to the soul to see a robustious periwig-pated fellow tear a
passion to tatters, to very rags, to split the ears of the

10   groundlings, who for the most part are capable of nothing
but inexplicable dumb shows and noise: I could have such a
fellow whipped for o'erdoing Termagant: it out-Herods
Herod. Pray you avoid it.

A PLAYER   I warrant your honour.

15 HAMLET   Be not too tame neither, but let your own discretion
be your tutor: suit the action to the word, the word to the

---

188 **round** blunt/severe   190 **find him not** fails to find the cause of his unhappiness
3.2   2 **trippingly** nimbly   **mouth** declaim, speak pompously   3 **as lief** as soon, rather
8 **robustious** boisterous/unruly   **periwig-pated** wig-wearing   10 **groundlings** members of
the audience standing in the yard in front of the stage, the cheapest place from which to watch
are capable of can understand   11 **dumb shows** mimes/unsophisticated spectacles
12 **Termagant** imaginary deity believed to have been worshipped by Muslims and represented
in the old mystery plays as a violent, overbearing person   13 **Herod** biblical king who
featured in the mystery plays as a raging tyrant   14 **warrant** assure   15 **discretion** judgment

action, with this special observance: that you o'erstep not
the modesty of nature; for anything so overdone is from the
purpose of playing, whose end, both at the first and now,
20 was and is to hold as 'twere the mirror up to nature, to show
virtue her own feature, scorn her own image, and the very
age and body of the time his form and pressure. Now this
overdone or come tardy off, though it make the unskilful
laugh, cannot but make the judicious grieve; the censure of
25 the which one must in your allowance o'erweigh a whole
theatre of others. O, there be players that I have seen play,
and heard others praise, and that highly — not to speak it
profanely — that, neither having the accent of Christians
nor the gait of Christian, pagan, nor no man, have so
30 strutted and bellowed that I have thought some of nature's
journeymen had made men and not made them well, they
imitated humanity so abominably.

A PLAYER   I hope we have reformed that indifferently with us,
sir.

35 **HAMLET**   O, reform it altogether. And let those that play your
clowns speak no more than is set down for them, for there be
of them that will themselves laugh, to set on some quantity
of barren spectators to laugh too, though in the meantime
some necessary question of the play be then to be
40 considered: that's villainous, and shows a most pitiful
ambition in the fool that uses it. Go, make you ready.—

Exeunt Players

Enter Polonius, Rosencrantz and Guildenstern

How now, my lord, will the king hear this piece of work?

POLONIUS   And the queen too, and that presently.

---

18 modesty restraints   **from** i.e. far from   **22 pressure** stamp, impression   **23 come tardy
off** performed inadequately   **unskilful** ignorant, unsophisticated   **24 censure** judgment/
criticism   **25 the which one** one of whom   **allowance** admission, acknowledgment
31 journeymen laborers   **32 abominably** plays on the popular misconception that the word
was derived from Latin *ab homine*, i.e. "away from man, unnatural" (previously spelled
"abhominably")   **33 indifferently** moderately well   **37 of** some among   **38 barren**
apathetic/dull-witted   **39 necessary question** important aspect   **41 uses** does, practices
43 presently imminently

HAMLET   Bid the players make haste.—   *Exit Polonius*

45   Will you two help to hasten them?

BOTH   We will, my lord.   *Exeunt [Rosencrantz and Guildenstern]*

Enter Horatio

HAMLET   What ho, Horatio!

HORATIO   Here, sweet lord, at your service.

HAMLET   Horatio, thou art e'en as just a man

50   As e'er my conversation coped withal.

HORATIO   O, my dear lord—

HAMLET   Nay, do not think I flatter,

For what advancement may I hope from thee

That no revenue hast but thy good spirits

55   To feed and clothe thee? Why should the poor be flattered?

No, let the candied tongue lick absurd pomp,

And crook the pregnant hinges of the knee

Where thrift may follow fawning. Dost thou hear?

Since my dear soul was mistress of her choice

60   And could of men distinguish, her election

Hath sealed thee for herself, for thou hast been

As one, in suffering all, that suffers nothing,

A man that fortune's buffets and rewards

Hath ta'en with equal thanks: and blest are those

65   Whose blood and judgement are so well commingled

That they are not a pipe for fortune's finger

To sound what stop she please. Give me that man

That is not passion's slave, and I will wear him

In my heart's core, ay, in my heart of heart,

70   As I do thee. Something too much of this.

There is a play tonight before the king:

One scene of it comes near the circumstance

Which I have told thee of my father's death:

---

50 As . . . withal as ever my dealings with people brought me into contact with   **56 candied** sugared (i.e. flattering)   **57 crook** bend   **pregnant** ready   **58 thrift** profit   **60 election** choice   **61 sealed** designated (literally, placed a legally binding seal upon)   **62 As . . . nothing** like one who endures everything with fortitude and is not wounded by any of it   **suffering** undergoing/enduring (the sense then shifts to "is hurt by")   **63 buffets** blows   **65 blood** passion   **67 stop** note produced by placing the finger over a hole in a wind instrument   **69 core** puns on the Latin *cor* meaning "heart"

I prithee, when thou see'st that act afoot,

75 Even with the very comment of thy soul

Observe mine uncle: if his occulted guilt

Do not itself unkennel in one speech,

It is a damnèd ghost that we have seen,

And my imaginations are as foul

80 As Vulcan's stithy. Give him heedful note,

For I mine eyes will rivet to his face,

And after we will both our judgements join

In censure of his seeming.

HORATIO   Well, my lord.

85 If he steal aught the whilst this play is playing

And scape detecting, I will pay the theft.

Enter King, Queen, Polonius, Ophelia, Rosencrantz, Guildenstern and
other Lords Attendant with his Guard carrying torches. Danish march.
Sound a flourish

HAMLET   They are coming to the play: I must be idle.

Get you a place.

KING   How fares our cousin Hamlet?

90 HAMLET   Excellent, i'faith, of the chameleon's dish: I eat the
air, promise-crammed: you cannot feed capons so.

KING   I have nothing with this answer, Hamlet: these
words are not mine.

HAMLET   No, nor mine now.— My lord, you   *To Polonius*

95 played once i'th'university, you say?

POLONIUS   That I did, my lord, and was accounted a good actor.

HAMLET   And what did you enact?

POLONIUS   I did enact Julius Caesar: I was killed i'th'Capitol:
Brutus killed me.

---

75 the . . . soul your most insightful, penetrating consideration   **76 occulted** hidden
77 unkennel reveal (as a fox is driven out of its hole)   **78 damnèd** i.e. evil, devilish   **79 foul**
black, grimy   **80 Vulcan's stithy** the forge of Vulcan, Roman god of fire and blacksmiths
heedful note careful attention   **83 censure . . . seeming** forming an opinion of his appearance
85 steal aught gets away with anything   *march* i.e. march played on drums   **87 idle**
unoccupied/mad   **89 fares** is (but Hamlet responds to the sense of "feeds")   **90 chameleon's**
dish supposedly these reptiles fed on **air**   **91 capons** castrated cockerels fattened to make their
meat more flavorsome   **92 have nothing with** gain nothing from   **93 not mine** nothing to do
with my question (Hamlet responds to the sense of "do not belong to me")   **98 i'th'Capitol** at
Capitoline Hill, site of the temple of supreme Roman god Jupiter

100 HAMLET   It was a brute part of him to kill so capital a calf
        there.— Be the players ready?

ROSENCRANTZ   Ay, my lord: they stay upon your patience.

GERTRUDE   Come hither, my good Hamlet, sit by me.

HAMLET   No, good mother, here's metal more attractive.

105 POLONIUS   O, ho! Do you mark that?   *To King*

HAMLET   Lady, shall I lie in your lap?

OPHELIA   No, my lord.

HAMLET   I mean, my head upon your lap?

OPHELIA   Ay, my lord.

110 HAMLET   Do you think I meant country matters?

OPHELIA   I think nothing, my lord.

HAMLET   That's a fair thought to lie between maids' legs.

OPHELIA   What is, my lord?

HAMLET   Nothing.

115 OPHELIA   You are merry, my lord.

HAMLET   Who, I?

OPHELIA   Ay, my lord.

HAMLET   O, God, your only jig-maker. What should a man do
        but be merry? For look you how cheerfully my mother looks,
120   and my father died within's two hours.

OPHELIA   Nay, 'tis twice two months, my lord.

HAMLET   So long? Nay then, let the devil wear black, for I'll
        have a suit of sables. O heavens! Die two months ago, and not
        forgotten yet? Then there's hope a great man's memory may
125   outlive his life half a year: but, by'r lady, he must build
        churches, then, or else shall he suffer not thinking on, with
        the hobby-horse, whose epitaph is 'For, O, for, O, the hobby-
        horse is forgot.'

---

100 brute brutal/stupid/animal (with obvious pun on **Brutus**)   **part** deed/role   **calf** fool
102 stay . . . patience await your permission (to start)   **104 metal more attractive** more
magnetic metal (**metal** puns on "mettle" for an additional sense of "one of a more pleasing
disposition")   **106 lie . . . lap** recline upon your lap/have sex with you   **110 country matters**
sex (**country** puns on "cunt")   **114 Nothing** i.e. "no thing" (vagina)   **118 your only jig-
maker** I'm your unrivaled composer of jigs (bawdy playlets)   **123 suit of sables** luxurious suit
trimmed with dark-colored sable fur   **126 suffer . . . on** be forgotten   **127 hobby-horse**
artificial horse fastened around the waist of one of the participants in a morris dance; **the
hobby-horse is forgot** was a popular phrase

Hautboys play. The dumb show enters
Enter a King and Queen very lovingly, the Queen embracing him. She
kneels, and makes show of protestation unto him. He takes her up, and
declines his head upon her neck: lays him down upon a bank of flowers:
she, seeing him asleep, leaves him. Anon comes in a fellow, takes off his
crown, kisses it, and pours poison in the King's ears, and exits. The
Queen returns, finds the King dead, and makes passionate action. The
Poisoner, with some two or three Mutes, comes in again, seeming to
lament with her. The dead body is carried away. The Poisoner woos the
Queen with gifts: she seems loath and unwilling awhile, but in the end
accepts his love.   *Exeunt*

OPHELIA   What means this, my lord?

130 HAMLET   Marry, this is miching malicho: that means mischief.

OPHELIA   Belike this show imports the argument of the play.

HAMLET   We shall know by these fellows: the players cannot
        keep counsel, they'll tell all.

OPHELIA   Will they tell us what this show meant?

135 HAMLET   Ay, or any show that you'll show him: be not you
        ashamed to show, he'll not shame to tell you what it means.

OPHELIA   You are naught, you are naught: I'll mark the play.

Enter Prologue

PROLOGUE   For us, and for our tragedy,
        Here stooping to your clemency,
140   We beg your hearing patiently.   [*Exit*]

HAMLET   Is this a prologue, or the posy of a ring?

OPHELIA   'Tis brief, my lord.

HAMLET   As woman's love.

Enter [two Players as] King and his Queen [Baptista]

PLAYER KING   Full thirty times hath Phoebus' cart gone round
145   Neptune's salt wash and Tellus' orbèd ground,

Hautboys oboe-like instruments   *protestation* solemn declaration (of love)   *passionate*
action gestures of extreme grief   *Mutes* i.e. other actors   **130 miching malicho** lurking
iniquity, skulking mischief   **131 Belike** presumably   **argument** plot   **133 counsel** a secret
135 show sexual display   **be not you** if you are not   **137 naught** indecent/offensive
141 posy of a ring short (usually clichéd) verse motto engraved on a ring   **144 Phoebus' cart**
the sun god's chariot   **145 Neptune's salt wash** i.e. the sea (of which Neptune was god)
Tellus' orbèd ground i.e. the earth (of which Tellus was goddess)

And thirty dozen moons with borrowed sheen
About the world have times twelve thirties been,
Since love our hearts and Hymen did our hands
Unite commutual in most sacred bands.

150 BAPTISTA   So many journeys may the sun and moon
Make us again count o'er ere love be done!
But, woe is me, you are so sick of late,
So far from cheer and from your former state,
That I distrust you: yet, though I distrust,
155 Discomfort you, my lord, it nothing must,
For women's fear and love holds quantity,
In neither aught, or in extremity.
Now, what my love is, proof hath made you know,
And as my love is sized, my fear is so.

160 PLAYER KING Faith, I must leave thee, love, and shortly too:
My operant powers my functions leave to do.
And thou shalt live in this fair world behind,
Honoured, beloved: and haply one as kind
For husband shalt thou—

165 BAPTISTA   O, confound the rest!
Such love must needs be treason in my breast:
In second husband let me be accurst!
None wed the second but who killed the first.

HAMLET   Wormwood, wormwood.   *Aside?*

170 BAPTISTA   The instances that second marriage move
Are base respects of thrift, but none of love:
A second time I kill my husband dead,
When second husband kisses me in bed.

146 **borrowed sheen** reflected radiance   148 **Hymen** god of marriage   149 **bands** bonds
154 **distrust** fear for   155 **Discomfort** dismay, discourage   156 **holds quantity** are to be found
in the same proportions   157 **In . . . extremity** they are either nonexistent or excessive
158 **proof** tried and tested experience   159 **as . . . so** my fear is just as great as my love
161 **operant** vital/active   **leave to do** cease to perform   165 **confound** destroy (i.e. do not
say)   168 **None** no woman   169 **Wormwood** i.e. that's bitter (the sharp-tasting plant was
also used to purge the digestive tract of worms, so there may also be a suggestion of bringing
forth gnawing guilt)   170 **instances** motives   **move** prompt   171 **respects of thrift**
considerations of personal profit

PLAYER KING I do believe you think what now you speak,
175   But what we do determine oft we break.
             Purpose is but the slave to memory,
             Of violent birth, but poor validity,
             Which now, like fruit unripe, sticks on the tree,
             But fall unshaken when they mellow be.
180   Most necessary 'tis that we forget
             To pay ourselves what to ourselves is debt:
             What to ourselves in passion we propose,
             The passion ending, doth the purpose lose.
             The violence of either grief or joy
185   Their own enactures with themselves destroy:
             Where joy most revels, grief doth most lament;
             Grief joys, joy grieves, on slender accident.
             This world is not for aye, nor 'tis not strange
             That even our loves should with our fortunes change,
190   For 'tis a question left us yet to prove,
             Whether love lead fortune, or else fortune love.
             The great man down, you mark his favourites flies:
             The poor advanced makes friends of enemies.
             And hitherto doth love on fortune tend,
195   For who not needs shall never lack a friend,
             And who in want a hollow friend doth try,
             Directly seasons him his enemy.
             But, orderly to end where I begun,
             Our wills and fates do so contrary run
200   That our devices still are overthrown:
             Our thoughts are ours, their ends none of our own.
             So think thou wilt no second husband wed,
             But die thy thoughts when thy first lord is dead.

---

176 Purpose . . . validity our intentions are subject to the weakness of memory, being
passionate at the outset, but lacking in endurance   **178 Which** i.e. **purpose**   **180 Most . . .
debt** it is inevitable that we should forget to fulfill our obligations to ourselves   **185 enactures**
fulfillments, performances   **187 Grief . . . accident** i.e. one extreme of emotion turns to its
opposite at the slightest event   **188 aye** ever   **192 down** fallen in fortune   **193 poor
advanced** poor man who improves his station in life   **194 hitherto** up to this point (in the
argument)   **tend** attend/serve   **195 who not needs** he who does not lack fortune
196 who in want he who, being in need   **try** test   **197 seasons him** ripens him into
200 devices plans   **still** continually   **201 ends** outcomes

	BAPTISTA	Nor earth to me give food, nor heaven light,

BAPTISTA   Nor earth to me give food, nor heaven light,
205   Sport and repose lock from me day and night,
              Each opposite that blanks the face of joy
              Meet what I would have well and it destroy!
              Both here and hence pursue me lasting strife,
              If, once a widow, ever I be wife!

210 HAMLET   If she should break it now!

PLAYER KING   'Tis deeply sworn. Sweet, leave me here awhile:
              My spirits grow dull, and fain I would beguile
              The tedious day with sleep.

BAPTISTA   Sleep rock thy brain,   *[He] sleeps*
215   And never come mischance between us twain.   *Exit*

HAMLET   Madam, how like you this play?

GERTRUDE   The lady protests too much, methinks.

HAMLET   O, but she'll keep her word.

KING   Have you heard the argument? Is there no offence
220   in't?

HAMLET   No, no, they do but jest, poison in jest: no offence
       i'th'world.

KING   What do you call the play?

HAMLET   *The Mousetrap.* Marry, how? Tropically. This play is
225   the image of a murder done in Vienna: Gonzago is the duke's
          name, his wife, Baptista. You shall see anon: 'tis a knavish
          piece of work, but what o'that? Your majesty and we that
          have free souls, it touches us not: let the galled jade wince,
          our withers are unwrung.

Enter Lucianus

230   This is one Lucianus, nephew to the king.

OPHELIA   You are a good chorus, my lord.

---

204 Nor let neither   **205 Sport . . . night** let me be barred from recreation during the day and
rest at night   **206 opposite** opposing force   **blanks** makes pale   **207 Meet . . . destroy** (may
it) encounter and destroy everything that I would like to see prosper   **208 here and hence** in
this and in the next world   **212 fain** willingly   **beguile** while away   **217 protests** makes
declarations, vows   **219 offence** offensive matter (Hamlet shifts the sense to "actual
injury/real crime")   **221 jest** pretend, act   **224 Tropically** figuratively   **225 duke's** i.e. king's
228 galled jade saddle-sore old horse   **wince** kick out from pain   **229 withers** part of the
horse's back between the shoulder blades   **unwrung** not pinched or chafed   **231 chorus**
actor who narrated or interpreted parts of a play

HAMLET   I could interpret between you and your love, if I could see the puppets dallying.

OPHELIA   You are keen, my lord, you are keen.

235   HAMLET   It would cost you a groaning to take off my edge.

OPHELIA   Still better, and worse.

HAMLET   So you mis-take your husbands.— Begin, murderer: pox, leave thy damnable faces, and begin. Come, the croaking raven doth bellow for revenge.

240   LUCIANUS   Thoughts black, hands apt, drugs fit and time agreeing,
Confederate season, else no creature seeing,
Thou mixture rank, of midnight weeds collected,
With Hecate's ban thrice blasted, thrice infected,
245   Thy natural magic and dire property,
On wholesome life usurp immediately.

Pours the poison in his ears

HAMLET   He poisons him i'th'garden for's estate. His name's Gonzago: the story is extant and writ in choice Italian. You shall see anon how the murderer gets the love of Gonzago's
250   wife.   *King stands*

OPHELIA   The king rises.

HAMLET   What, frighted with false fire?

GERTRUDE   How fares my lord?

POLONIUS   Give o'er the play.

255   KING   Give me some light. Away!

ALL   Lights, lights, lights!   *Exeunt. Hamlet and Horatio remain*

---

232 interpret provide dialogue as an actor does in a puppet show/act as a go-between
233 puppets possibly plays on a sense of "breasts/genitals"   . **dallying** spending idle time
together/flirting/having sex   **234 keen** quick/cutting   **235 groaning** the moans of a woman
losing her virginity (or possibly subsequently, in labor)   **take . . . edge** deter my sharp
wit/blunt my sexual appetite/cause me to lose my erection   **236 better, and worse** i.e. wittier,
yet more insulting   **237 So** in just such a manner   **mis-take your husbands** swear
insincerely to love and be faithful to your husbands (according to the marriage vow "for better
or for worse"); plays on the idea of "mistaking" another man for one's true husband, as Hamlet
deems Gertrude to have done   **238 pox** i.e. a plague on it   **239 the . . . revenge** refers to lines
from the anonymous *True Tragedy of Richard III*   **raven** considered a bird of ill omen whose cry
heralded death   **242 Confederate . . . seeing** the occasion itself an ally, there being no one else
to see me   **243 rank** virulent/pungent/foul   **244 Hecate's ban** the curse of Hecate, goddess of
witchcraft   **245 dire property** dreadful nature   **246 wholesome** healthy   **247 for's** for his
His i.e. the king's   **252 false fire** the discharge of blank cartridges from a firearm

HAMLET   Why, let the strucken deer go weep,
The hart ungallèd play,
For some must watch, while some must sleep:
260   So runs the world away.
Would not this, sir, and a forest of feathers — if the rest of
my fortunes turn Turk with me — with two Provincial
roses on my razed shoes, get me a fellowship in a cry of
players, sir?

265   HORATIO   Half a share.

HAMLET   A whole one, I.
For thou dost know, O Damon dear,
This realm dismantled was
Of Jove himself, and now reigns here
270   A very, very — pajock.

HORATIO   You might have rhymed.

HAMLET   O, good Horatio, I'll take the ghost's word for a
thousand pound. Didst perceive?

HORATIO   Very well, my lord.

275   HAMLET   Upon the talk of the poisoning?

HORATIO   I did very well note him.

HAMLET   O, ha! Come, some music. Come, the recorders.
For if the king like not the comedy,
Why then, belike, he likes it not, perdy.
280   Come, some music!

Enter Rosencrantz and Guildenstern

GUILDENSTERN   Good my lord, vouchsafe me a word with you.

HAMLET   Sir, a whole history.

---

257 strucken wounded   **258 hart ungallèd** uninjured male deer   **259 watch** remain awake
261 this the play/the verse just uttered   **feathers** i.e. elaborate plumes on a hat   **262 turn
Turk with** abandon (like one renouncing Christianity to become a Muslim)   **Provincial roses**
French roses from Provence (here rosettes, worn to hide the shoe fastenings and, like the
feathers, a feature of the actor's garb)   **263 razed shoes** shoes with ornamental cuts in the
leather   **fellowship . . . cry** partnership in a pack   **265 share** the major players in the
Chamberlain's Men had shares in the company's assets   **267 Damon** either an allusion to the
Greek tale of Damon and Pythias, famous for their great friendship, or used as a traditional
pastoral name   **268 dismantled** stripped/deprived   **269 Jove** supreme Roman god
270 pajock either "patchock" (i.e. base, ragged fellow) or "peacock"   **271 rhymed** the word
that might be expected to rhyme with **was** is "ass"   **279 perdy** corruption of the French *par
dieu* ("by God")   **281 vouchsafe** permit

GUILDENSTERN   The king, sir—

HAMLET   Ay, sir, what of him?

285   GUILDENSTERN   Is in his retirement marvellous distempered.

HAMLET   With drink, sir?

GUILDENSTERN   No, my lord, rather with choler.

HAMLET   Your wisdom should show itself more richer to
signify this to his doctor, for for me to put him to his
290   purgation would perhaps plunge him into far more choler.

GUILDENSTERN   Good my lord, put your discourse into some
frame and start not so wildly from my affair.

HAMLET   I am tame, sir: pronounce.

GUILDENSTERN   The queen, your mother, in most great affliction
295   of spirit, hath sent me to you.

HAMLET   You are welcome.

GUILDENSTERN   Nay, good my lord, this courtesy is not of the
right breed. If it shall please you to make me a wholesome
answer, I will do your mother's commandment: if not, your
300   pardon and my return shall be the end of my business.

HAMLET   Sir, I cannot.

GUILDENSTERN   What, my lord?

HAMLET   Make you a wholesome answer: my wit's diseased.
But, sir, such answers as I can make, you shall command, or
305   rather, as you say, my mother: therefore no more, but to the
matter: my mother, you say—

ROSENCRANTZ   Then thus she says: your behaviour hath struck
her into amazement and admiration.

HAMLET   O, wonderful son, that can so astonish a mother!
310   But is there no sequel at the heels of this mother's
admiration?

---

285 **retirement** withdrawal to his rooms   **distempered** out of humor (Hamlet chooses to understand the sense of "drunk")   287 **choler** anger (provoked by an excess of bile, one of the four bodily humours)   289 **signify** communicate   290 **purgation** cleansing the body through bloodletting or the use of emetics or laxatives (Hamlet plays on the idea of eliciting confession; the senses of legal and spiritual purging are also relevant)   292 **frame** order   **start** swerve/recoil   298 **breed** kind/courtly breeding   **wholesome** healthy, sane   300 **pardon** permission (to leave)   308 **amazement** bewilderment/alarm   **admiration** astonishment, wonder   309 **wonderful** astonishing/excellent

ROSENCRANTZ   She desires to speak with you in her closet ere
you go to bed.

HAMLET   We shall obey, were she ten times our mother. Have
315   you any further trade with us?

ROSENCRANTZ   My lord, you once did love me.

HAMLET   So I do still, by these pickers and stealers.

ROSENCRANTZ   Good my lord, what is your cause of distemper?
You do freely bar the door of your own liberty, if you deny
320   your griefs to your friend.

HAMLET   Sir, I lack advancement.

ROSENCRANTZ   How can that be, when you have the voice of the
king himself for your succession in Denmark?

HAMLET   Ay, but 'While the grass grows' — the proverb is
325   something musty.

Enter one with a recorder

O, the recorder! Let me see.   *Takes the recorder*
To withdraw with you: why do you go   *to Rosencrantz*
about to recover the wind of me, as if   *and Guildenstern*
you would drive me into a toil?

330   GUILDENSTERN   O, my lord, if my duty be too bold, my love is too
unmannerly.

HAMLET   I do not well understand that. Will you play upon
this pipe?

GUILDENSTERN   My lord, I cannot.

335   HAMLET   I pray you.

GUILDENSTERN   Believe me, I cannot.

HAMLET   I do beseech you.

GUILDENSTERN   I know no touch of it, my lord.

HAMLET   'Tis as easy as lying: govern these ventages with
340   your finger and thumb, give it breath with your mouth and it

---

312 **closet** private room   315 **trade** dealings (a deliberately derogatory term here)
317 **pickers and stealers** hands   319 **liberty** freedom from mental anguish (but a suggestive
image of literal imprisonment)   **deny** refuse to tell   324 **"While . . . grows"** the rest of the
proverb is "the horse starves"   327 **withdraw** speak privately   328 **recover . . . toil** a hunting
metaphor: the hunter would get to the windward side of the prey (**recover the wind**), allowing
it to scent him and thus driving the animal in the opposite direction and into a net (**toil**)
330 **if . . . unmannerly** i.e. if I am overly bold in my behavior it is my love for you that is to
blame   339 **ventages** holes (or **stops**)

will discourse most excellent music. Look you, these are the stops.

GUILDENSTERN   But these cannot I command to any utterance of harmony: I have not the skill.

345 HAMLET   Why, look you now, how unworthy a thing you make of me! You would play upon me; you would seem to know my stops, you would pluck out the heart of my mystery, you would sound me from my lowest note to the top of my compass, and there is much music, excellent voice, in

350 this little organ, yet cannot you make it speak. Why, do you think that I am easier to be played on than a pipe? Call me what instrument you will, though you can fret me, you cannot play upon me.— God bless you, sir! *To the entering Polonius*

Enter Polonius

POLONIUS   My lord, the queen would speak with you, and

355 presently.

HAMLET   Do you see that cloud that's almost in shape like a camel?

POLONIUS   By th'mass, and it's like a camel indeed.

HAMLET   Methinks it is like a weasel.

360 POLONIUS   It is backed like a weasel.

HAMLET   Or like a whale?

POLONIUS   Very like a whale.

HAMLET   Then will I will come to my mother by and by.— *Aside* They fool me to the top of my bent.— I will come by and by.

365 POLONIUS   I will say so.   *Exit*

HAMLET   'By and by' is easily said.

Leave me, friends.   [*Exeunt all but Hamlet*]

'Tis now the very witching time of night,

When churchyards yawn and hell itself breathes out

370 Contagion to this world: now could I drink hot blood

And do such bitter business as the day

---

348 mystery secret/craft, skill (playing an instrument)   **sound** question/produce music from
349 compass range   **352 fret** irritate/provide with frets (ridges for fingering on a lute)
355 presently straightaway   **358 By th'mass** by the Mass (a common oath)   **364 fool . . .**
bent indulge me in my foolishness to the limit/force me to play the fool to the limit of my ability
(or endurance)

Would quake to look on. Soft, now to my mother.
O heart, lose not thy nature; let not ever
The soul of Nero enter this firm bosom:
375   Let me be cruel, not unnatural.
I will speak daggers to her, but use none.
My tongue and soul in this be hypocrites:
How in my words somever she be shent,
To give them seals never my soul consent!   [*Exit*]

[Act 3 Scene 3]   *running scene 9*

Enter King, Rosencrantz and Guildenstern

KING   I like him not, nor stands it safe with us
To let his madness range. Therefore prepare you:
I your commission will forthwith dispatch,
And he to England shall along with you.
5   The terms of our estate may not endure
Hazard so dangerous as doth hourly grow
Out of his lunacies.
GUILDENSTERN   We will ourselves provide:
Most holy and religious fear it is
10   To keep those many many bodies safe
That live and feed upon your majesty.
ROSENCRANTZ   The single and peculiar life is bound
With all the strength and armour of the mind
To keep itself from noyance, but much more
15   That spirit upon whose weal depends and rests
The lives of many. The cease of majesty
Dies not alone, but like a gulf doth draw
What's near it with it: it is a massy wheel

---

373 nature natural feelings   **374 Nero** Roman emperor who murdered his mother
378 How . . . shent however much I rebuke and punish her verbally   **somever** to whatever
extent   **379 give them seals** i.e. by acting upon them   **3.3   1 him** i.e. his behavior
3 dispatch make ready/deal with promptly   **5 terms . . . estate** conditions or responsibilities
of my position as king   **8 provide** prepare, equip   **9 fear** concern, responsibility
12 single and peculiar individual and private   **14 noyance** vexation/harm   **15 weal** welfare
16 cease cessation/decease   **17 gulf** whirlpool   **18 massy** massive/weighty

Fixed on the summit of the highest mount,
20 To whose huge spokes ten thousand lesser things
Are mortised and adjoined, which, when it falls,
Each small annexment, petty consequence,
Attends the boist'rous ruin. Never alone
Did the king sigh, but with a general groan.
25 KING   Arm you, I pray you, to this speedy voyage,
For we will fetters put upon this fear,
Which now goes too free-footed.
BOTH   We will haste us.

Exeunt Gentlemen [Rosencrantz and Guildenstern]

Enter Polonius
POLONIUS   My lord, he's going to his mother's closet:
30 Behind the arras I'll convey myself
To hear the process. I'll warrant she'll tax him home,
And, as you said, and wisely was it said,
'Tis meet that some more audience than a mother,
Since nature makes them partial, should o'erhear
35 The speech, of vantage. Fare you well, my liege:
I'll call upon you ere you go to bed,
And tell you what I know.
KING   Thanks, dear my lord.—   [*Exit Polonius*]
O, my offence is rank, it smells to heaven:
40 It hath the primal eldest curse upon't,
A brother's murder. Pray can I not,
Though inclination be as sharp as will:
My stronger guilt defeats my strong intent,
And like a man to double business bound,
45 I stand in pause where I shall first begin,
And both neglect. What if this cursèd hand
Were thicker than itself with brother's blood,

---

21 **mortised** fastened securely   22 **annexment** adjunct, hanger-on   **petty consequence**
trivial attachment   23 **attends** accompanies   **boist'rous** massive/turbulent   25 **Arm you**
prepare yourselves   31 **process** proceedings   **tax him home** reprove him thoroughly
33 **meet** fitting   35 **of vantage** in addition/from an advantageous position   39 **rank** foul-
smelling/rotten   40 **primal eldest curse** God's curse on Cain, the first murderer, who killed
his brother Abel (biblical)   42 **inclination . . . will** my urge and determination to pray are
equally strong   44 **bound** directed/tied/sworn

Is there not rain enough in the sweet heavens
To wash it white as snow? Whereto serves mercy
50   But to confront the visage of offence?
And what's in prayer but this two-fold force,
To be forestallèd ere we come to fall,
Or pardoned being down? Then I'll look up:
My fault is past. But, O, what form of prayer
55   Can serve my turn? 'Forgive me my foul murder'?
That cannot be, since I am still possessed
Of those effects for which I did the murder:
My crown, mine own ambition and my queen.
May one be pardoned and retain th'offence?
60   In the corrupted currents of this world
Offence's gilded hand may shove by justice,
And oft 'tis seen the wicked prize itself
Buys out the law. But 'tis not so above:
There is no shuffling, there the action lies
65   In his true nature, and we ourselves compelled,
Even to the teeth and forehead of our faults,
To give in evidence. What then? What rests?
Try what repentance can. What can it not?
Yet what can it, when one cannot repent?
70   O, wretched state! O, bosom black as death!
O, limèd soul that, struggling to be free,
Art more engaged! Help, angels, make assay!
Bow, stubborn knees, and heart with strings of steel,   *Kneels*
Be soft as sinews of the newborn babe!
75   All may be well.
    Enter Hamlet

---

49 Whereto . . . offence? What is the point of mercy if not to confront sin face-to-face?
52 forestallèd prevented   **55 turn** need, purpose   **57 effects** benefits, acquisitions
59 th'offence i.e. the profits gained from committing the offense   **60 currents** courses,
practices   **61 gilded** golden/bearing bribes   **by** to one side   **64 There** i.e. above, in heaven
shuffling evasion, deceit   **the action lies** the sin is laid bare/the case is admissible (legal
metaphor, continued with **evidence**)   **66 to . . . forehead** in the very face   **67 give in** give,
submit   **rests** remains   **71 limèd** caught as a bird is trapped by bird-lime (sticky substance
spread on branches)   **72 assay** a great effort/an attempt

HAMLET   Now might I do it pat, now he is praying: *Draws*
And now I'll do't. And so he goes to heaven,
And so am I revenged. That would be scanned:
A villain kills my father, and for that,
80 I, his foul son, do this same villain send
To heaven.
O, this is hire and salary, not revenge.
He took my father grossly, full of bread,
With all his crimes broad blown, as fresh as May,
85 And how his audit stands who knows save heaven?
But in our circumstance and course of thought
'Tis heavy with him: and am I then revenged,
To take him in the purging of his soul,
When he is fit and seasoned for his passage?
90 No.   *Puts up his sword*
Up, sword, and know thou a more horrid hent:
When he is drunk asleep, or in his rage,
Or in th'incestuous pleasure of his bed,
At gaming, swearing, or about some act
95 That has no relish of salvation in't,
Then trip him, that his heels may kick at heaven,
And that his soul may be as damned and black
As hell, whereto it goes. My mother stays.
This physic but prolongs thy sickly days.   *Exit*
100 KING   My words fly up, my thoughts remain below:
Words without thoughts never to heaven go.   *Exit*

---

76 pat opportunely, conveniently   **78 would be scanned** needs to be examined/would be interpreted as follows   **80 foul** sinful/treacherous/shameful; most editors prefer Quarto's "sole"   **82 hire and salary** i.e. as if Hamlet had hired Claudius to do the murder and was now giving him his wages   **83 grossly . . . bread** i.e. in the grips of worldly pleasures, with no spiritual preparation (such as fasting)   **84 broad blown** in full bloom   **85 audit** account **86 circumstance . . . thought** situation and way of thinking/limited condition and way of thinking/indirect way of thinking   **87 heavy** grave/gloomy   **88 take him** kill Claudius **89 seasoned** prepared   **passage** journey into the next world   **91 hent** time to be seized at/opportunity   **92 drunk asleep** in a drunken stupor   **95 relish** trace, flavor   **98 stays** awaits   **99 physic** medicine (either Claudius' prayer or Hamlet's postponement of the murder)

[Act 3 Scene 4]

Enter Queen and Polonius

POLONIUS   He will come straight. Look you lay home to him:
Tell him his pranks have been too broad to bear with,
And that your grace hath screened and stood between
Much heat and him. I'll silence me e'en here.

5   Pray you, be round with him.

HAMLET   Mother, mother, mother!   *Within*

GERTRUDE   I'll warrant you,
Fear me not: withdraw, I hear him coming.

Enter Hamlet   *Polonius hides behind the arras*

10   HAMLET   Now, mother, what's the matter?

GERTRUDE   Hamlet, thou hast thy father much offended.

HAMLET   Mother, you have my father much offended.

GERTRUDE   Come, come, you answer with an idle tongue.

HAMLET   Go, go, you question with a wicked tongue.

15   GERTRUDE   Why, how now, Hamlet?

HAMLET   What's the matter now?

GERTRUDE   Have you forgot me?

HAMLET   No, by the rood, not so:
You are the queen, your husband's brother's wife,

20   But — would you were not so — you are my mother.

GERTRUDE   Nay, then, I'll set those to you that can speak.

HAMLET   Come, come, and sit you down, you shall not budge:
You go not till I set you up a glass
Where you may see the inmost part of you.

25   GERTRUDE   What wilt thou do? Thou wilt not murder me?
Help, help, ho!

POLONIUS   What, ho? Help, help, help!   *Behind the arras*

HAMLET   How now? A rat? Dead, for a ducat, dead!   *Draws*

POLONIUS   O, I am slain!   *[Hamlet] kills Polonius*

3.4   1 straight straightaway   **lay home** speak plainly, take to task   **2 broad** unrestrained
4 heat i.e. Claudius' anger   **5 round** blunt/severe   **18 rood** Christian cross   **19 queen**
perhaps this puns on "quean" (i.e. whore)   **23 glass** mirror   **28 Dead . . . ducat** i.e. I'll bet a
ducat (gold coin) he'll soon be dead/I'll kill him for a mere ducat

30	GERTRUDE	O me, what hast thou done?
	HAMLET	Nay, I know not: is it the king?
	GERTRUDE	O, what a rash and bloody deed is this!
	HAMLET	A bloody deed: almost as bad, good mother,
		As kill a king and marry with his brother.
35	GERTRUDE	As kill a king?
	HAMLET	Ay, lady, 'twas my word.— *Discovers Polonius*

Thou wretched, rash, intruding fool, farewell.
I took thee for thy better: take thy fortune;
Thou find'st to be too busy is some danger.—
40 Leave wringing of your hands. Peace. Sit you down,
And let me wring your heart, for so I shall,
If it be made of penetrable stuff,
If damnèd custom have not brazed it so
That it is proof and bulwark against sense.

45	GERTRUDE	What have I done, that thou dar'st wag thy tongue
		In noise so rude against me?
	HAMLET	Such an act

That blurs the grace and blush of modesty,
Calls virtue hypocrite, takes off the rose
50 From the fair forehead of an innocent love
And sets a blister there, makes marriage vows
As false as dicers' oaths: O, such a deed
As from the body of contraction plucks
The very soul, and sweet religion makes
55 A rhapsody of words. Heaven's face doth glow:
Yea, this solidity and compound mass
With tristful visage, as against the doom,
Is thought-sick at the act.

	GERTRUDE	Ay me, what act,
60		That roars so loud and thunders in the index?

---

39 **busy** interfering, prying   43 **brazed** covered with brass, hardened   44 **proof . . . sense**
fortified against feeling   **proof** armor   46 **rude** violent/harsh/offensive   53 **contraction**
binding agreement (specifically the marriage contract)   55 **rhapsody** confused mass   **glow**
i.e. blush for shame   56 **this . . . mass** i.e. the earth   57 **tristful** sorrowful   **as . . . doom** as if
in anticipation of doomsday   60 **index** table of contents that prefaces the body of a book

HAMLET   Look here, upon this picture, and on this,   *Shows her*
             The counterfeit presentment of two brothers.   *two pictures*
             See what a grace was seated on his brow:
             Hyperion's curls, the front of Jove himself,
65   An eye like Mars to threaten or command,
             A station like the herald Mercury
             New-lighted on a heaven-kissing hill,
             A combination and a form indeed
             Where every god did seem to set his seal
70   To give the world assurance of a man:
             This was your husband. Look you now, what follows:
             Here is your husband, like a mildewed ear,
             Blasting his wholesome brother. Have you eyes?
             Could you on this fair mountain leave to feed
75   And batten on this moor? Ha! Have you eyes?
             You cannot call it love, for at your age
             The heyday in the blood is tame, it's humble,
             And waits upon the judgement: and what judgement
             Would step from this to this? What devil was't
80   That thus hath cozened you at hoodman-blind?
             O, shame, where is thy blush? Rebellious hell,
             If thou canst mutine in a matron's bones,
             To flaming youth let virtue be as wax
             And melt in her own fire. Proclaim no shame
85   When the compulsive ardour gives the charge,
             Since frost itself as actively doth burn
             And reason panders will.

---

62 **counterfeit presentment** painted representation   64 **Hyperion** Greek god of the sun, and one of the Titans   **front** forehead/face   65 **Mars** Roman god of war   66 **station** manner of standing   **Mercury** winged messenger of the Roman gods   67 **New-lighted** newly alighted   69 **seal** i.e. mark of approval   72 **ear** i.e. of corn   73 **Blasting** withering   74 **leave** cease   75 **batten** feed greedily   **moor** marshland/waste ground (may play on the sense of "dark-skinned person" to contrast with the **fair mountain**)   77 **heyday . . . blood** (youthful) period of sexual excitement   80 **cozened** cheated   **hoodman-blind** blind-man's-buff (Hamlet imagines a blindfolded Gertrude being tricked into picking the wrong man)   82 **mutine** mutiny   **matron** mature married woman   85 **compulsive . . . charge** compelling sexual passion (of youth) attacks   86 **frost** i.e. age   87 **panders** acts as a go-between for/ministers to the gratification of   **will** sexual desire

GERTRUDE   O Hamlet, speak no more:
Thou turn'st mine eyes into my very soul,
90   And there I see such black and grainèd spots
As will not leave their tinct.

HAMLET   Nay, but to live
In the rank sweat of an enseamèd bed,
Stewed in corruption, honeying and making love
95   Over the nasty sty—

GERTRUDE   O, speak to me no more:
These words like daggers enter in mine ears.
No more, sweet Hamlet!

HAMLET   A murderer and a villain,
100   A slave that is not twentieth part the tithe
Of your precedent lord, a vice of kings,
A cutpurse of the empire and the rule,
That from a shelf the precious diadem stole,
And put it in his pocket!

105   GERTRUDE   No more!

Enter Ghost

HAMLET   A king of shreds and patches—
Save me, and hover o'er me with your wings,   *Sees the Ghost*
You heavenly guards!— What would you, gracious figure?

GERTRUDE   Alas, he's mad!

110   HAMLET   Do you not come your tardy son to chide,
That, lapsed in time and passion, lets go by
Th'important acting of your dread command? O, say!

GHOST   Do not forget: this visitation
Is but to whet thy almost blunted purpose.
115   But look, amazement on thy mother sits.

---

90 grainèd ingrained, indelible   **91 leave their tinct** abandon their color   **93 enseamèd**
saturated with grease or pig's fat, i.e. soiled from sexual activity   **94 Stewed** soaked/slowly
boiled (puns on "stew"—i.e. brothel)   **honeying** exchanging endearments   **making love**
talking amorously/having sex   **95 nasty** filthy/lewd/repellent   **sty** pigsty/place inhabited by
whores and lustful people   **100 tithe** tenth part   **101 precedent lord** previous husband
(**precedent** may have connotations of "exemplary/higher ranking")   **vice** epitome of
wickedness/buffoon or trickster from morality plays   **102 cutpurse** pickpocket   **103 diadem**
crown   **106 shreds and patches** paltry bits and pieces/the multicolored clothing of a fool or
clown   **112 important** urgent, pressing

O, step between her and her fighting soul:
Conceit in weakest bodies strongest works:
Speak to her, Hamlet.

HAMLET   How is it with you, lady?

120   GERTRUDE   Alas, how is't with you,
That you do bend your eye on vacancy
And with th'incorporal air do hold discourse?
Forth at your eyes your spirits wildly peep,
And, as the sleeping soldiers in th'alarm,

125   Your bedded hair, like life in excrements,
Start up and stand on end. O gentle son,
Upon the heat and flame of thy distemper
Sprinkle cool patience. Whereon do you look?

HAMLET   On him, on him! Look you how pale he glares!

130   His form and cause conjoined, preaching to stones,
Would make them capable.— Do not look upon me,   *To the*
Lest with this piteous action you convert   *Ghost*
My stern effects: then what I have to do
Will want true colour; tears perchance for blood.

135   GERTRUDE   To who do you speak this?

HAMLET   Do you see nothing there?

GERTRUDE   Nothing at all, yet all that is I see.

HAMLET   Nor did you nothing hear?

GERTRUDE   No, nothing but ourselves.

140   HAMLET   Why, look you there: look, how it steals away.
My father, in his habit as he lived!
Look where he goes even now out at the portal.   *Exit [Ghost]*

GERTRUDE   This is the very coinage of your brain:
This bodiless creation ecstasy is very cunning in.

---

117 **Conceit** imagination   122 **th'incorporal** the insubstantial   123 **spirits** vital spirits, a
bodily fluid thought to be vital for life   124 **as . . . th'alarm** like soldiers awoken abruptly by a
call to arms   125 **like . . . excrements** as if growths of hair had lives of their own
130 **His . . . conjoined** the combination of his appearance and his reason (for wanting revenge)
131 **capable** responsive   132 **piteous** pity-inspiring   **convert . . . effects** divert me from the
grim deeds I intend to carry out   134 **want** lack   **colour** character, quality/motive,
grounds/hue (colorless **tears** rather than red **blood**)   141 **habit** clothing/demeanor
as as when/as if   143 **coinage** invention   144 **cunning** skillful/crafty

145 **HAMLET**   Ecstasy?

My pulse as yours doth temperately keep time,

And makes as healthful music: it is not madness

That I have uttered. Bring me to the test,

And I the matter will reword, which madness

150 Would gambol from. Mother, for love of grace,

Lay not a flattering unction to your soul

That not your trespass, but my madness speaks:

It will but skin and film the ulcerous place,

Whilst rank corruption, mining all within,

155 Infects unseen. Confess yourself to heaven,

Repent what's past, avoid what is to come,

And do not spread the compost o'er the weeds

To make them ranker. Forgive me this my virtue,

For in the fatness of these pursy times

160 Virtue itself of vice must pardon beg,

Yea, curb and woo for leave to do him good.

GERTRUDE   O Hamlet, thou hast cleft my heart in twain.

HAMLET   O, throw away the worser part of it,

And live the purer with the other half.

165 Goodnight. But go not to mine uncle's bed:

Assume a virtue, if you have it not.

Refrain tonight,

And that shall lend a kind of easiness

To the next abstinence. Once more, goodnight:

170 And when you are desirous to be blessed,

I'll blessing beg of you. For this same lord,   *Points to the body*

I do repent, but heaven hath pleased it so

To punish me with this, and this with me,

That I must be their scourge and minister.

175 I will bestow him, and will answer well

---

149 **reword** repeat   150 **gambol** spring away   151 **unction** ointment   152 **trespass** sin
153 **skin and film** form a thin skin over   154 **mining** corroding/undermining/sapping
158 **ranker** more abundant   **virtue** i.e. virtuous talk and rebukes   159 **pursy** short-
winded/fat   161 **curb and woo** bow and entreat   174 **That** so that   **scourge and minister**
agent of retribution   175 **bestow** dispose of/stow away   **answer well** justify/pay for

The death I gave him. So, again, goodnight.
I must be cruel, only to be kind:
Thus bad begins and worse remains behind.

GERTRUDE   What shall I do?

180   HAMLET   Not this by no means that I bid you do:
Let the bloat king tempt you again to bed,
Pinch wanton on your cheek, call you his mouse,
And let him, for a pair of reechy kisses,
Or paddling in your neck with his damned fingers,

185   Make you to ravel all this matter out,
That I essentially am not in madness,
But mad in craft. 'Twere good you let him know,
For who that's but a queen, fair, sober, wise,
Would from a paddock, from a bat, a gib,

190   Such dear concernings hide? Who would do so?
No, in despite of sense and secrecy,
Unpeg the basket on the house's top,
Let the birds fly, and like the famous ape,
To try conclusions, in the basket creep,

195   And break your own neck down.

GERTRUDE   Be thou assured, if words be made of breath
And breath of life, I have no life to breathe
What thou hast said to me.

HAMLET   I must to England: you know that?

200   GERTRUDE   Alack,
I had forgot: 'tis so concluded on.

HAMLET   This man shall set me packing:
I'll lug the guts into the neighbour room.
Mother, goodnight. Indeed this counsellor

---

178 behind yet to come   **181 bloat** bloated/flabby/swollen with self-indulgence   **182 Pinch
wanton** in pinching your cheeks leave marks that proclaim you a wanton (lewd woman)
mouse common term of endearment   **183 reechy** filthy, squalid (literally "smoky")
185 ravel . . . out unravel (i.e. reveal) all this business   **187 in craft** through cunning, by
design   **189 paddock . . . gib** toad, bat, tomcat (creatures popularly supposed to be the
familiars of witches)   **190 dear concernings** important matters   **192 Unpeg** unfasten (thus
letting the **birds** out)   **193 famous . . . down** a reference to a lost story; presumably the ape
attempted to imitate the birds who had been released from the basket by climbing in, then
leaping out in the hope of flying, only to succeed in breaking his neck   **194 try conclusions**
experiment   **202 set me packing** cause me to be sent away at once/make me begin plotting

205 Is now most still, most secret and most grave,

Who was in life a foolish prating knave.—

Come, sir, to draw toward an end with you.—

Goodnight, mother.   *Exit Hamlet tugging in Polonius*

Enter King

 KING There's matter in these sighs, these profound heaves,

210 You must translate: 'tis fit we understand them.

Where is your son?

 GERTRUDE Ah, my good lord, what have I seen tonight!

 KING What, Gertrude? How does Hamlet?

 GERTRUDE Mad as the seas and wind when both contend

215 Which is the mightier: in his lawless fit,

Behind the arras hearing something stir,

He whips his rapier out and cries, 'A rat, a rat!'

And in his brainish apprehension kills

The unseen good old man.

220 KING O, heavy deed!

It had been so with us, had we been there.

His liberty is full of threats to all:

To you yourself, to us, to everyone.

Alas, how shall this bloody deed be answered?

225 It will be laid to us, whose providence

Should have kept short, restrained and out of haunt

This mad young man: but so much was our love,

We would not understand what was most fit,

But, like the owner of a foul disease,

230 To keep it from divulging, lets it feed

Even on the pith of life. Where is he gone?

 GERTRUDE To draw apart the body he hath killed,

O'er whom his very madness, like some ore

---

205 **still . . . grave** quiet, trustworthy and dignified/dead 206 **prating** prattling, chattering
207 **draw . . . you** finish my dealings with you/haul you to your grave 209 **matter**
significance 218 **brainish apprehension** headstrong conviction/deluded understanding
220 **heavy** sorrowful 224 **answered** accounted for 225 **providence** foresight/
arrangements 226 **short** on a tight leash **haunt** company 230 **divulging** becoming
apparent 232 **apart** away 233 **ore** precious metal

Among a mineral of metals base,
235   Shows itself pure: he weeps for what is done.
KING   O Gertrude, come away!
The sun no sooner shall the mountains touch,
But we will ship him hence, and this vile deed
We must with all our majesty and skill,
240   Both countenance and excuse.—

Enter Rosencrantz and Guildenstern

Ho, Guildenstern!
Friends both, go join you with some further aid.
Hamlet in madness hath Polonius slain,
And from his mother's closet hath he dragged him:
Go seek him out, speak fair, and bring the body
245   Into the chapel. I pray you haste in this.

Exeunt Gentlemen [Ros. and Guild.]

Come, Gertrude, we'll call up our wisest friends
To let them know, both what we mean to do
And what's untimely done. O, come away!
My soul is full of discord and dismay.   *Exeunt*

[Act 4 Scene 1]   *running scene 11*

Enter Hamlet

HAMLET   Safely stowed.
GENTLEMEN   Hamlet, Lord Hamlet!   *Within*
HAMLET   What noise? Who calls on Hamlet? O, here they come.

Enter Rosencrantz and Guildenstern   *With Attendants?*

ROSENCRANTZ   What have you done, my lord, with the dead body?
5   HAMLET   Compounded it with dust, whereto 'tis kin.
ROSENCRANTZ   Tell us where 'tis, that we may take it thence
and bear it to the chapel.
HAMLET   Do not believe it.

---

234 **mineral** mine or its products   240 **countenance** confront/bear out   248 **what's untimely done** i.e. Polonius' premature death   1 **Stowed** lodged (refers to Polonius' body); plays on slang sense of "kept quiet," "shut up"   5 **Compounded** united, mingled

ROSENCRANTZ   Believe what?

10   HAMLET   That I can keep your counsel and not mine own.
Besides, to be demanded of a sponge, what replication
should be made by the son of a king?

ROSENCRANTZ   Take you me for a sponge, my lord?

HAMLET   Ay, sir, that soaks up the king's countenance, his
15   rewards, his authorities. But such officers do the king best
service in the end: he keeps them, like an ape an apple, in the
corner of his jaw, first mouthed to be last swallowed: when
he needs what you have gleaned, it is but squeezing you,
and, sponge, you shall be dry again.

20   ROSENCRANTZ   I understand you not, my lord.

HAMLET   I am glad of it: a knavish speech sleeps in a foolish
ear.

ROSENCRANTZ   My lord, you must tell us where the body is, and
go with us to the king.

25   HAMLET   The body is with the king, but the king is not with
the body. The king is a thing—

GUILDENSTERN   A thing, my lord?

HAMLET   Of nothing. Bring me to him. Hide fox, and all after.

Exeunt   Running

[Act 4 Scene 2]   *running scene 11 continues*

Enter King

KING   I have sent to seek him and to find the body.
How dangerous is it that this man goes loose!
Yet must not we put the strong law on him:
He's loved of the distracted multitude,

---

10 keep . . . own keep your secrets and not my own/follow your advice (and tell you where the body is) and yet keep my own secret   **11 demanded of** questioned by   **replication** response   **14 countenance** favor   **15 authorities** power, influence   **17 mouthed** taken into the mouth   **21 sleeps in** i.e. is wasted on   **25 The . . . body** Claudius has a physical body, but he does not possess true kingship/the body is here in the castle, like Claudius; however he, not being dead, is not with Polonius/Polonius is with the true king, dead Hamlet senior, not with the usurping Claudius/Polonius is with God, rather than Claudius   **28 Hide . . . after** refers to a children's game in which one person (the fox) hides and the others pursue him   **4.2 4 of** by   **distracted** deranged/confused/foolish

5   Who like not in their judgement, but their eyes,
And where 'tis so, th'offender's scourge is weighed,
But ne'er the offence. To bear all smooth and even,
This sudden sending him away must seem
Deliberate pause. Diseases desperate grown
10   By desperate appliance are relieved,
Or not at all.

Enter Rosencrantz

                        How now? What hath befall'n?

ROSENCRANTZ   Where the dead body is bestowed, my lord,
We cannot get from him.

KING   But where is he?

15   **ROSENCRANTZ**   Without, my lord, guarded, to know your pleasure.

KING   Bring him before us.

ROSENCRANTZ   Ho, Guildenstern! Bring in my lord.   *Calls*

Enter Hamlet and Guildenstern   *With Attendants?*

KING   Now, Hamlet, where's Polonius?

HAMLET   At supper.

20   **KING**   At supper? Where?

HAMLET   Not where he eats, but where he is eaten: a certain
convocation of worms are e'en at him. Your worm is your
only emperor for diet: we fat all creatures else to fat us, and
we fat ourselves for maggots: your fat king and your lean
25   beggar is but variable service, two dishes, but to one table.
That's the end.

KING   Alas, alas!

HAMLET   A man may fish with the worm that hath eat of a
king, and eat of the fish that hath fed of that worm.

30   **KING**   What dost thou mean by this?

HAMLET   Nothing but to show you how a king may go a
progress through the guts of a beggar.

---

6 **scourge** punishment   **weighed** considered   7 **bear . . . even** manage matters smoothly
and evenly   9 **Deliberate pause** i.e. the result of careful consideration   10 **appliance** remedy
15 **Without** outside   22 **convocation . . . diet** a punning allusion to the Diet (i.e. assembly) of
the German city of Worms   22 **convocation** political assembly   **e'en** even now   25 **variable
service** different dishes in the same meal   28 **eat** eaten   32 **progress** official journey of state
undertaken by the monarch

KING   Where is Polonius?

HAMLET   In heaven, send thither to see. If your messenger
35   find him not there, seek him i'th'other place yourself. But
      indeed, if you find him not this month, you shall nose him as
      you go up the stairs into the lobby.

KING   Go seek him there.   *To Rosencrantz or Attendants*

HAMLET   He will stay till ye come. [*Exit Rosencrantz or Attendants*]

40 KING   Hamlet, this deed of thine, for thine especial safety —
      Which we do tender, as we dearly grieve
      For that which thou hast done — must send thee hence
      With fiery quickness: therefore prepare thyself.
      The bark is ready and the wind at help,
45   Th'associates tend and everything at bent
      For England.

HAMLET   For England?

KING   Ay, Hamlet.

HAMLET   Good.

50 KING   So is it, if thou knew'st our purposes.

HAMLET   I see a cherub that sees them. But come, for
      England! Farewell, dear mother.

KING   Thy loving father, Hamlet.

HAMLET   My mother. Father and mother is man and wife:
55   man and wife is one flesh, and so, my mother. Come, for
      England!   *Exit*

KING   Follow him at foot, tempt him with speed aboard:
      Delay it not, I'll have him hence tonight.
      Away! For everything is sealed and done
60   That else leans on th'affair: pray you make haste.

                          [*Exit Guildenstern and perhaps Rosencrantz*]

      And, England, if my love thou hold'st at aught —
      As my great power thereof may give thee sense,
      Since yet thy cicatrice looks raw and red
      After the Danish sword, and thy free awe

---

41 **tender** hold dear   44 **bark** ship   45 **tend** await   **at bent** ready   51 **cherub** angel
possessed of insight and knowledge   57 **at foot** closely   60 **leans on** appertains to
61 **aught** any worth   62 **thereof . . . sense** may give you an awareness of the value of my
love   63 **cicatrice** scar   64 **free awe** voluntary submission, uncompelled deference

65   Pays homage to us — thou mayst not coldly set
      Our sovereign process, which imports at full,
      By letters conjuring to that effect,
      The present death of Hamlet. Do it, England,
      For like the hectic in my blood he rages,
70   And thou must cure me. Till I know 'tis done,
      Howe'er my haps, my joys were ne'er begun.   *Exit*

[Act 4 Scene 3]   *running scene 12*

Enter Fortinbras with an army

FORTINBRAS   Go, captain, from me greet the Danish king:
      Tell him that by his licence Fortinbras
      Claims the conveyance of a promised march
      Over his kingdom. You know the rendezvous.
5   If that his majesty would aught with us,
      We shall express our duty in his eye,
      And let him know so.
CAPTAIN   I will do't, my lord.
FORTINBRAS   Go softly on.   *Exeunt*

[Act 4 Scene 4]   *running scene 13*

Enter Queen and Horatio

GERTRUDE   I will not speak with her.
HORATIO   She is importunate, indeed distract:
      Her mood will needs be pitied.

---

65 **coldly set** disregard/regard coolly   66 **process** command   **imports at full** is fully concerned with/conveys detailed instructions for   67 **conjuring** solemnly charging/conspiring   68 **present** immediate   69 **hectic** fever   71 **Howe'er my haps** whatever my fortunes   **4.3 *Location: the Danish border*** (see "Second Quarto Passages That Do Not Appear in the Folio," lines 81–139 [pp. 143–44], for a longer version of this scene, in which Hamlet witnesses the army's march and speaks his soliloquy "How all occasions do inform against me / And spur my dull revenge")   2 **licence** permission 3 **conveyance of** granting of/Danish escort for   6 **duty** respect   **eye** presence   9 **softly** slowly, carefully   **4.4 *Location: within the royal castle at Elsinore*** 2 **importunate** insistent, pressing   **distract** agitated/deranged

GERTRUDE   What would she have?

5   HORATIO   She speaks much of her father; says she hears
There's tricks i'th'world, and hems, and beats her heart,
Spurns enviously at straws, speaks things in doubt
That carry but half sense: her speech is nothing,
Yet the unshapèd use of it doth move
10   The hearers to collection; they aim at it,
And botch the words up fit to their own thoughts,
Which, as her winks and nods and gestures yield them,
Indeed would make one think there might be thought,
Though nothing sure, yet much unhappily.

15   GERTRUDE   'Twere good she were spoken with, for she may strew
Dangerous conjectures in ill-breeding minds.
Let her come in.   *Horatio goes to the door or may exit*
To my sick soul — as sin's true nature is —   *Aside*
Each toy seems prologue to some great amiss:
20   So full of artless jealousy is guilt,
It spills itself in fearing to be spilt.

Enter Ophelia, distracted   *With Horatio?*

OPHELIA   Where is the beauteous majesty of Denmark?

GERTRUDE   How now, Ophelia!

OPHELIA   How should I your true love know   *Sings*
25   From another one?
By his cockle hat and staff,
And his sandal shoon.

GERTRUDE   Alas, sweet lady, what imports this song?

OPHELIA   Say you? Nay, pray you, mark.

30   He is dead and gone, lady,   *Sings*

---

6 hems makes "hmm" noises   **7 Spurns . . . straws** strikes out spitefully at trifles
in doubt of unclear meaning   **9 use** manner/utterance   **10 collection** a gathering of
meaning   **aim** guess   **11 botch** patch, stitch clumsily together   **12 Which** which words
yield convey, deliver   **13 thought** intended   **14 unhappily** ominously near the truth/
maliciously   **16 ill-breeding** mischief-making   **19 toy** trifle   **amiss** wrong, calamity
20 artless jealousy unskilled suspicion   **21 It . . . spilt** its excessive fear of being revealed ends
up betraying it ("to spill" means both to destroy and to reveal)   **26 cockle hat** hat with a
cockle-shell on it, showing that the wearer had visited the Spanish shrine of Santiago (Saint
James) of Compostela; a **staff** and sandals were also typical of such a pilgrim   **27 shoon**
shoes

He is dead and gone.
At his head a grass-green turf,
At his heels a stone.

Enter King

GERTRUDE   Nay, but, Ophelia—

35   OPHELIA   Pray you, mark.
White his shroud as the mountain snow—   *Sings*

GERTRUDE   Alas, look here, my lord.

OPHELIA   Larded with sweet flowers   *Sings*
Which bewept to the grave did not go
40   With true-love showers.

KING   How do ye, pretty lady?

OPHELIA   Well, God yield you! They say the owl was a baker's
daughter. Lord, we know what we are, but know not what
we may be. God be at your table!

45   KING   Conceit upon her father.

OPHELIA   Pray you let's have no words of this, but when they
ask you what it means, say you this:
'Tomorrow is Saint Valentine's day,   *Sings*
All in the morning betime,
50   And I a maid at your window,
To be your Valentine.'
Then up he rose, and donned his clothes,
And dupped the chamber door:
Let in the maid, that out a maid
55   Never departed more.

KING   Pretty Ophelia.

OPHELIA   Indeed, la, without an oath, I'll make an end on't:
By Gis and by Saint Charity,   *Sings*

---

38 **Larded** strewn, covered   40 **showers** i.e. of tears   42 **yield** reward; a common way to
express thanks   **owl . . . daughter** refers to the tale of a baker's daughter who was turned into
an owl after she had been ungenerous to Jesus when he begged for bread   45 **Conceit upon**
fanciful thinking about/brooding on   49 **betime** early   51 **Valentine** sweetheart, supposedly
the first person of the opposite sex one saw on Valentine's Day   52 **rose** the sexual innuendo
of Ophelia's language suggests possible erectile connotations   53 **dupped** opened (perhaps
punning on "tupped," i.e. "had sex with")   **chamber door** playing on vaginal connotations
54 **maid** virgin   58 **Gis** Jesus

Alack, and fie for shame!

60   Young men will do't, if they come to't,
By cock, they are to blame.
Quoth she, 'Before you tumbled me,
You promised me to wed.'
'So would I ha' done, by yonder sun,
65   An thou hadst not come to my bed.'

KING   How long hath she been thus?

OPHELIA   I hope all will be well. We must be patient, but I
cannot choose but weep to think they should lay him
i'th'cold ground. My brother shall know of it: and so I thank
70   you for your good counsel. Come, my coach! Goodnight,
ladies, goodnight, sweet ladies, goodnight, goodnight.   *Exit*

KING   Follow her close: give her good watch,   *To Horatio*
I pray you.   [*Exit Horatio*]
O, this is the poison of deep grief: it springs
75   All from her father's death. O Gertrude, Gertrude,
When sorrows come, they come not single spies
But in battalions. First, her father slain:
Next, your son gone, and he most violent author
Of his own just remove: the people muddied,
80   Thick and unwholesome in their thoughts and whispers
For good Polonius' death, and we have done but greenly
In hugger-mugger to inter him: poor Ophelia
Divided from herself and her fair judgement,
Without the which we are pictures or mere beasts:
85   Last, and as much containing as all these,
Her brother is in secret come from France,
Feeds on his wonder, keeps himself in clouds,
And wants not buzzers to infect his ear
With pestilent speeches of his father's death,

---

60 do't have sex   **61 cock** euphemism for God, plays on sense of "penis"   **62 tumbled** had
sex with   **65 An** if   **76 spies** scouts sent ahead of the main army   **79 remove** removal
muddied stirred up   **81 greenly** foolishly   **82 hugger-mugger** secrecy   **85 as much
containing** of as much significance   **87 wonder** bewilderment/doubt (about his father's
death)   **in clouds** in a state of confusion (or suspicion)/aloof and inscrutable   **88 wants**
lacks   **buzzers** gossips, rumor-mongers

90   Wherein necessity, of matter beggared,
      Will nothing stick our persons to arraign
      In ear and ear. O, my dear Gertrude, this,
      Like to a murdering-piece, in many places
      Gives me superfluous death.

A noise within

Enter a Messenger

95   GERTRUDE   Alack, what noise is this?

      KING   Where are my Switzers? Let them guard the door.—
      What is the matter?

      MESSENGER   Save yourself, my lord.
      The ocean, overpeering of his list,
100   Eats not the flats with more impiteous haste
      Than young Laertes, in a riotous head,
      O'erbears your officers. The rabble call him lord,
      And, as the world were now but to begin,
      Antiquity forgot, custom not known,
105   The ratifiers and props of every word,
      They cry 'Choose we! Laertes shall be king.'
      Caps, hands and tongues, applaud it to the clouds:
      'Laertes shall be king, Laertes king!'

      GERTRUDE   How cheerfully on the false trail they cry!
110   O, this is counter, you false Danish dogs!

Noise within

Enter Laertes   *His followers remain at the door*

      KING   The doors are broke.

      LAERTES   Where is the king?— Sirs, stand you all without.

      ALL FOLLOWERS   No, let's come in.   *At the door*

      LAERTES   I pray you give me leave.

---

90 of matter beggared deprived of facts and solid evidence   **91 nothing . . . ear** not hesitate to
accuse me to one listener after another   **93 murdering-piece** small cannon which scattered
its shot and so could kill more people   **94 Gives . . . death** kills me over and over
96 Switzers Swiss guards (mercenaries commonly employed in royal households)
99 overpeering . . . list rising over its boundary   **100 flats** flat or low-lying land near the shore
101 head insurrection   **103 as** as if   **104 Antiquity** ancient tradition   **105 The . . . word**
(antiquity and custom are) the things that confirm and support every utterance   **107 Caps**
thrown into the air in support   **110 counter** following the scent in the wrong direction
(hunting term)   **false** disloyal/erring   **112 without** outside

115	**ALL** We will, we will.
	LAERTES I thank you: keep the door.— O thou vile king,
	Give me my father!
	GERTRUDE Calmly, good Laertes. *Restrains him or blocks his way*
	LAERTES That drop of blood that's calm proclaims me bastard,
120	Cries cuckold to my father, brands the harlot
	Even here, between the chaste unsmirchèd brow
	Of my true mother.
	KING What is the cause, Laertes,
	That thy rebellion looks so giant-like?—
125	Let him go, Gertrude: do not fear our person:
	There's such divinity doth hedge a king
	That treason can but peep to what it would,
	Acts little of his will.— Tell me, Laertes,
	Why thou art thus incensed.— Let him go, Gertrude.—
130	Speak, man.
	LAERTES Where's my father?
	KING Dead.
	GERTRUDE But not by him.
	KING Let him demand his fill.
135	**LAERTES** How came he dead? I'll not be juggled with:
	To hell, allegiance! Vows, to the blackest devil!
	Conscience and grace, to the profoundest pit!
	I dare damnation. To this point I stand,
	That both the worlds I give to negligence,
140	Let come what comes, only I'll be revenged
	Most throughly for my father.
	KING Who shall stay you?
	LAERTES My will, not all the world:
	And for my means, I'll husband them so well,
145	They shall go far with little.

---

116 keep guard   **120 cuckold** man with an unfaithful wife   **121 between** in the middle of
unsmirchèd unstained   **122 true** faithful   **125 fear** fear for   **126 hedge** protect
127 but . . . will only peep through at what it desires, and carry out little of its intention
135 juggled with tricked, deceived   **138 To . . . stand** I am fixed in this resolve   **139 both . . .**
negligence I disregard both this world and the next   **141 throughly** thoroughly, completely
142 stay prevent   **143 My . . . world** by my will, not all the world shall stop me
144 husband manage

KING   Good Laertes,
          If you desire to know the certainty
          Of your dear father's death, is't writ in your revenge,
          That, sweepstake, you will draw both friend and foe,
150   Winner and loser?
LAERTES   None but his enemies.
KING   Will you know them then?
LAERTES   To his good friends thus wide I'll ope my arms,
          And like the kind life-rend'ring pelican,
155   Repast them with my blood.
KING   Why, now you speak
          Like a good child and a true gentleman.
          That I am guiltless of your father's death,
          And am most sensible in grief for it,
160   It shall as level to your judgement pierce
          As day does to your eye.

A noise within

ALL FOLLOWERS   Let her come in!

Enter Ophelia

LAERTES   How now? What noise is that?
          O, heat dry up my brains, tears seven times salt   *Sees Ophelia*
165   Burn out the sense and virtue of mine eye!
          By heaven, thy madness shall be paid by weight,
          Till our scale turns the beam. O rose of May,
          Dear maid, kind sister, sweet Ophelia!
          O heavens, is't possible a young maid's wits
170   Should be as mortal as an old man's life?
          Nature is fine in love, and where 'tis fine,
          It sends some precious instance of itself
          After the thing it loves.

---

149 **sweepstake** indiscriminately (from gambling, where one person sweeps up all the stakes
on the table)   **draw** gather   154 **pelican** supposedly this bird fed its young with its own blood
155 **Repast** feed   159 **sensible** feeling   160 **level** directly   165 **virtue** power, efficacy
167 **turns the beam** tilts the crossbar of the scales (i.e. tips in our favor)   171 **Nature** human
nature   **fine in** refined by   172 **instance** sign, token   173 **After . . . loves** i.e. after Polonius,
to the grave

OPHELIA   They bore him barefaced on the bier,   *Sings*

175   Hey non nonny, nonny, hey nonny,

And on his grave rains many a tear—

Fare you well, my dove.

LAERTES   Hadst thou thy wits and didst persuade revenge,

It could not move thus.

180   OPHELIA   You must sing 'a-down a-down', and you call him
'a-down-a'. O, how the wheel becomes it! It is the false
steward that stole his master's daughter.

LAERTES   This nothing's more than matter.

OPHELIA   There's rosemary, that's for remembrance: pray,

185   love, remember: and there is pansies, that's for thoughts.

Gives real or imaginary flowers

LAERTES   A document in madness, thoughts and remembrance fitted.

OPHELIA   There's fennel for you, and columbines: there's rue
for you, and here's some for me: we may call it herb-grace

190   o'Sundays: O, you must wear your rue with a difference.
There's a daisy: I would give you some violets, but they
withered all when my father died: they say he made a good
end—

For bonny sweet Robin is all my joy.   *Sings*

195   LAERTES   Thought and affliction, passion, hell itself,

She turns to favour and to prettiness.

---

174 bier movable stand on which a corpse is carried to the grave   **175 Hey . . . nonny** a refrain
more usually associated with merry love songs   **179 move** affect (me)/persuade   **180 You**
Ophelia assigns parts to the individuals in the room   "**a-down . . . a-down-a**" well-known
refrains   **181 wheel** refrain   **false . . . daughter** refers to a story or ballad that remains
unidentified   **183 This . . . matter** this nonsense is actually more meaningful than sane
talk/this nonsense contains significance that is beyond the reach of sense   **184 rosemary**
herb symbolizing remembrance   **185 pansies** flowers symbolic of love, named from French
pensées (**thoughts**)   **186 document** lesson   **187 fitted** put together   **188 fennel** herb said to
symbolize flattery   **columbines** flowers symbolic of infidelity   **rue** herb symbolizing
repentance   **190 o'Sundays** on Sundays   **difference** variation on a coat of arms to
distinguish different members or branches of a family (or Ophelia may simply mean
"differently")   **191 daisy** possibly symbolic of deception; alternatively, a springtime flower
associated with love   **violets** flowers symbolic of faithfulness and of chastity   **194 For . . .
joy** a line from a well-known song   **195 Thought** melancholy   **passion** extreme grief
196 favour charm, attractiveness

OPHELIA   And will he not come again?   *Sings*

And will he not come again?

No, no, he is dead:

200   Go to thy death-bed,

He never will come again.

His beard as white as snow,

All flaxen was his poll:

He is gone, he is gone,

205   And we cast away moan.

Gramercy on his soul!

And of all Christian souls, I pray God. God buy ye.

Exeunt Ophelia [and Gertrude?]

LAERTES   Do you see this, you gods?

KING   Laertes, I must commune with your grief,

210   Or you deny me right. Go but apart,

Make choice of whom your wisest friends you will,

And they shall hear and judge 'twixt you and me:

If by direct or by collateral hand

They find us touched, we will our kingdom give,

215   Our crown, our life, and all that we call ours

To you in satisfaction. But if not,

Be you content to lend your patience to us,

And we shall jointly labour with your soul

To give it due content.

220   LAERTES   Let this be so:

His means of death, his obscure burial —

No trophy, sword, nor hatchment o'er his bones,

No noble rite nor formal ostentation —

Cry to be heard, as 'twere from heaven to earth,

225   That I must call in question.

---

203 **flaxen** white   **poll** head, i.e. hair   205 **cast away moan** waste our laments
206 **Gramercy** great mercy   207 **God buy ye** goodbye (literally, "God be with you")
211 **whom** whichever of   212 **'twixt** between   213 **collateral** indirect   214 **touched**
implicated   222 **trophy** memorial   **hatchment** tablet bearing the coat of arms of the dead
person, placed over the tomb   223 **ostentation** ceremony   225 **That** so that   **call in
question** demand an explanation

KING   So you shall,
And where th'offence is, let the great ⸱
I pray you go with me.

[Act 4 Scene 5]

Enter Horatio with an Attendant

HORATIO   What are they that would speak with me?

SERVANT   Sailors, sir: they say they have letters for you.

HORATIO   Let them come in.   [*Exit Servant*]
I do not know from what part of the world
5   I should be greeted, if not from Lord Hamlet.

Enter Sailor

SAILOR   God bless you, sir.

HORATIO   Let him bless thee too.

SAILOR   He shall, sir, an't please him. There's a   *Gives a letter*
letter for you, sir: it comes from th'ambassador that was
10   bound for England, if your name be Horatio, as I am let to
know it is.

HORATIO   *Reads the letter*   'Horatio, when thou shalt have
overlooked this, give these fellows some means to the king:
they have letters for him. Ere we were two days old at sea, a
15   pirate of very warlike appointment gave us chase. Finding
ourselves too slow of sail, we put on a compelled valour, in
the grapple I boarded them: on the instant they got clear of
our ship, so I alone became their prisoner. They have dealt
with me like thieves of mercy, but they knew what they did: I
20   am to do a good turn for them. Let the king have the letters I
have sent, and repair thou to me with as much haste as thou
wouldst fly death. I have words to speak in your ear will
make thee dumb, yet are they much too light for the bore of
the matter. These good fellows will bring thee where I am.

4.5 8 an't if it   **13 overlooked** looked over, read   **means** means of access   **15 appointment**
equipment   **16 compelled** necessary   **17 grapple** forcible seizing of a ship for the purpose of
boarding   **19 thieves of mercy** merciful thieves   **21 repair** come   **23 too . . . matter** i.e.
inadequate to convey the importance of the issue   **bore** caliber of a gun (Hamlet's words are
bullets that are too small to fit)

sencrantz and Guildenstern hold their course for England:
f them I have much to tell thee. Farewell. He that thou
knowest thine, Hamlet.'—
Come, I will give you way for these your letters,
And do't the speedier that you may direct me
30   To him from whom you brought them.   *Exeunt*

[Act 4 Scene 6]   *running scene 15*

Enter King and Laertes

KING   Now must your conscience my acquittance seal,
And you must put me in your heart for friend,
Sith you have heard, and with a knowing ear,
That he which hath your noble father slain
5   Pursued my life.

LAERTES   It well appears. But tell me
Why you proceeded not against these feats
So crimeful and so capital in nature,
As by your safety, wisdom, all things else,
10   You mainly were stirred up.

KING   O, for two special reasons,
Which may to you, perhaps, seem much unsinewed,
And yet to me they are strong. The queen his mother
Lives almost by his looks, and for myself —
15   My virtue or my plague, be it either which —
She's so conjunctive to my life and soul,
That, as the star moves not but in his sphere,
I could not but by her. The other motive,
Why to a public count I might not go,
20   Is the great love the general gender bear him,

---

28 way access   **4.6 1 my acquittance seal** confirm my innocence   **3 Sith** since   **knowing** understanding/knowledgeable   **7 proceeded not** did not take legal proceedings   **feats** deeds/crimes   **8 capital** punishable by death   **9 As . . . up** i.e. given that it was greatly in the interests of safety and prudence to do so   **12 unsinewed** weak   **16 conjunctive** closely united (an astronomical term referring to proximity between planets)   **17 sphere** orbit; individual stars and planets were thought to be contained within concentric hollow spheres that revolved around the earth   **18 but** except, unless I were   **19 count** account, reckoning, indictment   **20 general gender** common people   **gender** kind, sort

Who, dipping all his faults in their affection,
Would like the spring that turneth wood to stone,
Convert his gyves to graces, so that my arrows,
Too slightly timbered for so loud a wind,
25   Would have reverted to my bow again
And not where I had aimed them.

LAERTES   And so have I a noble father lost,
A sister driven into desperate terms,
Who has — if praises may go back again —
30   Stood challenger on mount of all the age
For her perfections: but my revenge will come.

KING   Break not your sleeps for that: you must not think
That we are made of stuff so flat and dull
That we can let our beard be shook with danger
35   And think it pastime. You shortly shall hear more:
I loved your father, and we love ourself,
And that, I hope, will teach you to imagine—

Enter a Messenger

How now? What news?

MESSENGER   Letters, my lord, from Hamlet:
40   This to your majesty, this to the queen.   *Gives letters*

KING   From Hamlet? Who brought them?

MESSENGER   Sailors, my lord, they say: I saw them not.
They were given me by Claudio: he received them.

KING   Laertes, you shall hear them.— Leave us.

Exit Messenger

45   'High and mighty, you shall know I am set naked on your
kingdom. Tomorrow shall I beg leave to see your kingly
eyes, when I shall, first asking your pardon thereunto,
recount th'occasions of my sudden and more strange
return. Hamlet.'

---

22 **spring . . . stone** a spring with high levels of lime in its water would petrify a piece of wood placed in it   23 **gyves** fetters   24 **Too slightly timbered** i.e. too light   28 **terms** circumstances   29 **go back again** i.e. recall her as she was   30 **on mount** on high   34 **shook with** tugged (contemptuously) by   43 **Claudio** a bluff, an intermediary, or Shakespeare's slip when he meant "Horatio"   45 **naked** destitute   47 **pardon** permission

50   What should this mean? Are all the rest come back?
        Or is it some abuse? Or no such thing?
LAERTES   Know you the hand?
KING   'Tis Hamlet's character. 'Naked' —
        And in a postscript here, he says 'alone'.
55   Can you advise me?
LAERTES   I'm lost in it, my lord. But let him come:
        It warms the very sickness in my heart
        That I shall live and tell him to his teeth,
        'Thus diest thou.'
60 KING   If it be so, Laertes —
        As how should it be so? How otherwise? —
        Will you be ruled by me?
LAERTES   If so you'll not o'errule me to a peace.
KING   To thine own peace. If he be now returned,
65   As checking at his voyage, and that he means
        No more to undertake it, I will work him
        To an exploit, now ripe in my device,
        Under the which he shall not choose but fall;
        And for his death no wind of blame shall breathe,
70   But even his mother shall uncharge the practice
        And call it accident. Some two months since,
        Here was a gentleman of Normandy.
        I've seen myself, and served against, the French,
        And they can well on horseback; but this gallant
75   Had witchcraft in't; he grew into his seat,
        And to such wondrous doing brought his horse
        As had he been incorpsed and demi-natured
        With the brave beast: so far he passed my thought,
        That I in forgery of shapes and tricks
80   Come short of what he did.

---

51 abuse deceit   **no such thing** not what it seems, a trick   **53 character** handwriting   **63 If**
so so long as   **65 As checking at** as a result of deviating from or aborting (a falconry term
referring to the hawk turning away from its pursuit in mid-flight)   **67 device** devising
70 uncharge the practice acquit the plot from blame   **74 can well** are skilled   **gallant** fine
young man   **77 As** as if   **incorpsed** of one body   **demi-natured** half of the same nature
78 brave splendid   **passed my thought** surpassed anything I could have imagined
79 forgery . . . tricks imagining feats of horsemanship

LAERTES	A Norman was't?
KING	A Norman.
LAERTES	Upon my life, Lamond.
KING	The very same.

85 LAERTES   I know him well: he is the brooch indeed
  And gem of all our nation.

KING   He made confession of you,
  And gave you such a masterly report
  For art and exercise in your defence,
90 And for your rapier most especially,
  That he cried out, 'twould be a sight indeed
  If one could match you. Sir, this report of his
  Did Hamlet so envenom with his envy
  That he could nothing do but wish and beg
95 Your sudden coming o'er, to play with him.
  Now, out of this—

LAERTES   What out of this, my lord?

KING   Laertes, was your father dear to you?
  Or are you like the painting of a sorrow,
100 A face without a heart?

LAERTES   Why ask you this?

KING   Not that I think you did not love your father,
  But that I know love is begun by time,
  And that I see, in passages of proof,
105 Time qualifies the spark and fire of it.
  Hamlet comes back: what would you undertake
  To show yourself your father's son in deed
  More than in words?

LAERTES   To cut his throat i'th'church.

110 KING   No place, indeed, should murder sanctuarize;
  Revenge should have no bounds. But, good Laertes,

---

83 **Lamond** some editors prefer Quarto's *Lamord*, with its hint of death (*la mort*, French for "death")   85 **brooch** jewel/ornament   87 **made . . . you** testified to your skill   89 **For . . . defence** with regard to your skill and performance in self-defense   93 **envenom** embitter/ poison   95 **sudden** immediate   **play** compete   103 **begun by time** generated by particular circumstances   104 **passages of proof** events that have proved it   105 **qualifies** weakens, diminishes   110 **sanctuarize** give sanctuary to, protect

Will you do this, keep close within your chamber.
Hamlet returned shall know you are come home:
We'll put on those shall praise your excellence
115 And set a double varnish on the fame
The Frenchman gave you, bring you in fine together
And wager on your heads: he, being remiss,
Most generous and free from all contriving,
Will not peruse the foils, so that with ease,
120 Or with a little shuffling, you may choose
A sword unbated, and in a pass of practice
Requite him for your father.

LAERTES   I will do't,
And for that purpose I'll anoint my sword.
125 I bought an unction of a mountebank
So mortal I but dipped a knife in it,
Where it draws blood no cataplasm so rare,
Collected from all simples that have virtue
Under the moon, can save the thing from death
130 That is but scratched withal: I'll touch my point
With this contagion, that if I gall him slightly,
It may be death.

KING   Let's further think of this,
Weigh what convenience both of time and means
135 May fit us to our shape: if this should fail,
And that our drift look through our bad performance,
'Twere better not assayed: therefore this project
Should have a back or second, that might hold,

---

112 **Will you** if you are to   **close** secluded   114 **put on** encourage/organize   116 **in fine** in
conclusion, finally   117 **remiss** negligent, not vigilant   118 **generous** noble-minded
119 **peruse** examine carefully   **foils** light swords, blunted for use in fencing   121 **unbated**
not blunted   **pass of practice** treacherous thrust/deliberately planned thrust   122 **Requite**
repay, have revenge on   125 **unction** ointment   **mountebank** quack doctor who traveled
around selling various remedies   126 **I . . . it** Laertes leaves unfinished the account of what
happened when he did this; or perhaps he means "one need but dip a knife in it"; some editors
prefer Quarto's "so mortal that, but dip"   127 **cataplasm** medicated plaster, poultice   **rare**
excellent   128 **simples** medicinal herbs   129 **Under the moon** i.e. anywhere, though
gathering herbs by moonlight was thought to lend them extra potency   130 **withal** with it
131 **contagion** poison   **gall** graze   135 **fit . . . shape** suit our plan/fit us for the roles we are
going to play   136 **drift** scheme, intention   **look** becomes visible

If this should blast in proof. Soft, let me see:
140　We'll make a solemn wager on your cunnings.
I ha't:
When in your motion you are hot and dry —
As make your bouts more violent to the end —
And that he calls for drink, I'll have prepared him
145　A chalice for the nonce, whereon but sipping,
If he by chance escape your venomed stuck,
Our purpose may hold there.—

Enter Queen

　　　　　　　　　　How now, sweet queen?

GERTRUDE　One woe doth tread upon another's heel,
So fast they'll follow: your sister's drowned, Laertes.

150　LAERTES　Drowned? O, where?

GERTRUDE　There is a willow grows aslant a brook,
That shows his hoar leaves in the glassy stream:
There with fantastic garlands did she come
Of crow-flowers, nettles, daisies and long purples
155　That liberal shepherds give a grosser name,
But our cold maids do dead men's fingers call them:
There on the pendent boughs her coronet weeds
Clamb'ring to hang, an envious sliver broke,
When down the weedy trophies and herself
160　Fell in the weeping brook. Her clothes spread wide,
And mermaid-like awhile they bore her up,
Which time she chanted snatches of old tunes,
As one incapable of her own distress,
Or like a creature native and indued

---

139 blast in proof explode when put to the test　**140 cunnings** skills (i.e. Laertes' and Hamlet's)　**141 ha't** have it　**143 As** i.e. you should　**bouts** rounds in a fight **145 nonce** purpose　**146 stuck** thrust　**151 willow** a tree associated with sadness and forsaken love　**152 hoar** grayish white　**153 fantastic** elaborate/fanciful　**154 crow-flowers** buttercups/ragged robins (both types of wildflower)　**long purples** a type of purple orchid; the roots resemble testicles, hence the **grosser name**　**155 liberal** freely spoken/licentious **grosser** coarser/more vulgar　**156 cold** chaste　**157 pendent** drooping, overhanging **158 envious sliver** malicious part of a branch　**159 weedy** made of wildflowers **163 incapable** uncomprehending/insensible　**distress** affliction, calamity　**164 indued** adapted

165   Unto that element: but long it could not be
       Till that her garments, heavy with their drink,
       Pulled the poor wretch from her melodious lay
       To muddy death.

LAERTES   Alas, then, is she drowned?

170 GERTRUDE   Drowned, drowned.

LAERTES   Too much of water hast thou, poor Ophelia,
       And therefore I forbid my tears. But yet
       It is our trick: nature her custom holds,
       Let shame say what it will: when these are gone,   *Weeps*

175   The woman will be out.— Adieu, my lord:
       I have a speech of fire that fain would blaze,
       But that this folly douts it.   *Exit*

KING   Let's follow, Gertrude:
       How much I had to do to calm his rage!

180   Now fear I this will give it start again;
       Therefore let's follow.   *Exeunt*

[Act 5 Scene 1]   *running scene 16*

Enter two Clowns   *With a spade and a pickax*

FIRST CLOWN Is she to be buried in Christian burial that wilfully
       seeks her own salvation?

SECOND CLOWN   I tell thee she is: and therefore make her
       grave straight: the crowner

5   hath sat on her, and finds it Christian burial.

FIRST CLOWN How can that be, unless she drowned herself in her
       own defence?

SECOND CLOWN   Why, 'tis found so.

---

167 lay song   **173 trick** way, habit   **174 these** i.e. his tears   **175 woman . . . out** the woman
in me will be finished   **177 folly** i.e. his weeping   **douts** extinguishes   **5.1 *Location: a
graveyard near the royal castle at Elsinore***   ***Clowns*** rustics   **1 Christian burial** suicides
were not allowed Christian burial rites   **2 salvation** probably a malapropism for "damnation,"
though perhaps the Clown suggests Ophelia was trying to get to heaven early   **4 straight**
straightaway (plays on the sense of "not crooked")   **crowner** coroner   **5 sat** held an inquest
(with a play on the literal sense)

FIRST CLOWN It must be *se offendendo*, it cannot be else. For here
10   lies the point: if I drown myself wittingly, it argues an act,
and an act hath three branches: it is to act, to do and to
perform: argal, she drowned herself wittingly.

SECOND CLOWN   Nay, but hear you, goodman delver—

FIRST CLOWN Give me leave: here lies the water; good: here stands
15   the man; good: if the man go to this water, and drown
himself, it is, will he, nill he, he goes — mark you that. But if
the water come to him and drown him, he drowns not
himself: argal, he that is not guilty of his own death shortens
not his own life.

20 SECOND CLOWN   But is this law?

FIRST CLOWN Ay, marry, is't: crowner's quest law.

SECOND CLOWN   Will you ha' the truth on't? If this had not been
a gentlewoman, she should have been buried out of
Christian burial.

25 FIRST CLOWN Why, there thou say'st: and the more pity that great
folk should have countenance in this world to drown or
hang themselves, more than their even Christian. Come, my
spade. There is no ancient gentlemen but gardeners, ditchers
and grave-makers: they hold up Adam's profession.

30 SECOND CLOWN   Was he a gentleman?

FIRST CLOWN He was the first that ever bore arms.

SECOND CLOWN   Why, he had none.

FIRST CLOWN What, art a heathen? How dost thou understand
the Scripture? The Scripture says 'Adam digged'. Could he
35   dig without arms? I'll put another question to thee: if thou
answerest me not to the purpose, confess thyself—

SECOND CLOWN   Go to.

---

9 *se offendendo* perversion of *se defendendo* (Latin for "in self-defense," a legal term); literally
"in self-offense"   **12 argal** perversion of *ergo* (Latin for "therefore")   **13 goodman** title for a
person below the rank of gentleman and often followed by the individual's occupation (here a
delver or digger)   **16 will . . . he** whether he will or no   **21 quest** inquest   **25 there thou
say'st** i.e. how right you are   **26 countenance** authority, permission   **27 even Christian**
fellow Christians   **28 ditchers** ditch-makers   **29 Adam's profession** in the Bible, Adam's job
was to look after the Garden of Eden   **31 bore arms** had a coat of arms (the sign of a
gentleman); with obvious play on sense of "limbs"   **36 confess thyself** the saying continues
"and be hanged"

FIRST CLOWN What is he that builds stronger than either the mason, the shipwright, or the carpenter?

40 SECOND CLOWN   The gallows-maker, for that frame outlives a thousand tenants.

FIRST CLOWN I like thy wit well, in good faith: the gallows does well; but how does it well? It does well to those that do ill: now thou dost ill to say the gallows is built stronger than the

45 church: argal, the gallows may do well to thee. To't again, come.

SECOND CLOWN   Who builds stronger than a mason, a shipwright, or a carpenter?

FIRST CLOWN Ay, tell me that, and unyoke.

50 SECOND CLOWN   Marry, now I can tell.

FIRST CLOWN To't.

SECOND CLOWN   Mass, I cannot tell.

Enter Hamlet and Horatio afar off   *Hamlet cloaked?*

FIRST CLOWN Cudgel thy brains no more about it, for your dull ass will not mend his pace with beating; and when you are asked

55 this question next, say 'A grave-maker: the houses that he makes lasts till doomsday.' Go, get thee to Yaughan: fetch me a stoup of liquor.   [*Exit Second Clown*]

In youth, when I did love, did love,   *Sings*
Methought it was very sweet,

60 To contract-O-the time, for-a-my behove,
O, methought there was nothing meet.

HAMLET   Has this fellow no feeling of his business that he sings at grave-making?

HORATIO   Custom hath made it in him a property of easiness.

65 HAMLET   'Tis e'en so: the hand of little employment hath the daintier sense.

---

42 does well i.e. as an answer (the sense then shifts to "serves well")   **49 unyoke** give up, stop laboring (literally, unyoke the oxen)   **54 mend** improve   **56 Yaughan** variant spelling of Vaughan, presumably the name of the local innkeeper, perhaps based on one near the Globe **57 stoup** tankard   **58 In . . . love** this and the following stanza are loose versions of parts of Thomas Vaux's poem "The Aged Lover Renounceth Love," printed in 1557; **O** and **a** may be the gravedigger's grunts as he goes about his work   **60 contract . . . behove** pass away the time to my own advantage   **61 meet** (more) fitting   **64 property of easiness** something he can undertake with indifference   **65 hath . . . sense** is more sensitive/fastidious

FIRST CLOWN   But age with his stealing steps   *Sings*
    Hath caught me in his clutch,
    And hath shipped me intil the land,
70   As if I had never been such.   *Throws up a skull*

HAMLET   That skull had a tongue in it and could sing once:
how the knave jowls it to th'ground, as if it were Cain's jawbone, that did the first murder. It might be the pate of a
politician, which this ass o'er-offices, one that could
75   circumvent God, might it not?

HORATIO   It might, my lord.

HAMLET   Or of a courtier, which could say 'Good morrow,
sweet lord! How dost thou, good lord?' This might be my lord
Such-a-one, that praised my lord Such-a-one's horse when
80   he meant to beg it, might it not?

HORATIO   Ay, my lord.

HAMLET   Why, e'en so, and now my lady Worm's, chapless,
and knocked about the mazzard with a sexton's spade: here's
fine revolution, if we had the trick to see't. Did these bones
85   cost no more the breeding, but to play at loggats with 'em?
Mine ache to think on't.

FIRST CLOWN   A pickaxe and a spade, a spade,   *Sings*
    For and a shrouding sheet:
    O, a pit of clay for to be made
90   For such a guest is meet.   *Throws up another skull*

HAMLET   There's another: why may not that be the skull of a
lawyer? Where be his quiddities now, his quillets, his cases,
his tenures, and his tricks? Why does he suffer this rude

---

69 shipped . . . land dispatched me into the earth (i.e. my grave/dust)   **intil** into   **70 been such** been a young man in love   **72 jowls** strikes, dashes (puns on "jowl"–i.e. jawbone)   **Cain** in the Bible, the first murderer; he killed his brother Abel   **74 politician** crafty schemer   **o'er-offices** lords it over (on account of his office as gravedigger)   **75 circumvent** cheat, outwit   **82 chapless** jawless   **83 mazzard** head (from the term for a drinking bowl)   **84 revolution** change/turn of the wheel of fortune   **trick** knack   **Did . . . 'em?** Did these people cost so little to bring up that we may play games with their bones?   **85 loggats** a game where pieces of wood shaped like bowling pins were thrown at a stake fixed in the ground   **88 For and** and furthermore   **shrouding sheet** sheet in which the corpse was wrapped   **92 quiddities . . . quillets** subtleties, verbal distinctions, quibbling arguments   **93 tenures** (documents or cases relating to) conditions on which property is held   **rude** ignorant/rough

knave now to knock him about the sconce with a dirty shovel,
95   and will not tell him of his action of battery? Hum. This fellow
might be in's time a great buyer of land, with his statutes, his
recognizances, his fines, his double vouchers, his recoveries:
is this the fine of his fines and the recovery of his recoveries,
to have his fine pate full of fine dirt? Will his vouchers vouch
100   him no more of his purchases, and double ones too, than the
length and breadth of a pair of indentures? The very
conveyances of his lands will hardly lie in this box; and must
the inheritor himself have no more, ha?

HORATIO   Not a jot more, my lord.

105   HAMLET   Is not parchment made of sheepskins?

HORATIO   Ay, my lord, and of calf-skins too.

HAMLET   They are sheep and calves that seek out assurance in
that. I will speak to this fellow.— Whose grave's this, sirrah?

FIRST CLOWN Mine, sir.

110   O, a pit of clay for to be made   *Sings*
For such a guest is meet.

HAMLET   I think it be thine, indeed, for thou liest in't.

FIRST CLOWN You lie out on't, sir, and therefore it is not yours. For
my part, I do not lie in't, and yet it is mine.

115   HAMLET   Thou dost lie in't, to be in't and say 'tis thine: 'tis for
the dead, not for the quick: therefore thou liest.

FIRST CLOWN 'Tis a quick lie, sir: 'twill away again, from me to
you.

---

94 sconce head   **95 action of battery** litigation concerning physical assault   **96 statutes**
legal documents that secured a debt on land and property (similar to a mortgage)
97 recognizances legal documents that formally acknowledged a debt   **fines . . . recoveries**
legal processes concerned with securing the outright ownership of land; **double vouchers**
refers to the practice of having two people vouch for a claimant's ownership of the land
98 fine . . . fines end of his fines (the sense of **fine** then shifts to "elegant, handsome" and then
to "finely powdered")   **99 vouch** guarantee   **100 the . . . indentures** land (i.e. his grave) only
as long and wide as a legal document   **101 pair of indentures** two copies of an agreement
drawn up on the same sheet of paper, which was then halved along a zigzag line to form
documents that, when placed together, were a unique match   **102 conveyances** deeds
relating to the transfer of land and property (plays on the sense of "light-fingered theft/sleight
of hand")   **box** deed-box/coffin   **103 inheritor** i.e. owner   **107 assurance in that** security in
legal documents   **108 sirrah** sir (used to a social inferior)   **114 not lie** the First Clown begins
a series of puns on the senses of "dwell/fib"   **116 quick** living (in his reply, the First Clown
plays on the senses of "quick-witted/speedy")

	HAMLET	What man dost thou dig it for?
120	FIRST CLOWN	For no man, sir.
	HAMLET	What woman, then?
	FIRST CLOWN	For none, neither.
	HAMLET	Who is to be buried in't?

FIRST CLOWN One that was a woman, sir; but, rest her soul, she's
125   dead.

HAMLET   How absolute the knave is! We must speak by the card, or equivocation will undo us. By the Lord, Horatio, these three years I have taken note of it: the age is grown so picked that the toe of the peasant comes so near the heels of
130   our courtier, he galls his kibe.— How long hast thou been a grave-maker?

FIRST CLOWN Of all the days i'th'year, I came to't that day that our last king Hamlet o'ercame Fortinbras.

HAMLET   How long is that since?

135 FIRST CLOWN Cannot you tell that? Every fool can tell that: it was the very day that young Hamlet was born — he that was mad and sent into England.

HAMLET   Ay, marry, why was he sent into England?

FIRST CLOWN Why, because he was mad: he shall recover his wits
140   there, or if he do not, it's no great matter there.

HAMLET   Why?

FIRST CLOWN 'Twill not be seen in him: there the men are as mad as he.

HAMLET   How came he mad?

145 FIRST CLOWN Very strangely, they say.

HAMLET   How strangely?

FIRST CLOWN Faith, e'en with losing his wits.

HAMLET   Upon what ground?

FIRST CLOWN Why, here in Denmark: I have been sexton here,
150   man and boy, thirty years.

---

126 absolute strictly accurate   **by the card** precisely (literally, according to either the sailor's map or compass)   **127 equivocation** verbal ambiguity   **129 picked** over-refined/fastidious **130 galls his kibe** chafes his chilblain   **148 ground** cause (but the First Clown responds to the literal sense of the word)

HAMLET   How long will a man lie i'th'earth ere he rot?

FIRST CLOWN   I'faith, if he be not rotten before he die — as we have many pocky corpses now-a-days, that will scarce hold the laying in — he will last you some eight year or nine year: a
155   tanner will last you nine year.

HAMLET   Why he more than another?

FIRST CLOWN   Why, sir, his hide is so tanned with his trade that he will keep out water a great while, and your water is a sore decayer of your whoreson dead body. Here's a skull now: this
160   skull has lain in the earth three-and-twenty years.

HAMLET   Whose was it?

FIRST CLOWN   A whoreson mad fellow's it was: whose do you think it was?

HAMLET   Nay, I know not.

165   FIRST CLOWN   A pestilence on him for a mad rogue! A poured a flagon of Rhenish on my head once. This same skull, sir, this same skull, sir, was Yorick's skull, the king's jester.

HAMLET   This?

FIRST CLOWN   E'en that.

170   HAMLET   Let me see.—Alas, poor Yorick!   *Takes the skull* I knew him, Horatio: a fellow of infinite jest, of most excellent fancy. He hath borne me on his back a thousand times — and how abhorred my imagination is! My gorge rises at it. Here hung those lips that I have kissed I know not
175   how oft.— Where be your gibes now, your gambols, your songs, your flashes of merriment that were wont to set the table on a roar? No one now to mock your own jeering? Quite chop-fallen? Now get you to my lady's chamber and tell her, let her paint an inch thick, to this favour she must come.

153 **pocky** diseased, especially with the pox i.e. syphilis   **hold . . . in** hold together long enough to be buried   155 **tanner** one who converts animal hides into leather by tanning (infusing with an astringent liquid)   159 **whoreson** wretched (an abusive intensifier used in a jocular manner)   **Here's a skull** presumably one of the two thrown up earlier, but conceivably a third if he is still digging   165 **A** he   166 **Rhenish** German wine from the area around the River Rhine   172 **fancy** imagination   173 **abhorred** filled with horror   **My gorge rises** i.e. I feel like vomiting   **gorge** stomach contents   177 **No . . . jeering?** There's no one left to laugh at the way you mocked and made fun of people?   178 **chop-fallen** downcast/lacking the lower jaw   179 **favour** facial appearance

180 Make her laugh at that.— Prithee, Horatio, tell me one
thing.

HORATIO   What's that, my lord?

HAMLET   Dost thou think Alexander looked o'this fashion
i'th'earth?

185 HORATIO   E'en so.

HAMLET   And smelt so? Puh!   *Places the skull on the ground or*

HORATIO   E'en so, my lord.   *throws it down*

HAMLET   To what base uses we may return, Horatio! Why
may not imagination trace the noble dust of Alexander till
190 he find it stopping a bung-hole?

HORATIO   'Twere to consider too curiously to consider so.

HAMLET   No, faith, not a jot, but to follow him thither with
modesty enough, and likelihood to lead it, as thus:
Alexander died, Alexander was buried, Alexander returneth
195 into dust; the dust is earth; of earth we make loam, and why
of that loam whereto he was converted might they not stop a
beer-barrel?
Imperial Caesar, dead and turned to clay,
Might stop a hole to keep the wind away.
200 O, that that earth, which kept the world in awe,
Should patch a wall t'expel the winter's flaw!
But soft, but soft, aside: here comes the king.

Enter King, Queen, Laertes, [a Priest] and a coffin with Lords Attendant
The queen, the courtiers — who is that they follow?
And with such maimèd rites? This doth betoken
205 The corpse they follow did with desperate hand
Fordo it own life: 'twas of some estate.
Couch we awhile and mark.   *They hide*

LAERTES   What ceremony else?

---

183 Alexander Alexander the Great, fourth-century king of Macedonia and one of the world's
most successful military leaders   **190 bung-hole** hole in a barrel stoppered with a bung
191 too curiously too closely/overly ingeniously   **193 modesty** moderation   **195 loam**
mortar made of clay, sand and straw   **201 flaw** squall, violent gust of wind   **204 maimèd**
truncated, insufficient   **205 desperate** filled with spiritual despair, suicidal   **206 Fordo**
destroy   **estate** status   **207 Couch** hide

HAMLET	That is Laertes, a very noble youth. Mark.	*Aside to*
210 LAERTES	What ceremony else?	*Horatio*

PRIEST   Her obsequies have been as far enlarged
As we have warrantise: her death was doubtful,
And but that great command o'ersways the order
She should in ground unsanctified have lodged
215   Till the last trumpet. For charitable prayer,
Shards, flints and pebbles should be thrown on her.
Yet here she is allowed her virgin rites,
Her maiden strewments and the bringing home
Of bell and burial.

220   LAERTES   Must there no more be done?

PRIEST   No more be done:
We should profane the service of the dead
To sing sage requiem and such rest to her
As to peace-parted souls.

225   LAERTES   Lay her i'th'earth:
And from her fair and unpolluted flesh
May violets spring! I tell thee, churlish priest,
A minist'ring angel shall my sister be
When thou liest howling.

230   HAMLET   What, the fair Ophelia!   *Aside to Horatio*

GERTRUDE   Sweets to the sweet. Farewell!   *Scatters flowers*
I hoped thou shouldst have been my Hamlet's wife:
I thought thy bride-bed to have decked, sweet maid,
And not t'have strewed thy grave.

235   LAERTES   O, treble woe
Fall ten times treble on that cursèd head
Whose wicked deed thy most ingenious sense

---

211 **obsequies** commemorative rites for the dead   212 **warrantise** authorization
doubtful suspicious   213 **o'ersways** overrules   214 **unsanctified** not consecrated by the
Church   215 **last trumpet** i.e. Doomsday, which would, according to the Bible, be heralded by
the sound of a trumpet   **For** instead of   216 **Shards** fragments of broken pottery
218 **strewments** flowers strewn on the coffin or grave   **bringing . . . burial** bringing her to her
final resting place accompanied by the funeral bell and burial rites   223 **sage requiem** a
solemn funeral chant · **such rest** pray for the same rest   224 **peace-parted** peacefully
departed   227 **violets** the flower was associated with chastity   229 **howling** i.e. in hell
237 **ingenious sense** quick, intelligent mind

Deprived thee of!— Hold off the earth awhile,
Till I have caught her once more in mine arms:

Leaps in the grave

240   Now pile your dust upon the quick and dead,
Till of this flat a mountain you have made,
To o'ertop old Pelion or the skyish head
Of blue Olympus.

HAMLET   What is he whose grief   *Comes forward*

245   Bears such an emphasis? Whose phrase of sorrow
Conjures the wand'ring stars, and makes them stand
Like wonder-wounded hearers? This is I,   *Removes cloak?*
Hamlet the Dane.   *Leaps into the grave*

LAERTES   The devil take thy soul!   *They fight*

250 **HAMLET**   Thou pray'st not well.
I prithee take thy fingers from my throat,
Sir: though I am not splenitive and rash,
Yet have I something in me dangerous,
Which let thy wiseness fear: away thy hand!

255 **KING**   Pluck them asunder.

GERTRUDE   Hamlet, Hamlet!

HORATIO   Good my lord, be quiet. *Attendants part them, and they come out*

HAMLET   Why I will fight with him upon this theme *of the grave*
Until my eyelids will no longer wag.

260 **GERTRUDE**   O my son, what theme?

HAMLET   I loved Ophelia: forty thousand brothers
Could not — with all their quantity of love —
Make up my sum. What wilt thou do for her?

KING   O, he is mad, Laertes.

265 **GERTRUDE**   For love of God, forbear him.

HAMLET   Come, show me what thou'lt do:
Woo't weep? Woo't fight? Woo't fast? Woo't tear thyself?

---

240 quick living (i.e. Laertes)   **242 Pelion** the mountain in Thessaly that, in Greek mythology, the warring giants piled on top of Mount Ossa in their attempt to scale **Olympus**, the mountain home of the gods   **245 emphasis** strength of expression (a rhetorical term)   **246 Conjures . . . stars** casts a spell on the planets   **252 splenitive** hot-tempered (the spleen was thought to be the seat of the passions)   **257 quiet** calm   **259 wag** open and shut   **265 forbear him** leave him alone   **267 Woo't** wilt thou   **tear** tear violently at (hair, clothing)/injure/destroy

Woo't drink up eisel? Eat a crocodile?
I'll do't. Dost thou come here to whine?
270   To outface me with leaping in her grave?
Be buried quick with her, and so will I:
And if thou prate of mountains, let them throw
Millions of acres on us, till our ground,
Singeing his pate against the burning zone,
275   Make Ossa like a wart! Nay, an thou'lt mouth,
I'll rant as well as thou.

KING   This is mere madness,
And thus awhile the fit will work on him:
Anon, as patient as the female dove
280   When that her golden couplets are disclosed,
His silence will sit drooping.

HAMLET   Hear you, sir: *To Laertes*
What is the reason that you use me thus?
I loved you ever: but it is no matter.
285   Let Hercules himself do what he may,
The cat will mew and dog will have his day.   *Exit*

KING   I pray you, good Horatio, wait upon him.—

[*Exit Horatio*]

Strengthen your patience in our last night's speech: *To Laertes*
We'll put the matter to the present push.—
290   Good Gertrude, set some watch over your son.—
This grave shall have a living monument:
An hour of quiet shortly shall we see;
Till then, in patience our proceeding be.   *Exeunt*

---

268 **eisel** vinegar   **crocodile** i.e. something tough and dangerous, the creature that was supposed to shed copious hypocritical tears   270 **outface** defy/defeat   273 **our ground** the piled-up earth above us   274 **burning zone** sun's orbit between the tropics   275 **Ossa** in Greek mythology, the mountain on which the giants piled Pelion in their attempt to reach Olympus   **an** if   **mouth** grimace/rant   277 **mere** complete   280 **golden couplets** baby birds covered in golden down   **disclosed** hatched   283 **use** treat   285 **Let . . . day** i.e. even Hercules could not stop Laertes from his tiresome rant/my turn will come and even Hercules (or the ranting Laertes) cannot stop me   288 **in** i.e. by remembering   289 **present push** immediate test (**push** may also be suggestive of the thrust of a weapon)   291 **living** lasting (but also implies that murdering Hamlet will serve as a memorial)

[Act 5 Scene 2]

Enter Hamlet and Horatio

HAMLET   So much for this, sir; now let me see the other:
You do remember all the circumstance?

HORATIO   Remember it, my lord?

HAMLET   Sir, in my heart there was a kind of fighting
5   That would not let me sleep: methought I lay
Worse than the mutines in the bilboes. Rashly —
And praise be rashness for it — let us know
Our indiscretion sometimes serves us well,
When our dear plots do pall, and that should teach us
10   There's a divinity that shapes our ends,
Rough-hew them how we will—

HORATIO   That is most certain.

HAMLET   Up from my cabin,
My sea-gown scarfed about me, in the dark
15   Groped I to find out them, had my desire,
Fingered their packet, and in fine withdrew
To mine own room again, making so bold —
My fears forgetting manners — to unseal
Their grand commission, where I found, Horatio —
20   O, royal knavery! — an exact command,
Larded with many several sorts of reason
Importing Denmark's health and England's too,
With, ho, such bugs and goblins in my life,
That on the supervise, no leisure bated,

5.2 Location: within the royal castle at Elsinore   **1 this** the pair enter mid-conversation;
this refers to what Hamlet has just been telling Horatio   **see the other** hear the other news
2 circumstance details   **6 mutines . . . bilboes** mutineers in shackles   **Rashly** on impulse
(Hamlet then digresses before returning to his tale in line 13)   **7 know** acknowledge
8 indiscretion lack of forethought and prudence   **9 dear** important   **pall** weaken/become
flat and stale   **11 Rough-hew** carve roughly   **14 sea-gown** short-sleeved, calf-length sailor's
gown made of coarse material   **scarfed** wrapped loosely   **15 them** i.e. Rosencrantz and
Guildenstern   **16 Fingered** stole   **in fine** finally, in conclusion   **21 Larded** garnished,
interspersed   **several** various   **22 Importing** concerning   **23 bugs . . . life** terrors to be
feared were I to be allowed to continue living   **bug** hobgoblin, bogeyman   **24 supervise**
reading (of the commission)   **leisure bated** time wasted

25   No, not to stay the grinding of the axe,
            My head should be struck off.
HORATIO   Is't possible?
HAMLET   Here's the commission: read it at more leisure.   *Gives*
            But wilt thou hear me how I did proceed?   *a paper*
30 HORATIO I beseech you.
HAMLET   Being thus benetted round with villainies —
            Ere I could make a prologue to my brains,
            They had begun the play — I sat me down,
            Devised a new commission, wrote it fair:
35   I once did hold it, as our statists do,
            A baseness to write fair and laboured much
            How to forget that learning, but, sir, now
            It did me yeoman's service. Wilt thou know
            The effect of what I wrote?
40 HORATIO Ay, good my lord.
HAMLET   An earnest conjuration from the king,
            As England was his faithful tributary,
            As love between them as the palm should flourish,
            As peace should still her wheaten garland wear
45   And stand a comma 'tween their amities,
            And many such-like 'As'es of great charge,
            That on the view and know of these contents,
            Without debatement further, more or less,
            He should the bearers put to sudden death,
50   Not shriving-time allowed.
HORATIO   How was this sealed?

---

25 stay await   **31 benetted round** snared, surrounded as if in a net   **32 Ere . . . play** i.e.
before my brain could begin to consider the issue, I had already taken action   **34 fair** in
elegant handwriting   **35 statists** statesmen   **38 yeoman's** i.e. efficient, loyal (a yeoman was
an attendant in a royal household)   **39 effect** nature   **41 conjuration** entreaty
42 tributary country owing him a tribute (a regular payment after defeat in war)   **44 still**
always (i.e. continue)   **wheaten garland** symbolic of peace   **45 comma** the mark of
punctuation that indicated only a slight break between words, thus a symbol of closeness and
connection between the two countries   **amities** friendship   **46 'As'es** phrases beginning
with "as" (puns on "asses")   **charge** importance/burden (continuing the play on "asses")
50 shriving-time time for confession and absolution from sin

HAMLET	Why, even in that was heaven ordinant.
	I had my father's signet in my purse,
	Which was the model of that Danish seal:
55	Folded the writ up in form of the other,
	Subscribed it, gave't th'impression, placed it safely,
	The changeling never known. Now, the next day
	Was our sea-fight, and what to this was sequent
	Thou know'st already.
60 HORATIO	So Guildenstern and Rosencrantz go to't.
HAMLET	Why, man, they did make love to this employment:
	They are not near my conscience; their defeat
	Doth by their own insinuation grow.
	'Tis dangerous when the baser nature comes
65	Between the pass and fell incensèd points
	Of mighty opposites.
HORATIO	Why, what a king is this!
HAMLET	Does it not, think'st thee, stand me now upon —
	He that hath killed my king and whored my mother,
70	Popped in between th'election and my hopes,
	Thrown out his angle for my proper life,
	And with such cozenage — is't not perfect conscience
	To quit him with this arm? And is't not to be damned,
	To let this canker of our nature come
75	In further evil?
HORATIO	It must be shortly known to him from England
	What is the issue of the business there.

---

52 ordinant in control   **53 signet** signet ring which acted as a seal   **54 model . . . seal**
exactly the same as the seal used to secure the commission   **55 writ** letter/written command
56 Subscribed signed (in Claudius' name)   **th'impression** the seal   **57 changeling**
substitution, i.e. false letter (literally a fairy child substituted for a human one)   **58 to . . .**
sequent followed this   **61 make love to** court, entreat   **62 defeat** destruction
63 insinuation ingratiating behavior/intrusive involvement   **64 baser** of lower social
status/inferior   **65 pass** sword thrust   **fell** fierce   **points** swords   **66 opposites** opponents,
enemies   **68 Does . . . upon** do you not think that it is now incumbent upon me
70 th'election i.e. the designation as king   **71 angle** fishing-hook and line   **proper** own
72 cozenage deception (puns on "cousinage"—i.e. kinship)   **73 quit** requite, repay
74 canker spreading ulcer   **come in** spread to, generate   **77 issue** outcome

HAMLET   It will be short: the interim is mine,
           And a man's life's no more than to say 'one'.
80   But I am very sorry, good Horatio,
           That to Laertes I forgot myself;
           For by the image of my cause I see
           The portraiture of his. I'll count his favours.
           But, sure, the bravery of his grief did put me
85   Into a tow'ring passion.

HORATIO   Peace, who comes here?

Enter young Osric   *Takes off his hat*

OSRIC   Your lordship is right welcome back to Denmark.

HAMLET   I humbly thank you, sir.— Dost know this water-fly?

HORATIO   No, my good lord.

90 HAMLET   Thy state is the more gracious, for 'tis a vice to know
           him. He hath much land, and fertile: let a beast be lord of
           beasts, and his crib shall stand at the king's mess; 'tis a
           chough, but, as I say, spacious in the possession of dirt.

OSRIC   Sweet lord, if your friendship were at leisure, I
95   should impart a thing to you from his majesty.

HAMLET   I will receive it with all diligence of spirit. Put your
           bonnet to his right use: 'tis for the head.

OSRIC   I thank your lordship, 'tis very hot.

HAMLET   No, believe me, 'tis very cold: the wind is northerly.

100 OSRIC   It is indifferent cold, my lord, indeed.

HAMLET   Methinks it is very sultry and hot for my complexion.

OSRIC   Exceedingly, my lord: it is very sultry, as 'twere, I
           cannot tell how. But, my lord, his majesty bade me signify to
           you that he has laid a great wager on your head: sir, this is
105   the matter—

---

79 no . . . 'one' is only as brief as the time it takes to say "one"   **82 by . . . his** i.e. in my
situation (having a murdered father) I recognize his also   **84 bravery** extravagance,
ostentatious display   **88 water-fly** i.e. buzzing insect   **90 gracious** blessed, fortunate
91 let . . . mess even if you are an animal yourself, provided that you own a lot of livestock you
shall eat at the king's table (**mess**)   **crib** animal's food receptacle   **93 chough** jackdaw (i.e.
chatterer)/chuff (i.e. rustic, churl)   **94 if . . . leisure** i.e. if the two of you have finished talking
97 bonnet hat (usually worn indoors when in company)   **100 indifferent** moderately
101 complexion constitution

HAMLET   I beseech you remember—   *Gestures towards hat*

OSRIC   Nay, in good faith, for mine ease, in good faith. Sir, you are not ignorant of what excellence Laertes is at his weapon.

110 HAMLET   What's his weapon?

OSRIC   Rapier and dagger.

HAMLET   That's two of his weapons; but, well.

OSRIC   The king, sir, has waged with him six Barbary horses, against the which he imponed, as I take it, six French 115 rapiers and poniards, with their assigns, as girdle, hangers or so. Three of the carriages, in faith, are very dear to fancy, very responsive to the hilts, most delicate carriages, and of very liberal conceit.

HAMLET   What call you the carriages?

120 OSRIC   The carriages, sir, are the hangers.

HAMLET   The phrase would be more germane to the matter, if we could carry cannon by our sides: I would it might be hangers till then. But, on: six Barbary horses against six French swords, their assigns, and three liberal-conceited 125 carriages: that's the French bet against the Danish. Why is this 'imponed' as you call it?

OSRIC   The king, sir, hath laid, that in a dozen passes between you and him, he shall not exceed you three hits: he

---

106 remember probably "remember your courtesy," a way of asking someone to put on their hat   **107 for mine ease** a polite way of resisting Hamlet's request   **111 Rapier** long, pointed, double-edged sword (the flexible épée of modern fencing had not yet been invented)   **112 well** very well, never mind   **113 Barbary horses** valued North African horses, noted for their speed   **114 imponed** wagered (impawned; or an affected coinage from the Latin *imponere*, meaning "to pile or lay on")   **115 poniards** daggers   **assigns** accessories   **as such as**   **girdle** sword belt   **hangers** loops on sword belts, from which the sword was hung; often richly ornamented   **116 carriages** an affected word for **hangers**   **dear to fancy** pleasing to the fancy/delightfully tasteful   **117 responsive . . . hilts** well-matched to the sword handle   **delicate** finely made   **118 liberal conceit** elaborate design   **119 call you** do you mean by   **121 germane** relevant   **122 cannon . . . sides** "carriage" is the word for the wheeled support on which a cannon is mounted   **127 laid** wagered   **in . . . nine** famously incomprehensible and much-debated wager; Claudius bets that, in a series of twelve rounds, Laertes' total number of hits will not exceed Hamlet's by three or more, but it is unclear what is meant by "twelve for nine," where "he" may be Claudius or Laertes   **passes** rounds   **128 him** i.e. Laertes

130   hath laid on twelve for nine, and that would come to
immediate trial, if your lordship would vouchsafe the answer.

HAMLET   How if I answer 'no'?

OSRIC   I mean, my lord, the opposition of your person in
trial.

HAMLET   Sir, I will walk here in the hall: if it please his
135   majesty, 'tis the breathing time of day with me; let the foils be
brought, the gentleman willing, and the king hold his
purpose, I will win for him if I can: if not, I'll gain nothing
but my shame and the odd hits.

OSRIC   Shall I redeliver you e'en so?

140   HAMLET   To this effect, sir, after what flourish your nature
will.

OSRIC   I commend my duty to your lordship.

HAMLET   Yours, yours.—   [Exit Osric]
He does well to commend it himself, there are no tongues
145   else for's turn.

HORATIO   This lapwing runs away with the shell on his head.

HAMLET   He did comply with his dug, before he sucked it.
Thus has he — and many more of the same bevy that I know
the drossy age dotes on — only got the tune of the time and
150   outward habit of encounter, a kind of yeasty collection,
which carries them through and through the most fond and
winnowed opinions; and do but blow them to their trials, the
bubbles are out.

---

130 vouchsafe the answer be pleased to accept the challenge (Hamlet interprets **answer** more
literally as "reply")   **132 opposition . . . trial** presenting of yourself as an opponent in a
contest   **135 breathing time** time for exercise   **138 odd** occasional/extra three   **139 redeliver you** report back what you say   **140 after what flourish** according to whatever lavish
gesture or manner of speaking you choose   **142 commend** entrust (part of a standard
phrase, but Hamlet responds to the sense of "recommend, praise")   **145 for's turn** to do it for
him   **146 lapwing** bird proverbial for youthful precocity as it left the nest soon after being
hatched; **shell . . . head** may suggest that Osric has just put his hat on   **147 comply . . . dug**
pay courteous compliments to his mother's (or nurse's) nipple   **148 bevy** company/group of
birds   **149 drossy** worthless, impure   **tune** i.e. fashionable speech/general style   **150 habit
of encounter** custom of social interaction/fashionable dress   **yeasty** frothy   **collection** i.e. of
fashionable words and manners   **151 carries them through** enables them to successfully pass
off/enables them to hold their own among   **fond** foolish   **152 winnowed** selective (literally
refers to the blowing away of chaff from grain)   **and . . . out** yet test them by blowing on
them and the bubbles will burst/test their opinions and they are lost for words

HORATIO	You will lose this wager, my lord.
155 HAMLET	I do not think so: since he went into France, I have been in continual practice; I shall win at the odds. But thou wouldst not think how ill all's here about my heart, but it is no matter.
HORATIO	Nay, good my lord—
160 HAMLET	It is but foolery; but it is such a kind of gain-giving as would perhaps trouble a woman.
HORATIO	If your mind dislike anything, obey it: I will forestall their repair hither, and say you are not fit.
HAMLET	Not a whit, we defy augury: there's a special
165	providence in the fall of a sparrow. If it be now, 'tis not to come: if it be not to come, it will be now: if it be not now, yet it will come: the readiness is all. Since no man has aught of what he leaves, what is't to leave betimes?

Enter King, Queen, Laertes and Lords, with [Osric and] other Attendants with foils and gauntlets, a table and flagons of wine on it

KING	Come, Hamlet, come and take this hand from me.

Puts Laertes' hand into Hamlet's

170 HAMLET	Give me your pardon, sir: I've done you wrong,
	But pardon't, as you are a gentleman.
	This presence knows,
	And you must needs have heard, how I am punished
	With sore distraction. What I have done
175	That might your nature, honour and exception
	Roughly awake, I here proclaim was madness.
	Was't Hamlet wronged Laertes? Never Hamlet:
	If Hamlet from himself be ta'en away,
	And when he's not himself does wrong Laertes,
180	Then Hamlet does it not, Hamlet denies it.

---

156 at the odds given the odds that have been laid   **160 gain-giving** misgiving, foreboding   **163 repair** coming   **164 augury** prophecy (literally, making predictions based on an interpretation of the behavior of birds)   **there's . . . sparrow** i.e. God's hand is in every slightest thing—alluding to Matthew 10:29   **165 it** i.e. his own death   **167 readiness** i.e. to meet death   **has aught of** really owns, can take with him   **168 betimes** early   *gauntlets* protective gloves used for fencing   **172 presence** assembly/royal company   **175 nature** natural feeling/filial loyalty   **exception** disapproval, objection

Who does it, then? His madness. If't be so,
Hamlet is of the faction that is wronged,
His madness is poor Hamlet's enemy.
Sir, in this audience,
185   Let my disclaiming from a purposed evil
Free me so far in your most generous thoughts
That I have shot mine arrow o'er the house,
And hurt my brother.

LAERTES   I am satisfied in nature,
190   Whose motive in this case should stir me most
To my revenge: but in my terms of honour
I stand aloof, and will no reconcilement
Till by some elder masters, of known honour
I have a voice and precedent of peace,
195   To keep my name ungored. But till that time,
I do receive your offered love like love,
And will not wrong it.

HAMLET   I do embrace it freely,
And will this brother's wager frankly play.—
200   Give us the foils. Come on.

LAERTES   Come, one for me.

HAMLET   I'll be your foil, Laertes: in mine ignorance
Your skill shall, like a star i'th'darkest night,
Stick fiery off indeed.

205   LAERTES   You mock me, sir.

HAMLET   No, by this hand.

KING   Give them the foils, young Osric. Cousin Hamlet,
You know the wager?

HAMLET   Very well, my lord:
210   Your grace hath laid the odds o'th'weaker side.

---

182 faction party   **185 disclaiming from** disavowal, denial of   **purposed** intentional
186 generous noble-minded/magnanimous   **187 That I have** as to think that I have
191 my . . . honour where my honor is concerned   **192 will** want, will have   **194 voice**
(authoritative) endorsement   **peace** reconciliation   **195 name ungored** reputation
uninjured   **199 frankly** freely, with no ill will   **202 foil** background material used to set off
the luster of a jewel (shifting the sense away from "sword")   **204 Stick fiery off** stand out and
sparkle brilliantly   **210 laid the odds** backed

KING   I do not fear it: I have seen you both:
       But since he is bettered, we have therefore odds.

LAERTES   This is too heavy, let me see another.   *Looks over the foils*

HAMLET   This likes me well. These foils have all a length?

Prepare to play

215 OSRIC   Ay, my good lord.

KING   Set me the stoups of wine upon that table:
       If Hamlet give the first or second hit,
       Or quit in answer of the third exchange,
       Let all the battlements their ordnance fire:
220   The king shall drink to Hamlet's better breath,
       And in the cup an union shall he throw
       Richer than that which four successive kings
       In Denmark's crown have worn. Give me the cups,
       And let the kettle to the trumpets speak,
225   The trumpet to the cannoneer without,
       The cannons to the heavens, the heaven to earth,
       'Now the king drinks to Hamlet.' Come, begin:
       And you, the judges, bear a wary eye.

HAMLET   Come on, sir.

230 LAERTES   Come on, sir.   *They play*

HAMLET   One.

LAERTES   No.

HAMLET   Judgement.

OSRIC   A hit, a very palpable hit.

235 LAERTES   Well, again.

KING   Stay, give me drink.— Hamlet, this   *Drinks, then puts*
       pearl is thine: Here's to thy health.—   *the pearl in the cup?*
       Give him the cup.

Trumpets sound and shot goes off

---

212 he is bettered Laertes is considered to be better   **odds** the advantage (Laertes is handicapped by having to score three hits over Hamlet)   **214 likes** pleases   **have . . . length** are all of the same length   **216 stoups** cups   **218 quit . . . exchange** repays Laertes (for winning the first two bouts) by scoring a hit in the third bout   **219 ordnance** cannon   **220 better breath** increased energy and vigor   **221 union** valuable pearl   **224 kettle** kettle-drum

HAMLET	I'll play this bout first: set by awhile.— Come.	
240	Another hit; what say you?	*They play*
LAERTES	A touch, a touch, I do confess.	
KING	Our son shall win.	
GERTRUDE	He's fat, and scant of breath.—	
	Here's a napkin, rub thy brows:	*To Hamlet*
245	The queen carouses to thy fortune, Hamlet.	
HAMLET	Good madam.	
KING	Gertrude, do not drink!	
GERTRUDE	I will, my lord; I pray you, pardon me.	*Drinks*
KING	It is the poisoned cup: it is too late.	*Aside*
250	HAMLET I dare not drink yet, madam: by and by.	
GERTRUDE	Come, let me wipe thy face.	
LAERTES	My lord, I'll hit him now.	*To the King*
KING	I do not think't.	
LAERTES	And yet 'tis almost gainst my conscience.	*Aside*
255	HAMLET Come, for the third: Laertes, you but dally.	
	I pray you pass with your best violence:	
	I am afeard you make a wanton of me.	
LAERTES	Say you so? Come on.	*Play*
OSRIC	Nothing, neither way.	
260	LAERTES Have at you now!	*In scuffling they change rapiers*
KING	Part them: they are incensed.	
HAMLET	Nay, come, again.	*Gertrude falls?*
OSRIC	Look to the queen there, ho!	*To Hamlet*
HORATIO	They bleed on both sides.— How is it, my lord?	
265	OSRIC How is't, Laertes?	
LAERTES	Why, as a woodcock to mine own springe, Osric:	
	I am justly killed with mine own treachery.	
HAMLET	How does the queen?	
KING	She swoons to see them bleed.	

---

243 fat may suggest greasy/sweaty, but primary sense is corpulent, overweight   **244 napkin**
handkerchief   **245 carouses to** toasts   **256 pass** thrust   **257 make . . . me** toy with
me/indulge me   **wanton** spoiled child   **260** *scuffling* fighting at close quarters   *change*
exchange, probably via the maneuver known as "left-hand seizure" (see Introduction,
p. xv)   **266 woodcock** proverbially stupid, easily caught birds   **springe** snare

270   **GERTRUDE**   No, no, the drink, the drink — O my dear Hamlet —
The drink, the drink! I am poisoned.   *Dies*

HAMLET   O, villainy! Ho! Let the door be locked:
Treachery! Seek it out.

LAERTES   It is here, Hamlet. Hamlet, thou art slain:
275   No medicine in the world can do thee good,
In thee there is not half an hour of life;
The treacherous instrument is in thy hand,
Unbated and envenomed. The foul practice
Hath turned itself on me: lo, here I lie,
280   Never to rise again. Thy mother's poisoned.
I can no more. The king, the king's to blame.

HAMLET   The point envenomed too!
Then, venom, to thy work.   *Hurts the King*

ALL   Treason! Treason!

285   **KING**   O, yet defend me, friends, I am but hurt.

HAMLET   Here, thou incestuous, murd'rous, damnèd Dane,
Drink off this potion. Is thy union here?
Follow my mother.   *King dies*

LAERTES   He is justly served:
290   It is a poison tempered by himself.
Exchange forgiveness with me, noble Hamlet:
Mine and my father's death come not upon thee,
Nor thine on me.   *Dies*

HAMLET   Heaven make thee free of it! I follow thee.—
295   I am dead, Horatio.— Wretched queen, adieu!—
You that look pale and tremble at this chance,
That are but mutes or audience to this act,
Had I but time — as this fell sergeant, death,
Is strict in his arrest — O, I could tell you.
300   But let it be.— Horatio, I am dead:

---

278 practice plot   **287 Drink off** drink up, drain   **union** pearl (plays on the sense of
"marriage")   **290 tempered** mixed   **296 chance** mischance/event   **297 mutes** silent
onlookers/actors without speaking parts   **act** event/theatrical performance   **298 fell** cruel
299 strict rigorously just/unrelenting, stern   **arrest** taking into custody/halting (of my words)

Thou liv'st: report me and my causes right
To the unsatisfied.

HORATIO   Never believe it.
I am more an antique Roman than a Dane:
305   Here's yet some liquor left.

HAMLET   As thou'rt a man,
Give me the cup: let go, by heaven, I'll have't.
O, good Horatio, what a wounded name —
Things standing thus unknown — shall live behind me!
310   If thou didst ever hold me in thy heart,
Absent thee from felicity awhile,
And in this harsh world draw thy breath in pain,
To tell my story.

March afar off and shot within

What warlike noise is this?

Enter Osric

OSRIC   Young Fortinbras, with conquest come from Poland,
315   To th'ambassadors of England gives
This warlike volley.

HAMLET   O, I die, Horatio:
The potent poison quite o'er-crows my spirit.
I cannot live to hear the news from England,
320   But I do prophesy th'election lights
On Fortinbras: he has my dying voice,
So tell him, with the occurrents more and less
Which have solicited. The rest is silence. O, o, o, o!   *Dies*

HORATIO   Now cracks a noble heart. Goodnight, sweet prince,
325   And flights of angels sing thee to thy rest!—
Why does the drum come hither?

*Enter Fortinbras and English Ambassador, with Drum, Colours
and Attendants*

---

301 causes grievances, grounds for revenge   **302 unsatisfied** uninformed/those who wish to
know   **304 antique Roman** one of the ancient Romans, who viewed suicide as a noble
alternative to an unworthy life   **311 felicity** happiness, bliss   **318 o'er-crows** triumphs over
(an image from cockfighting)   **320 th'election** i.e. the selection of the next king of Denmark
321 voice vote/support   **322 occurrents** events   **323 solicited** prompted this   **O . . . o!** a
dying groan is represented thus in several plays of the period   ***Colours*** battle flags

FORTINBRAS Where is this sight?

HORATIO   What is it ye would see?
If aught of woe or wonder, cease your search.

330 FORTINBRAS This quarry cries on havoc. O proud death,
What feast is toward in thine eternal cell,
That thou so many princes at a shot
So bloodily hast struck?

AMBASSADOR The sight is dismal,
335 And our affairs from England come too late:
The ears are senseless that should give us hearing,
To tell him his commandment is fulfilled,
That Rosencrantz and Guildenstern are dead.
Where should we have our thanks?

340 HORATIO   Not from his mouth,
Had it th'ability of life to thank you:
He never gave commandment for their death.
But since, so jump upon this bloody question,
You from the Polack wars, and you from England,
345 Are here arrived, give order that these bodies
High on a stage be placèd to the view,
And let me speak to th'yet unknowing world
How these things came about: so shall you hear
Of carnal, bloody and unnatural acts,
350 Of accidental judgements, casual slaughters,
Of deaths put on by cunning and forced cause,
And, in this upshot, purposes mistook
Fall'n on the inventors' heads: all this can I
Truly deliver.

355 FORTINBRAS Let us haste to hear it,
And call the noblest to the audience.

---

328 would wish to   **330 quarry . . . havoc** mound of bodies proclaims total slaughter and
destruction   **quarry** pile of dead game after a hunt   **331 toward** imminent/being prepared
cell small dwelling   **334 dismal** ominous/calamitous/depressing   **336 The ears** i.e. Claudius'
ears   **343 jump** precisely   **question** dispute/affair   **346 stage** platform   **view** general view
350 accidental judgements punishments happening by chance   **casual** occurring by chance
351 put on instigated/arranged   **forced cause** deliberate contrivance/false grounds
352 upshot conclusion, outcome   **354 deliver** report

For me, with sorrow I embrace my fortune:
I have some rights of memory in this kingdom,
Which now to claim my vantage doth invite me.

360 HORATIO   Of that I shall have also cause to speak,
And from his mouth whose voice will draw on more:
But let this same be presently performed,
Even while men's minds are wild, lest more mischance
On plots and errors happen.

365 FORTINBRAS   Let four captains
Bear Hamlet, like a soldier, to the stage,
For he was likely, had he been put on,
To have proved most royally: and for his passage,
The soldiers' music and the rites of war

370 Speak loudly for him.
Take up the body: such a sight as this
Becomes the field, but here shows much amiss.
Go, bid the soldiers shoot.

Exeunt marching. After the which a peal of ordnance are shot off

---

358 of memory old/traditional/unforgotten   **359 vantage** advantage, favorable opportunity
361 voice speaking voice/vote   **draw on** encourage, rally the support of   **362 this same** i.e.
the displaying of the bodies and explanation of events   **presently** immediately   **363 wild**
bewildered/agitated   **364 On** on top of/as a result of   **367 put on** put to the test (as king)
368 passage journey into death   **370 Speak** i.e. let them speak   **372 Becomes the field**
suits the battlefield   **shows much amiss** is very out of place

TEXTUAL NOTES

Q1 = First Quarto text of 1603 (of uncertain authority)
Q2 = Second Quarto text of 1604–05
Q1/Q2 = a reading in which the First Quarto and Second Quarto texts agree
F = First Folio text of 1623
F2 = a correction introduced in the Second Folio text of 1632
Ed = a correction introduced by a later editor
SD = stage direction
SH = speech heading (i.e. speaker's name)

List of parts = Ed

1.1.70 he = Q1/Q2. *Not in* F **72 steelèd** = Ed. Q1/Q2 = sleaded. F = sledded **pole-axe** = F *(Pollax). Sometimes emended to* Polacks **104 designed** = F2. F = designe **126 haply** *spelled* happily *in* F **151 say** = Q1/Q2. F = sayes **167 Let's** = Q1/Q2. F= Let
1.2.8 sometime = Q2. F = sometimes **67 SH GERTRUDE** = Ed. F = *Queen.* **129 solid** = F. Q2 = sallied, *sometimes emended to* sullied **134 Seem** = Q2. F = Seemes **141 beteem** = Q2. F = beteene **207 distilled** = Q1/Q2. F = bestil'd **212 Where, as** = Ed. F = Whereas **221 its** = Q4. F = it **232 SH MARCELLUS *and* BARNARDO** = Ed. F = *Both.* **249 SH MARCEL-LUS *and* BARNARDO** = Ed. F = *All.* **254 walk** = Q1/Q2. F = wake **260 tenable** = Q1/Q2. F = treble
1.3.18 will = Q2. F = feare **23 sanctity** = F. Q2 = safety. Ed = sanity **whole** = Q2. F = weole **48 watchman** Q2. F = watchmen **68 new-hatched** = Q2. F = vnhatch't **77 chief** *spelled* cheff *in* F **113 Running** = Ed. F = Roaming **121 Lends** = Q1/Q2. F = Giues **132 dye** = Q2. F = eye **134 bawds** = Ed. F = bonds
1.4.10 wassail = Q1/Q2. F = wassels **23 intents** = Q1/Q2. F = euents **37 the** = Q1/Q2. F = thee; **54 summit** = Ed. F = Sonnet **64 artery** = Ed. F = Artire
1.5.23 on *spelled* an *in* F **33 I** = Q2. *Not in* F **38 roots** = Q1/Q2. F = rots **48 wit** = Ed. F = wits **with** = Q1/Q2. F = hath **50 to his** = Q1/Q2. F = to to this **74 eager** *spelled* Aygre *in* F **76 barked** = Q1/Q2. F = bak'd **112–13 My tables, My tables** = F *(in one line).* Q1/Q2 *does not repeat* **122 SH HAMLET** = Q2. F = *Mar.* **123 Hillo** *spelled* Ilio *in* F **146 whirling** *spelled*

hurling *in* F **150 Horatio** = Q2. F = my Lord **174 our** = Q1/Q2. F = for
194 they = Q1/Q2. F = there

2.1.1 this = Q1/Q2. F = his **3 marvellous** *spelled* maruels *in* F **15 As** = Q2.
F = And **67 carp** = Q2. F = Cape **121 feared** = Q2. F = feare

2.2.0 SD *with others* F *has the Latin* "*Cum alijs*" **17 Whether . . . thus** = Q2.
Not in F *(compositor's eyeskip?)* **46 lord? I** = Q2. F = lord? **48 and** =
Q1/Q2. F = one **55 fruit** = Q2. F = Newes **129 solicitings** = Q2. F =
soliciting **169 does** = Q2. F = ha's **204 that you read** = Q2. F = you
meane **208 lack** = Q2. F = locke **226 SD *Enter . . . Guildenstern*** *placed*
one line later in F **239 favours** = Q2. F = fauour **283 of** = Q1/Q2. *Not in*
F **297 discovery, and** = Q2. F = discouery of **300 heavily** = Q2. F =
heauenly **303 firmament** = Q2. *Not in* F **339 berattle** = F2. F = be-
ratled **345 most like** = Ed. F = like most **384 Roscius, an** = F *(Rossius*
an). Q1/Q2 = *Rossius* was an **388 came** = Q2. F = can **392 individable**
= Q2. F = indiuible **411 pious** = Q2. F = *Pons* **415 valanced** = Q2. F =
valiant **427 caviar** *spelled Caviarie in* F **434–35 as . . . fine** = Q2. *Not in* F
435 One = Q2. F = One cheefe **447 total** = Q1/Q2. F = to take **455 So,**
proceed you. = Q2. *Not in* F **461 matched** = Q2. F = match **465 this** =
Q2. F = his **485 fellies** *spelled* Fallies *in* F **492 mobled** = Q1/Q2. F = ino-
bled *(throughout)* **539 wanned** = Q2. F = warm'd **566 bawdy** = Q2. F =
a Bawdy **569 Why** = Q2. F = Who

3.1.33 here = Q2. F = there **48 please you** = Q2. F = please ye **53 sugar** =
Q2. F = surge **77 proud** = Q2. F = poore **83 would these** = F. Q2 =
would **93 away** = F. Q2 = awry **104 I know** = F. Q2 = you know **106**
their perfume lost = Q2. F = then perfume left **117 with** = Q1/Q2. F =
your **138 nowhere** = Q2. F = no way **147 paintings** = Q1/Q2. F =
pratlings **148 face** = Q1/Q2. F = pace **149 jig** *spelled* gidge *in* F **160**
And = Q2. F = Haue **182 this** = F. Q2 = his

3.2.4 with = Q2. *Not in* F **17 o'erstep** = Q2. F = ore-stop **29 nor no man** =
Ed. F = or Norman **56 lick** = Q2. F = like **58 fawning** = Q2. F = faining
59 her = Q2. F = my **75 thy** = Q2. F = my **80 stithy** *spelled* Stythe *in* F
heedful = Q2. F = needfull **94 mine now.** = Ed. F = mine. Now **138 SH**
PROLOGUE = Ed. *Not in* F **144 SH PLAYER KING** = Ed. F = *King.* **153**
former = Q2. F = forme **174 you think** = Q2. F = you. Think **184 either**
= Q2. F = other **185 enactures** = Q2. F= ennactors **228 wince** *spelled*
winch *in* F **237 mis-take** = Ed. F = mistake **your** = Q1/Q2. *Not in* F **280**
SD *Enter . . . Guildenstern* *occurs four lines earlier in* F **305 as you** = Q2.
F = you **350 speak** = Q2. *Not in* F **358 mass** = Q2. F = Misse

3.3.15 weal = Q2. F = spirit **19 summit** = Ed. F = Somnet

3.4.4 silence = F. *Sometimes emended to* sconce = conceal **14 a wicked** =
Q2. F = an idle *(probably picked up by compositor from previous line)* **38**
better = Q2. F = Betters **51 sets** = Q2. F = makes **73 brother** = Q2. F =
breath **87 And** = Q2. F = As **121 do** = Q2. *Not in* F **122 th'incorporal** =

Q2. F = their corporall **126 on** = Ed. F = an **151 a** = F. Q2 = that **158 ranker** = Q2. F = ranke **159 these** = Q2. F = this **181 bloat** = Ed. F = blunt. Q2 = blowt **243 mother's closet** = Q2. F = Mother Clossets

4.1.16 ape an apple = Ed. F = Ape. Q = an apple

4.2.7 ne'er *spelled* neerer *in* F **24 ourselves** = Q2. F = our selfe **27–29 SH KING Alas . . . worm** = Q2. *Not in* F *(probably due to printer's error)* **51 them** = Q2. F = him

4.4.13 might = Q2. F = would **42 yield** *spelled* dil'd *in* F **76 sorrows come** = Q2. F = sorrows comes **77 battalions** = Q2. F = Battaliaes **87 Feeds** = Q2. F = Keepes **113 SH ALL FOLLOWERS** = Ed. F = *All.* **119 that's calm** = Q2. F = that calmes **148 is't** = Q2. F = if **149 sweepstake** *spelled* Soop-stake *in* F **154 pelican** = Q2. F = Politician **163 SH ALL FOLLOWERS** = Ed. *Not in* F **180 sing 'a-down** = Q2. F = sing downe **185 pansies** = Q2. F = Paconcies **209 commune** = Q2. F = common

4.5.9 ambassador = Q2. F = Ambassadours **12 SH HORATIO** = Ed. *Not in* F

4.6.26 aimed = Q2. F = arm'd **29 has** = Ed. F = was **59 diest** = Ed. F = diddest **71 since** = Q2. F = hence **74 can** = Q2. F = ran **97 What** = Q2. F = Why **140 cunnings** = Q2. F = commings **147 How now** = F2. F = how **166 their** = Q1/Q2. F = her **167 lay** = Q2. F = buy

5.1.1 SH FIRST CLOWN = Ed. F = *Clown* **3 SH SECOND CLOWN** = Ed. F = *Other* **11 to** = Q2. F = an **91 of** = Q2. F = of of **92 quiddities** = Q2. F = Quiddits **108 sirrah** = Q2. F = Sir **149 sexton** = Q2. F = sixteene **206 of** = Q2. *Not in* F **235 treble woe** = Q2. F = terrible woer **244 grief** = Q2. F = griefes **246 Conjures** = Q2. F = Coniure **257 SH HORATIO** = Q2. F = *Gen.* **267 Woo't fast?** = Q2. *Not in* F **280 couplets** = Q2. F = Cuplet **288 your** = Q2. F = you

5.2.31 villainies = Ed. F = Villaines **39 effect** = Q2. F = effects **52 ordinant** = Q2. F = ordinate **58 sequent** = Q2. F = sement **62 defeat** = Q2. F = debate **78 interim is** = Q2. F = *interim's* **93 say** = Q2. F = saw **113 king, sir** = Q2. F = sir King **125 bet** = Q2. F = but **129 laid on** = Q2. F = one **nine** = Q2. F = mine **145 turn** = Q2. F = tongue **148 has** = Q2. F = had **many** = Q2. F = mine **157 ill all's** = Q2. F = all **162 it** = Q2. *Not in* F **188 brother** = Q2. F = Mother **195 ungored** = Q2. F = vngorg'd **266 own** = Q2. *Not in* F **269 swoons** *spelled* sounds *in* F **272 Ho!** *spelled* How! *in* F **313 SD shot** = Ed. F = *shout* **324 cracks** = Q2. F = cracke **330 This** = Q2. F = His **332 shot** = Q2. F = shoote **339 now** = Q1/Q2. F = are **340 also** = Q2. F = alwayes **343 while** = Q2. F = whiles

SECOND QUARTO PASSAGES THAT DO NOT APPEAR IN THE FOLIO

Lines are numbered continuously, for ease of reference.

Following 1.1.117:

BARNARDO I think it be no other but e'en so:
Well may it sort that this portentous figure
Comes armèd through our watch, so like the king
That was and is the question of these wars.

5 **HORATIO** A mote it is to trouble the mind's eye.
In the most high and palmy state of Rome,
A little ere the mightiest Julius fell,
The graves stood tenantless and the sheeted dead
Did squeak and gibber in the Roman streets:
10 As stars with trains of fire and dews of blood,
Disasters in the sun, and the moist star
Upon whose influence Neptune's empire stands
Was sick almost to doomsday with eclipse:
And even the like precurse of feared events,
15 As harbingers preceding still the fates
And prologue to the omen coming on,
Have heaven and earth together demonstrated
Unto our climatures and countrymen.—

Following 1.2.59:

wrung from me my slow leave
20 By laboursome petition, and at last
Upon his will I sealed my hard consent.

---

1 e'en even, i.e. exactly   **2 sort** fit   **4 question** cause (of dispute)   **5 mote** speck, irritating particle   **6 palmy** triumphant, flourishing   **7 ere** before   **Julius** Julius Caesar, murdered by conspirators in 44 BC   **8 sheeted** shrouded   **9 squeak** ghosts were traditionally supposed to have thin high-pitched voices   **10 As** editors have speculated that a preceding line is missing   **stars . . . fire** i.e. comets, signs of ill omen   **11 Disasters** unfavorable aspects (astrological term)   **moist star** i.e. the moon, which controls the tides   **12 Neptune** Roman god of the sea   **stands** depends   **13 to doomsday** as if it were Judgment Day (when, according to the Bible, the moon would grow dark)   **14 even . . . precurse** exactly the same foreshadowing   **15 As harbingers** like forerunners   **still** always   **16 omen** calamity   **18 climatures** regions   **20 petition** entreaty   **21 will** plays on the sense of "legal document" (which Polonius fixed his seal on)   **hard** reluctant

Following 1.4.18:

This heavy-headed revel east and west
Makes us traduced and taxed of other nations:
They clepe us drunkards, and with swinish phrase
25 Soil our addition: and indeed it takes
From our achievements, though performed at height,
The pith and marrow of our attribute.
So, oft it chances in particular men
That for some vicious mole of nature in them,
30 As in their birth—wherein they are not guilty,
Since nature cannot choose his origin—
By their o'ergrowth of some complexion,
Oft breaking down the pales and forts of reason,
Or by some habit that too much o'erleavens
35 The form of plausive manners, that these men,
Carrying, I say, the stamp of one defect,
Being nature's livery, or fortune's star,
His virtues else—be they as pure as grace,
As infinite as man may undergo—
40 Shall in the general censure take corruption
From that particular fault: the dram of eale
Doth all the noble substance often douse,
To his own scandal.

Following 1.4.58:

The very place puts toys of desperation,
45 Without more motive, into every brain
That looks so many fathoms to the sea
And hears it roar beneath.

Following 3.2.159:

Where love is great, the littlest doubts are fear:
Where little fears grow great, great love grows there.

---

22 **east and west** i.e. everywhere   23 **traduced . . . of** dishonored and censured by
24 **clepe** call   **with swinish phrase** by calling us pigs   25 **addition** name, reputation   **takes**
removes   26 **though . . . height** even though they are outstanding   27 **pith . . . attribute** very
essence of our distinguished reputation   29 **for** because of   **mole** blemish   30 **As** for
example   32 **o'ergrowth . . . complexion** excessive growth of some natural trait   33 **pales**
fences, safeguards   34 **too much o'erleavens** spoils (as too much leaven ruins dough)
35 **plausive** pleasing, praiseworthy   37 **nature's livery** uniform designating one's servitude to
nature   38 **virtues else** other virtues   39 **undergo** sustain   40 **general censure** public
opinion/view of the man as a whole   41 **the . . . scandal** unclear; the general sense is "even a
tiny portion (**dram**) of polluting matter can bring a **noble substance** into disrepute" (or perhaps
". . . corrupt a **noble substance** to its own shameful nature")   **eale** ale   44 **toys** wild
thoughts   **desperation** the hopelessness or spiritual despair preceding suicide
46 **fathoms** a fathom is approximately six feet

Following 3.2.205:

50   To desperation turn my trust and hope!
      An anchor's cheer in prison be my scope,

Following 3.4.79 (before "What devil was't"):

        Sense sure, you have,
      Else could you not have motion: but sure that sense
      Is apoplexed, for madness would not err
55   Nor sense to ecstasy was ne'er so thralled
      But it reserved some quantity of choice,
      To serve in such a difference.

Following 3.4.80:

      Eyes without feeling, feeling without sight,
      Ears without hands or eyes, smelling sans all,
60   Or but a sickly part of one true sense
      Could not so mope.

Following 3.4.166:

      That monster, custom, who all sense doth eat
      Of habits devil, is angel yet in this,
      That to the use of actions fair and good
65   He likewise gives a frock or livery,
      That aptly is put on.

Following 3.4.170 (before "Once more, goodnight"):

        the next more easy,
      For use almost can change the stamp of nature,
      And either [ ] the devil, or throw him out
70   With wondrous potency.

Following 3.4.178:

      One word more, good lady.

Following 3.4.201:

HAMLET There's letters sealed: and my two schoolfellows,
      Whom I will trust as I will adders fanged,

---

51 anchor's cheer the provisions or lifestyle of an anchorite (i.e. hermit)   **scope** limit
52 Sense senses, feeling (in the following line the sense shifts to "reason")   **53 motion** the
power of movement/emotions and impulses   **54 apoplexed** paralyzed   **err** err in this
manner/err to this degree   **55 ecstasy** madness   **thralled** enslaved   **56 quantity** small
amount   **57 serve . . . difference** enable it to distinguish between the two men   **59 *sans***
without   **61 mope** be stupefied/wander aimlessly   **62 sense . . . devil** destroys all sensitivity
to devilish practices   **64 use** habit/undertaking   **65 frock** monk's clothing/man's coat/dress
livery uniform   **66 aptly** readily   **68 use** habit   **69 [ ]** a verb is missing here; editors often
insert "master" or, more recently, "shame"   **70 wondrous potency** extraordinary power

They bear the mandate, they must sweep my way,
75 And marshal me to knavery. Let it work:
For 'tis the sport to have the enginer
Hoist with his own petard: and't shall go hard
But I will delve one yard below their mines
And blow them at the moon. O, 'tis most sweet
80 When in one line two crafts directly meet.

Following 4.3.9:

Exeunt all [but the Captain]

Enter Hamlet, Rosencrantz and others

HAMLET Good sir, whose powers are these?
CAPTAIN They are of Norway, sir.
HAMLET How purposed, sir, I pray you?
CAPTAIN Against some part of Poland.
85 HAMLET Who commands them, sir?
CAPTAIN The nephew to old Norway, Fortinbras.
HAMLET Goes it against the main of Poland, sir,
Or for some frontier?
CAPTAIN Truly to speak, and with no addition,
90 We go to gain a little patch of ground
That hath in it no profit but the name.
To pay five ducats, five, I would not farm it:
Nor will it yield to Norway or the Pole
A ranker rate, should it be sold in fee.
95 HAMLET Why, then the Polack never will defend it.
CAPTAIN Yes, it is already garrisoned.
HAMLET Two thousand souls and twenty thousand ducats
Will not debate the question of this straw!
This is th'imposthume of much wealth and peace,
100 That inward breaks, and shows no cause without
Why the man dies. I humbly thank you, sir.
CAPTAIN God buy you, sir.   *[Exit]*
ROSENCRANTZ Will't please you go, my lord?
HAMLET I'll be with you straight: go a little before.

[Exeunt all but Hamlet]

105 How all occasions do inform against me,
And spur my dull revenge. What is a man,
If his chief good and market of his time

---

74 sweep my way clear my path   **75 marshal** guide   **76 enginer** constructor of military
engines (weaponry)/plotter   **77 Hoist . . . petard** blown up by his own bomb   **and't . . . But**
unless luck is against me   **78 delve . . . mines** i.e. countermine by digging deeper than and
intercepting the enemy mines   **80 crafts** cunning plots   **81 powers** troops   **87 main** main
part   **89 addition** exaggeration   **92 farm** rent   **94 ranker** higher   **fee** fee simple, i.e. sold
outright, with no conditions   **98 Will . . . straw** are not enough to fight out this trifling issue
99 th'imposthume abscess   **102 buy** i.e. be with   **104 straight** straightaway   **105 inform**
against betray/bring a charge against   **107 market** profit

Be but to sleep and feed? A beast, no more.
Sure he that made us with such large discourse,
110   Looking before and after, gave us not
That capability and godlike reason
To fust in us unused. Now, whether it be
Bestial oblivion, or some craven scruple
Of thinking too precisely on th'event—
115   A thought which, quartered, hath but one part wisdom
And ever three parts coward—I do not know
Why yet I live to say this thing's to do,
Sith I have cause and will and strength and means
To do't. Examples gross as earth exhort me:
120   Witness this army of such mass and charge
Led by a delicate and tender prince,
Whose spirit with divine ambition puffed
Makes mouths at the invisible event,
Exposing what is mortal and unsure
125   To all that fortune, death and danger dare,
Even for an eggshell. Rightly to be great
Is not to stir without great argument,
But greatly to find quarrel in a straw
When honour's at the stake. How stand I then,
130   That have a father killed, a mother stained,
Excitements of my reason and my blood,
And let all sleep, while to my shame I see
The imminent death of twenty thousand men
That, for a fantasy and trick of fame,
135   Go to their graves like beds, fight for a plot
Whereon the numbers cannot try the cause,
Which is not tomb enough and continent
To hide the slain? O, from this time forth,
My thoughts be bloody, or be nothing worth!   *Exit*

Following 4.6.43:
140   Of him that brought them.

---

109 discourse powers of reasoning   **110 Looking . . . after** able to look ahead and to assess
what is past   **112 fust** molder   **113 oblivion** forgetfulness   **craven** cowardly   **114 Of**
resulting from   **precisely** scrupulously   **th'event** outcome   **117 to do** i.e. yet to be done
118 Sith since   **119 gross** obvious/large/material, earthly   **120 mass and charge** size and
cost   **121 delicate** fine/skilled/elegant   **tender** youthful   **123 Makes mouths** makes faces,
i.e. is scornful   **invisible event** unforseeable outcome   **125 dare** can do/can threaten
126 Rightly . . . great i.e. true greatness   **127 stir** i.e. take up arms   **great argument** a noble
cause   **128 greatly . . . straw** to find great cause for contention over a trifle   **131 Excitements**
incitements, provocations   **blood** anger/passion   **134 fantasy and trick** illusory and
deceptive whim   **fame** reputation, honor   **135 plot** plot of land   **136 Whereon . . . cause**
which is not big enough to hold the soldiers who are to fight for it   **137 continent** (sufficiently
large) container; plays on the sense of "land"

Following 4.6.71 (before "Some two months since"):

LAERTES My lord, I will be ruled,
  The rather, if you could devise it so
  That I might be the organ.
 KING It falls right.
145 You have been talked of since your travel much,
  And that in Hamlet's hearing, for a quality
  Wherein they say you shine: your sum of parts
  Did not together pluck such envy from him
  As did that one, and that, in my regard,
150 Of the unworthiest siege.
 LAERTES What part is that, my lord?
 KING A very ribbon in the cap of youth,
  Yet needful too, for youth no less becomes
  The light and careless livery that it wears
155 Than settled age his sables and his weeds
  Importing health and graveness.

Following 4.6.92 (before "Sir, this report"):

  The scrimers of their nation,
  He swore had neither motion, guard, nor eye,
  If you opposed them.

Following 4.6.105:

160 There lives within the very flame of love
  A kind of wick or snuff that will abate it:
  And nothing is at a like goodness still,
  For goodness, growing to a pleurisy,
  Dies in his own too much. That we would do,
165 We should do when we would, for this 'would' changes
  And hath abatements and delays as many
  As there are tongues, are hands, are accidents,
  And then this 'should' is like a spendthrift sigh
  That hurts by easing. But, to the quick of th'ulcer:

---

143 organ instrument, agent (of Hamlet's death)   **144 falls right** fits well   **147 your . . . parts** all of your other qualitites   **150 unworthiest siege** least importance   **152 ribbon** i.e. mere adornment/crowning accomplishment   **153 becomes** suits   **155 sables** garments trimmed with sable fur   **weeds** clothing/mourning garments   **156 health** well-being/prosperity   **157 scrimers** fencers (from the French *escrimeur*)   **158 motion** skilled and trained movements   **eye** quick perception   **162 is . . . still** remains always at the same degree of goodness   **163 pleurisy** excess/chest inflammation   **164 too much** excess   **That** that which   **would** wish to   **167 tongues . . . accidents** i.e. tongues to dissuade one, hands to prevent one and chance events to get in the way   **168 spendthrift** i.e. wasteful; each **sigh** was thought to drain a drop of blood from the heart   **169 hurts by easing** harms the heart at the same time as it eases the immediate emotional pain of the sufferer   **quick** tender central part

Following 5.2.107:

170   Sir, here is newly come to court Laertes—believe me, an absolute gentleman, full of most excellent differences, of very soft society and great showing: indeed, to speak feelingly of him, he is the card or calendar of gentry, for you shall find in him the continent of what part a gentleman would see.

175   HAMLET Sir, his definement suffers no perdition in you, though I know, to divide him inventorially would dizzy the arithmetic of memory, and yet but yaw neither, in respect of his quick sail. But, in the verity of extolment, I take him to be a soul of great article and his infusion of such dearth and rareness as, to make true diction of him, his semblable is his mirror and who
180   else would trace him his umbrage, nothing more.

  OSRIC Your lordship speaks most infallibly of him.

  HAMLET The concernancy, sir? Why do we wrap the gentleman in our more rawer breath?

  OSRIC Sir?

185   HORATIO Is't not possible to understand in another tongue? You will do't, sir, really.

  HAMLET What imports the nomination of this gentleman?

  OSRIC Of Laertes?

  HORATIO His purse is empty already: all's golden words are spent.

190   HAMLET Of him, sir.

  OSRIC I know you are not ignorant—

  HAMLET I would you did, sir. Yet in faith if you did, it would not much approve me. Well, sir?

  OSRIC You are not ignorant of what excellence Laertes is—

195   HAMLET I dare not confess that, lest I should compare with him in excellence: but to know a man well were to know himself.

---

170 absolute perfect, accomplished   **171 differences** fine qualities   **soft society** pleasant company/sociable manners   **great showing** fine appearance   **172 feelingly** to the purpose, with just perception   **card or calendar** map or guide   **173 the . . . see** one who contains any quality a gentleman would wish to see   **175 definement** definition (Hamlet begins to mock Osric's affected language)   **perdition** loss   **you** i.e. your account of him   **to . . . inventorially** to list his qualities, to itemize him   **176 but . . . sail** merely swing unsteadily off course in comparison to his speedy sailing (i.e. Laertes outstrips attempts to define his virtues) **177 in . . . extolment** to praise him truthfully   **178 of great article** highly accomplished, with many qualities to list in an inventory   **infusion** essence (literally, what has been infused into him)   **dearth** rarity/costliness   **179 make . . . diction** speak truly   **his mirror** the only person truly like him is his reflection in a mirror   **who** whoever   **180 trace** follow/imitate **his umbrage** is his shadow   **181 infallibly** absolutely truly   **182 The concernancy, sir?** Why is all this relevant?   **183 rawer breath** crude words that cannot do him justice   **185 in another tongue** i.e. when someone speaks your own elaborate language   **do't** get there in the end   **187 nomination** naming   **192 approve me** commend me, be to my credit **195 I . . . himself** I do not dare to admit that I know just how excellent a man Laertes is lest I should seem to be comparing myself favorably with him: to know a man well one must first know oneself

OSRIC I mean, sir, for his weapon: but in the imputation laid on him, by them in his meed, he's unfellowed.

Following 5.2.119:

HORATIO I knew you must be edified by the margent ere you had done.

Following 5.2.153:

Enter a Lord

200 LORD My lord, his majesty commended him to you by young Osric, who brings back to him that you attend him in the hall: he sends to know if your pleasure hold to play with Laertes or that you will take longer time.

HAMLET I am constant to my purposes, they follow the king's pleasure: if his fitness speaks, mine is ready. Now or whensoever, provided I be so able as

205 now.

LORD The king and queen and all are coming down.

HAMLET In happy time.

LORD The queen desires you to use some gentle entertainment to Laertes before you fall to play.

210 HAMLET She well instructs me.

[*Exit Lord*]

---

197 for i.e. with   **in . . . meed** in the estimation of those in his pay (i.e. servants/fencing-masters), he is unparalleled/in the estimation of others, he's unmatched by any man of comparable worth and honor   **199 edified . . . margent** instructed by the explanatory notes in the margin   **201 that** if   **203 if . . . ready** my readiness waits on his convenience   **207 In happy time** at an opportune moment   **208 use . . . entertainment** give a courteous reception

TEXTUAL NOTES

Q2 = Second Quarto text of 1604/5
Q3 = a correction introduced in the Third Quarto text of 1611
Ed = a correction introduced by a later editor

5 mote *spelled* moth *in* Q2   **14 feared** = Ed. Q2 = feare   **24 clepe** *spelled* clip *in* Q2   **42 often douse** = Ed. Q2 = of a doubt   **51 An anchor's** = Ed. Q2 = And Anchors   **168 spendthrift** = Ed. Q2 = spend thirsts   **172 feelingly** = Q3. Q2 = fellingly *(in some copies)* sellingly *(in other copies)*   **176 dizzy** = Q3. Q2 = dosie *(in some copies)* dazzie *(in other copies)*

SCENE-BY-SCENE ANALYSIS

ACT 1 SCENE 1

Lines 1–14: The play begins with a question, as the guards Barnardo and Francisco swap shifts and Barnardo asks "Who's there?," evoking the themes of identity, uncertainty and existence which indicate that this is a reflective play, often with more emphasis on thought and speech than on action. The information that it is midnight reinforces setting, with ideas of night and darkness and the associated themes of secrecy/deception. It also introduces the concept of "balance" between two opposites: the play begins at the point between one day and another, a literal representation of this "balance" between key themes and motifs such as day/night, words/actions, physical/spiritual and appearance/reality.

Lines 15–117: Marcellus brings Horatio to witness an "apparition" that he and the sentinels have previously seen, as Horatio thinks they have imagined the whole thing. Barnardo begins to describe a previous encounter when the ghost appears. Commenting on its resemblance to the late king, they urge it to speak, but the ghost leaves in silence. Shaken, Horatio says that he would not believe it "Without the sensible and true avouch" of his "own eyes," a statement that raises the theme of sight/perception. He adds that the appearance of the ghost "bodes some strange eruption to our state," establishing that the play functions on a national/public level, often in tension with the individual/personal. Marcellus asks why Denmark appears to be preparing for war. Horatio explains that the late king conquered lands belonging to Norway and that the young Norwegian prince, Fortinbras, is preparing to take them back.

Lines 118–168: The ghost reappears and, as Horatio attempts to make it speak, a cock crows. Horatio instructs Marcellus to "Stop it" and Marcellus strikes at the ghost, which leaves again. Horatio suggests that they tell Prince Hamlet what they have seen, as, if it really is the ghost of his father, it will speak to him.

ACT 1 SCENE 2

Lines 1–128: King Claudius (whose name is never mentioned in the dialogue) makes a speech to court, expressing his grief at the death of his brother and announcing that he has married his brother's widow, Queen Gertrude: "With mirth in funeral and with dirge in marriage, / In equal scale weighing delight and dole," again suggesting balance between opposites. The speech is formal and ceremonious, as Claudius emphasizes his new role as king, but it seems awkward as well: it is difficult to reconcile his apparent grief with his happiness at his marriage. Claudius also announces that Fortinbras is demanding the "surrender" of the captured Norwegian lands, and he sends two ambassadors to inform the king of Norway, Fortinbras' elderly uncle, of his nephew's actions. Laertes asks for permission to return to his studies in France now that he has shown his duty in attending Claudius' coronation. Claudius agrees, provided Laertes has Polonius' permission, which is given. Three sets of father/son relationships have now been established, emphasizing the importance of this particular family dynamic to the play. Claudius turns to Hamlet, addressing him as "my son," and asks him why "the clouds still hang" on him, to which Hamlet replies that he is "too much i'th'sun." This pun on "son/sun" establishes the wordplay that is a key feature of this play, particularly in Hamlet's speeches. Language/words are focused on and explored throughout in terms of the complexities of "meaning," and also as an opposition to action. Gertrude asks Hamlet to stop wearing mourning for his father, but Hamlet responds that his grief goes much deeper than "the trappings and the suits of woe," reinforcing the theme of appearance and reality and the motif of clothing. He argues that there is a difference between what is "within" and external appearances, which are something a "man might play," an expression that raises the theme of performance/theater. Claudius accuses Hamlet of "impious stubbornness," and calls his grief "unmanly," one of several reflections on gender. In a more conciliatory tone, he asks Hamlet to think of him as a father, and says that he would prefer him to remain in court rather than returning to university in Wittenberg. Gertrude adds her "prayers" that Hamlet will remain, and he agrees.

Lines 129–271: Alone, Hamlet embarks on the first of the many soliloquies that reveal his introspective nature. He wishes that he could die and that his "too solid flesh would melt," emphasizing the opposing elements of physical and spiritual as he also regrets that suicide is a sin against God. He contemplates the "stale" nature of the world, comparing it to an "unweeded garden" filled with "things rank and gross in nature," establishing the recurring motif of decay/infection. He reveals his disgust at his mother's remarriage and the "wicked speed" with which she moved between "incestuous sheets." He recalls how much she appeared to love his father, blaming her behavior on the fickle nature of her sex: "frailty, thy name is woman!" Horatio, Barnardo and Marcellus arrive. Horatio tells Hamlet about seeing his father's ghost. Hamlet resolves to watch that night and to try to speak to it. After they leave, he contemplates what the appearance of the "armed" ghost means, suspecting "some foul play."

ACT 1 SCENE 3

Laertes says goodbye to his sister, Ophelia. He warns her against "Hamlet and the trifling of his favours," saying that, while Hamlet may love her now, their difference of rank is too great for him to marry Ophelia and so she must not open her "chaste treasure" to him. Ophelia says that she will do as he asks, but reminds him that he must not preach virtue to her and then behave immorally himself. Polonius arrives and urges his son to board the ship, which is ready to sail. He kindly, but pompously, gives Laertes a great deal of advice and bids him farewell. Laertes urges Ophelia to remember what he has said and leaves. Polonius asks Ophelia what Laertes meant and, hearing that it concerns Hamlet, repeats Laertes' advice in harsher, more realistic terms. He forbids Ophelia to "give words or talk with the Lord Hamlet," and Ophelia obeys with a readiness that demonstrates her father's authority over her.

ACT 1 SCENE 4

Hamlet, Horatio and Marcellus wait for the ghost as sounds of revelry from the court are heard in the background. The Ghost appears and Hamlet declares his intention to speak to it, whether it is "a spirit of health or goblin damned," raising the possibility that the Ghost is a malevolent force and reminding us that appearances are subjective. The Ghost beckons and Hamlet follows, despite Horatio and Marcellus' attempts to stop him.

ACT 1 SCENE 5

Lines 1–118: The Ghost tells Hamlet that he is his father's spirit, "Doomed for a certain time to walk the night," and asks Hamlet to revenge his murder. The ghostly request for revenge is a key element of the "revenge tragedy," a genre that is acknowledged throughout the play, but also consciously explored and challenged. Hamlet begs to hear more, so that he may "sweep" to his revenge. The Ghost explains that Hamlet's father was not, as everyone believes, killed by a snake's bite. He tells Hamlet that Claudius first seduced the "seeming virtuous queen," Gertrude, and then killed him by pouring poison in his ear as he slept (a literal representation of the rumor and plotting in the play). He urges Hamlet to kill Claudius, but says that he must spare Gertrude, who will be punished by her own guilt: "the thorns that in her bosom lodge." Morning approaches and the ghost leaves, urging Hamlet to remember him. Alone, Hamlet swears that he will remember nothing else.

Lines 119–207: Horatio and Marcellus find Hamlet and question him, but he reveals nothing except that "There's ne'er a villain dwelling in all Denmark / But he's an arrant knave," a statement that is both true and meaningless, showing the ambiguity of language and Hamlet's control over it. Hamlet asks his companions to swear on his sword that they will never reveal what they have seen that night. The voice of the Ghost repeats "swear," and Horatio and Marcellus do so. Hamlet's disjointed speech reveals his state of mind as he thinks about what he has heard. Establishing the theme of sanity/madness, he hints that he may in the future pretend to be mad: "put an antic disposition on," and asks them not to reveal what they know, whatever happens.

ACT 2 SCENE 1

Polonius sends Reynaldo to Paris with messages and money for his son, but tells him that first he is to spy on Laertes and spread rumors about him to the effect that he is "very wild." Ironically, he explains the purpose behind these lies is to discover the truth about Laertes' behavior. He shows Reynaldo how to subtly generate rumors, demonstrating the potential distance between words and truth. The conversation reveals tensions in the characterization of Polonius: his instructions to Reynaldo show cunning, but the reason for them seems nonsensical and foolish. The latter aspect to his character is emphasized by his long-windedness and temporary forgetfulness mid-speech, requiring Reynaldo to "prompt" him in a moment that becomes almost metatheatrical. Reynaldo leaves and Ophelia enters, telling Polonius that she has been "affrighted" by Hamlet, who appeared in her chamber half-dressed and looking "As if he had been loosèd out of hell." She reports that Hamlet did not speak, but just held her arm and stared at her face. Polonius decides that Hamlet has gone mad with love for Ophelia and goes to tell Claudius.

ACT 2 SCENE 2

Lines 1–89: Claudius greets Rosencrantz and Guildenstern, for-mer schoolfellows of Hamlet. He explains that he is worried about Hamlet and suggests that they might spend time with him and find out whether there is anything "unknown" afflicting him. Although Claudius presents this as kindly concern, revealing his capacity as an "actor," we are reminded of Polonius' attempts to spy on Laertes. Rosencrantz and Guildenstern agree to help, and are taken to find Hamlet. Polonius brings the news that the ambassadors have arrived back from Norway and adds that he has found the "very cause of Hamlet's lunacy." He insists that Claudius sees the ambassadors first, however, and goes to fetch them. The ambassadors report that the king of Norway believed Fortinbras was preparing for war on Poland,

but found out that it was really against Denmark. He ordered Fortinbras to cease plotting against Denmark and genuinely prepare to
fight Poland. The king of Norway sends a request that Claudius will
grant him "quiet pass" through his lands, and Claudius promises to
consider it.

Lines 90–227: Despite declaring that he will be brief, Polonius
embarks on a lengthy and rambling explanation of Hamlet's madness that demonstrates his obsequious attitude to the king and
queen. He reads out a love letter from Hamlet to Ophelia and
explains that he instructed Ophelia not to encourage Hamlet
because of the difference in their status. He explains that Hamlet's
madness stems from being "repulsèd" by Ophelia. Claudius and
Gertrude ask Polonius if he is certain and he offers to prove it, suggesting a plan: he will "loose" Ophelia to Hamlet, and then hide
behind an arras with Claudius to watch the encounter. His choice
of vocabulary reduces Ophelia to the level of an animal, demonstrating her powerlessness and her status as one her father's pos-
sessions. Claudius agrees to the plan and, as Hamlet enters, he and
Gertrude leave. Polonius greets Hamlet, who appears not to recognize him. Hamlet's disjointed and nonsensical speech suggests
madness, but many of his remarks contain implicit comments/
criticisms on Polonius' character. This uncertainty as to the extent
and veracity of Hamlet's madness has been the subject of much
debate in the play's critical history, as the audience remains uncertain as to whether he is really mad or merely acting, or, perhaps,
there is a genuine disturbance due to his father's death that he is
exaggerating for his own purposes. Rosencrantz and Guildenstern
arrive and Polonius leaves.

Lines 228–372: Hamlet seems pleased to see Rosencrantz and
Guildenstern, but asks them why they have come to the "prison" of
Denmark. They cheerfully claim that they have come solely to see
Hamlet, but he tells them that he knows that Claudius and Gertrude
sent for them. Our perception of Hamlet's sanity is further confused
during this exchange, as his manner toward Rosencrantz and
Guildenstern is introspective and melancholy, but shows nothing of
the "madness" he portrayed to Polonius. Rosencrantz tells him that

they have engaged a group of "Players," "the tragedians of the city," that Hamlet has previously enjoyed watching. The presence of the Players further develops the theme of theater/performance and the conversation about them establishes a metatheatrical commentary on the conventions of genre, as Hamlet lists various recognizable "roles" (the "adventurous knight," the "lover" and the "clown," for example). A flourish announces the arrival of the Players and Hamlet tells Rosencrantz and Guildenstern that they are "welcome to Elsinore," adding that his "uncle-father and aunt-mother are deceived" about his madness, a description that emphasizes the "incestuous" nature of Claudius and Gertrude's relationship, and the uncomfortably close nature of various family dynamics in the play.

Lines 373–533: Polonius returns, and Hamlet switches back to a more disjointed pattern of speech. He breaks off to welcome the Players and asks one man to recite a speech about the fall of Troy, which he begins and which is then taken up by the player, emphasizing Hamlet's potential role as an "actor." Pleased with the recital, Hamlet asks Polonius to "see the players well bestowed" and asks for a performance of *The Murder of Gonzago* the next day, adding that he has written "some dozen or sixteen lines" that he would like them to add.

Lines 534–591: Hamlet's soliloquy reveals his anguish at his own inaction, a factor that conflicts with his potential role of revenge-hero and one of the ways in which the play challenges expectations of genre. He comments that the player who gave the speech was able to summon emotion for a character in a play, whereas he himself is a "dull and muddy-mettled rascal" who remains unmotivated by a genuine "cue for passion." The tensions between actions and words are explored again, as Hamlet comments that, despite being "Prompted to [his] revenge by heaven and hell," all he does is "unpack" his heart "with words." He outlines his plan to establish Claudius' guilt: the players will act out "something like" the death of his father, while he watches Claudius' reaction. This will give him proof that Claudius really did commit the murder and allay his concern that the spirit might have been "the devil," working to damn him, rather than the genuine ghost of his father.

ACT 3 SCENE 1

Lines 1–61: Claudius questions Rosencrantz and Guildenstern. They report that they cannot find out what is troubling Hamlet, who has evaded their questions "with a crafty madness." The king tells them to encourage Hamlet's interest in the players and they leave. Claudius asks Gertrude to leave, so that he and Polonius may secretly observe the arranged meeting between Ophelia and Hamlet. Polonius "directs" Ophelia in how she is to act, drawing attention once more to theater/performance and appearance/reality as he comments on how a "pious action" can "sugar o'er / The devil himself." This prompts an aside about his "conscience" from Claudius, the first implicit acknowledgment of his guilt that he has made. Hearing Hamlet approach, they withdraw, forming a dual audience to the action, further revealing the play's self-conscious theatricality.

Lines 62–166: Hamlet appears to be contemplating suicide as he asks himself: "To be, or not to be," although the question can be considered in a more abstract way than just Hamlet's choice over whether to live or die, and can potentially transcend the action of the play as a philosophical argument. It returns us to the concept of "balance," between flesh/spirit and action/inaction, as Hamlet is torn between a passive acceptance of life's events, "to suffer / The slings and arrows of outrageous fortune," and definitive resistance to them: "to take arms against a sea of troubles, / And by opposing end them." Hamlet breaks off as he sees Ophelia, who tries to return some love-tokens that he has previously given her. Hamlet's disjointed responses become a wild verbal attack on Ophelia that further complicates our understanding of his mental state, seeming too extreme to be merely acting. It is also difficult to distinguish whether Hamlet's outburst is personal and related directly to his feelings for Ophelia, or an attack on all women and their sexuality, possibly generated by his disgust at his mother's relationship with his uncle. He repeatedly tells Ophelia to go "to a nunnery," and then leaves abruptly. Ophelia laments the loss of Hamlet's "sovereign reason."

Lines 167–194: Claudius and Polonius discuss what they have overheard. Claudius is not convinced that Hamlet's madness is the result of love, nor, indeed, that Hamlet is actually mad. He says that there is something in Hamlet's soul "O'er which his melancholy sits on brood" and that he is worried that the "hatch and the disclose" of this thing will be "some danger" (although he does not acknowledge aloud the fear that the danger will be to himself). He resolves to send Hamlet to England, claiming that the change might "expel" the "something-settled matter" from his heart. Polonius agrees, but still insists that Hamlet's problem is "neglected love." He suggests a further test of this: Queen Gertrude will speak "all alone" to her son, and "entreat him / To show his griefs," while Polonius will conceal himself again and listen to the exchange.

ACT 3 SCENE 2

The performance of the play-within-the-play makes the theme of theater/performance explicit and focuses attention on the nature of "reality." The presence of a dual audience also emphasizes the theme of sight/perception, as we watch the characters watching a play, and, more specifically, Hamlet secretly observing Claudius (neatly reversing their roles of observed/observer from the previous scene).

Lines 1–129: Hamlet directs the players as to how he wants them to deliver the lines he has written, urging them to "suit the action to the word, the word to the action"—an ironic instruction given the apparent disparity between words and actions in the wider play. The players go to prepare and Hamlet sends Polonius, Rosencrantz and Guildenstern to "hasten" them. Horatio arrives and Hamlet excitedly explains his plan and tells him to watch Claudius. Horatio agrees, and the king and queen enter in a formal procession with other members of the court, accompanied by guards and torchbearers. This ceremony emphasizes the public setting for this scene, which contrasts with the concealed secrets, emotions and intentions of the various characters. Hamlet continues to disconcert everyone with his changeable speech, including some bawdy wordplay directed at Ophelia that emphasizes his fixation with women in terms of their sexuality. Music sounds, and the dumb show begins.

Lines 130–256: The dumb show establishes the plot of the play-within-the-play, and the events surrounding the death of Hamlet's father in the wider play. This paralleling of storylines creates meta-theatrical awareness, emphasized by Ophelia's comment, "Belike this show imports the argument of the play." The full performance begins, with asides from Hamlet as he comments on and explains the action for the others. Ophelia says that he makes a "good chorus," emphasizing his capacity as an "actor" but also highlighting that, despite this, he is often slightly distanced from the action, observing and commenting rather than participating. Hamlet responds to Ophelia with his usual harsh, deliberately sexual, wordplay. As we reach the point in the play-within-the-play where "Lucianus" kills "Gonzago" by pouring poison in his ear, Claudius rushes out, calling for light and throwing the court into confusion.

Lines 257–379: Hamlet and Horatio discuss Claudius' behavior and Horatio's more measured response contrasts with Hamlet's wild exclamations of conviction as to his uncle's guilt. Rosencrantz and Guildenstern come to report that the king is "marvellous distempered" and that they have been sent by Gertrude to fetch Hamlet. Despite their attempts to make Hamlet respond in a more reasoned way and put his "discourse into some frame," he continues to disconcert them with his unpredictable speech and behavior. He accuses them of trying to "play" him as they might play a musical instrument. Polonius interrupts and tells Hamlet to go to his mother. When he is left alone, Hamlet prepares himself to see Gertrude, declaring that he will be "cruel," but "not unnatural" and that although he will "speak daggers" he will "use none."

ACT 3 SCENE 3

Claudius tells Rosencrantz and Guildenstern that he is sending Hamlet to England immediately as he does not feel that it is safe "To let his madness range." He instructs them that they are to accompany Hamlet, and they go to prepare for the voyage. Polonius brings the news that Hamlet is going to speak to Gertrude and that he intends to conceal himself so as to "hear the process." Once alone, Claudius makes his first direct admission of guilt: he has committed an act that has "the primal eldest curse upon't, / A brother's murder." Claudius' conscience appears to be troubling him as he tries to pray but cannot and, although he wishes to be forgiven for his sin, he does not wish to give up the "effects" it has brought him: his "crown," his "ambition" and his "queen." He wonders whether it is possible to "be pardoned and retain th'offence." He kneels and attempts to pray. Hamlet enters and, seeing Claudius, prepares to kill him. Once more, however, the expected progress of the revenge tragedy is frustrated as Hamlet shifts from a definite declaration of action, "now I'll do't," to further uncertainty. Emphasizing the opposing concepts of the physical/spiritual aspects to humanity, he considers the spiritual consequences of killing Claudius. He argues that, if he kills Claudius while he is at prayer, then Claudius' soul will go to heaven, which would be more of a reward than a punishment. Deciding to wait until Claudius is "about some act / That has no relish of salvation in't" so that "his soul may be as damned and black / As hell, whereto it goes," Hamlet puts up his sword and leaves. Claudius, unaware of his presence, rises and ironically announces that he could not pray, as "Words without thoughts never to heaven go."

ACT 3 SCENE 4

Lines 1–44: Polonius arranges with Gertrude that he will conceal himself behind the arras to overhear her conversation with Hamlet. Hamlet arrives, and Gertrude accuses him of offending his father (meaning Claudius). He responds that it is she who has offended, referring to his actual father. He continues to parry her attempts to question him, demonstrating his characteristic verbal dexterity, and then insists that she sit down so that he may show her "the inmost part" of herself. Frightened that Hamlet intends to attack her, Gertrude cries out and Polonius responds, calling for help from behind the arras. In an unusual moment of spontaneous action, Hamlet stabs the concealed figure, believing it to be Claudius. When he discovers that he has killed Polonius, he is unmoved, merely saying "Thou wretched, rash, intruding fool, farewell," before turning once more to his mother.

Lines 45–105: Gertrude asks what she has done to deserve Hamlet's anger. He shows her two pictures, one of his father and one of Claudius, "The counterfeit presentment of two brothers," a visual symbol of the theme of identity. He urges her to look at the picture of his father, "Jove himself," and to compare it with a picture of Claudius, who is "like a mildewed ear" of corn. He asks her how she could "step" from one to the other, showing his bitterness and disgust. Despite Gertrude's attempts to stop him, he continues to accuse her, focusing particularly on the sexual aspect of her betrayal. Distressed, Gertrude claims that Hamlet has revealed her "very soul," which has "such black and grained spots." As she begs "No more!" the Ghost appears.

Lines 106–208: Hamlet fears that the Ghost has come to "chide" him for not taking revenge on Claudius, and the Ghost urges him to act, claiming that he is there "to whet" Hamlet's "almost blunted purpose." As they talk, it becomes clear that Gertrude cannot see the Ghost. Hamlet urges her to "look" as the Ghost leaves them, but Gertrude takes this as a sign of his insanity. Hamlet insists that he is "But mad in craft" and urges his mother to repent of her sins and avoid any further relationship with Claudius. He asks her to keep his feigned madness a secret and she agrees. He leaves, dragging Polonius' body with him.

Lines 209–249: Gertrude tells Claudius that Hamlet is "Mad as the seas and wind" in a storm, although it is uncertain whether she is lying to Claudius or still believes this to be true. She reports how Hamlet killed Polonius, and Claudius uses this as his excuse to send Hamlet to England. Sustaining his performance of grief at his nephew's behavior, he orders Rosencrantz and Guildenstern to find Hamlet and take Polonius' body to the chapel.

ACT 4 SCENE 1

Hamlet enters, commenting that Polonius is "safely stowed." Rosencrantz and Guildenstern come to ask what he has done with the body and Hamlet accuses them of being "sponges" out of which Claudius may squeeze information. He agrees to see the king, but leaves, running, with Rosencrantz and Guildenstern following.

ACT 4 SCENE 2

Claudius contemplates the danger he is in while Hamlet "goes loose," but says that he cannot "put the strong law on him" because Hamlet is loved by Denmark's people. He compares sending Hamlet away to ridding himself of a disease, reinforcing previous references to infection/decay. Rosencrantz arrives and reports that Hamlet will not reveal the whereabouts of the body, but that they have managed to get him to come to Claudius. Guildenstern brings Hamlet in and Claudius demands Polonius' body. Hamlet gives a nonsensical, macabre response, but eventually tells them that they will "nose him" in the lobby, another image of decay that emphasizes the corporeal, rather than spiritual, aspect of death. Claudius sends someone to find the body and, pretending great sorrow, informs Hamlet that he must go to England immediately as a result of his actions. Hamlet apparently agrees and Claudius sends Rosencrantz and Guildenstern to hurry Hamlet on board the ship. When they have left, Claudius' soliloquy reveals that he is sending letters to the English, instructing them to kill Hamlet.

ACT 4 SCENE 3

Fortinbras, marching across stage with his army, sends a messenger to tell Claudius that he is claiming safe passage across Denmark. In the Quarto version of the play (see "Second Quarto Passages That Do Not Appear in the Folio"), Hamlet witnesses the march and contrasts Fortinbras' willingness to "find quarrel in a straw" when his honor is affronted to his own inaction in the face of monstrous provocation.

ACT 4 SCENE 4

Lines 1–110: Horatio persuades Gertrude to see Ophelia, who has been sent mad by the death of her father. Ophelia is shown in and reveals a genuine, pitiful madness that contrasts with the potentially more contrived or exaggerated moments of Hamlet's insanity. She speaks mostly in rhyme and, while her ideas are disjointed and largely nonsensical, they focus on death and sex. Ophelia leaves and Claudius sends Horatio to watch over her. He laments recent events, and comments to Gertrude that the people of Denmark are stirred up by Polonius' death and have become "Thick and unwholesome in their thoughts and whispers." They are interrupted by a messenger, bringing the news that Laertes has stormed Elsinore.

Lines 111–228: Laertes breaks in, demanding vengeance for his father's death, creating parallels and contrasts with Hamlet, as Laertes also becomes a potential "revenge hero." In contrast to Hamlet's hesitant and thoughtful approach, Laertes is intent on action and his assertion that he will "dare damnation" shows that he has less consideration for the moral/spiritual issues raised by revenge. The king and queen explain that Claudius is not responsible for Polonius' death and Laertes is calmer, until Ophelia returns. He is aghast at the change in his sister, who continues to sing in a distracted way and distributes flowers (possibly imaginary) such as "rosemary" for "remembrance" and "pansies" for "thoughts." She sings a lament, and leaves. Laertes calls on the gods as Claudius tries to calm him. He promises to help Laertes get revenge, saying that "where th'offence is, let the great axe fall."

ACT 4 SCENE 5

Sailors bring Horatio a letter from Hamlet. Hamlet explains that he was captured by pirates who have returned him to Denmark, while Rosencrantz and Guildenstern are still bound for England. He asks Horatio to see that some enclosed letters are given to Claudius and then to come to him.

ACT 4 SCENE 6

Laertes asks why Claudius did not take public action against Hamlet for Polonius' death. Claudius persuades him that it was because both the queen and the Danish people love Hamlet and he did not wish to upset her or cause trouble. A messenger brings the letter from Hamlet, announcing that he has returned to Denmark and asking to see Claudius the next day. The king is confused, but Laertes is pleased as it means he can confront and kill Hamlet. Claudius sees a way to rid himself of Hamlet and urges Laertes to take his revenge and show that he is his father's son "in deed / More than in words," again forcing a comparison with Hamlet, who generally seems more concerned with words than deeds. Claudius reminds Laertes that Hamlet has always been jealous of his abilities with a sword, and has long wished to fence with him. Claudius suggests that they tempt Hamlet into fencing with Laertes but that Laertes use an "unbated" sword rather than a blunted one. Laertes agrees and announces his intention to anoint the tip of the sword with poison. Claudius further suggests poisoning a cup of wine to give to Hamlet if he should win the duel. Gertrude interrupts with the news that Ophelia has drowned, describing how she went to a "glassy stream," dressed in a crown of flowers, and fell in. Gertrude seems to suggest that the fall was an accident, but Ophelia sang serenely as the weight of her clothes dragged her down. Laertes leaves, distraught.

ACT 5 SCENE 1

Lines 1–207: Two rustics are digging Ophelia's grave and discussing the fact that she is to have a Christian burial, despite appearing to have committed suicide. Their witty exchange creates dark humor when juxtaposed with their task. Hamlet and Horatio approach, unaware of who the grave is for. Hamlet observes that the gravedigger has no finer feelings as he sings while he digs and unceremoniously throws down any skulls that he unearths. Hamlet muses that status has no meaning once you are dead. He banters with the gravedigger, sustaining the witty wordplay that began the scene and ironically discussing the madness of "young Hamlet" as the gravedigger does not recognize him. Hamlet's discussion of himself in the third person emphasizes the divisions in his character that have been evident throughout. The banter continues until the rustic identifies one of the skulls as belonging to Yorick, a court jester that Hamlet knew as a child. Hamlet immediately becomes more introspective, philosophizing on the inevitability of death and commenting that no matter how great the man, he will eventually die and decompose: "Alexander [the Great] died, Alexander was buried, Alexander returneth into dust." This seems to mark a new turn in Hamlet's thoughts concerning death: until now he has largely been concerned with the spiritual, rather than corporeal, aspects of dying. He sees a funeral procession approach, led by the king, queen and Laertes, and notes that the funeral rites have been shortened, guessing that it is for a suicide. He and Horatio conceal themselves to watch.

Lines 208–293: Hamlet recognizes Laertes, who is asking the priest why the ceremony is so short. The priest explains that because Ophelia's death "was doubtful," she should really have been buried in "ground unsanctified" and that he has done as much as he has "warrantise" to do. Furious, Laertes retorts that his sister will become "a minist'ring angel" and Hamlet realizes that the funeral is for Ophelia. Gertrude scatters flowers in the grave, emphasizing the repeated association between Ophelia and flowers, which represent the transience and beauty of nature. Overcome, Laertes curses Hamlet for sending Ophelia mad and leaps into her grave, demanding to be buried with her. Hamlet steps forward and reveals his identity, also jumping into the grave. Laertes and Hamlet fight and Hamlet declares that he did love Ophelia. He rushes off, followed by Horatio. Claudius speaks to Laertes, obliquely reassuring him that the subject of their "last night's speech" will be put "to the present push."

ACT 5 SCENE 2

Lines 1–168: Hamlet tells Horatio the circumstances of his return to Denmark. He explains that while on board the ship he crept from his cabin and took the letter entrusted to Rosencrantz and Guildenstern by Claudius, containing the instructions for his execution. He explains how he forged a replacement letter from Claudius, asking that the English put Rosencrantz and Guildenstern "to sudden death." The next day he was captured by the pirates, leaving Rosencrantz and Guildenstern to sail to their deaths, a fate he feels that they deserved. He repeats his intention to kill Claudius and expresses regret at his behavior toward Laertes, acknowledging the similarities in their circumstances. They are interrupted by Osric, whose long-winded and obsequious manner is mocked by Hamlet. Osric explains that he has been sent to tell Hamlet that the king has placed a bet that he will win a fencing match against Laertes and to ask if Hamlet will take up the challenge. Hamlet agrees and Osric goes to report this. Horatio warns Hamlet that he will "lose this wager," but Hamlet says that he has been in "continual practice" and, anyway, it does not matter if he is killed as everyone must die: it is not important when, but "the readiness is all."

Lines 169–230: Claudius and Gertrude enter with Laertes, other courtiers and attendants, emphasizing the public nature of the duel in contrast to the secret intentions of Claudius and Laertes. The king joins Hamlet's and Laertes' hands and Hamlet asks for Laertes' pardon, explaining that his actions were "Never Hamlet," but the result of "madness" which caused "Hamlet from himself [to] be taken away," again reinforcing the fragmented nature of his identity. Laertes will not consider "reconcilement" until he has consulted "some elder masters" on the matter of honor, but he accepts Hamlet's "offered love." They begin to fence.

Lines 231–325: The fight signifies a shift from "words" to "action." After all the contemplation and conversation, we are presented with fast and confusing activity, added to by the various characters' brief comments and asides. There is a switch of rapiers, resulting in both Hamlet and Laertes being stabbed with the poisoned blade. Gertrude, meanwhile, mistakenly drinks the poisoned wine. She dies and Hamlet demands that they seek out the treachery that killed her. Laertes, realizing that he and Hamlet are both dying, explains everything and blames Claudius. Hamlet kills Claudius with the poisoned sword, finally fulfilling his quest for revenge. Laertes begs Hamlet to "exchange forgiveness" with him and dies. Hamlet forgives Laertes and curses the courtiers who stand around and watch as "but mutes or audience to this act," sustaining the theatrical awareness to the end. Horatio wishes to drink the poison and die, but Hamlet begs him to remain alive "in this harsh world," so as to tell Hamlet's story. A "warlike noise" is heard, and Osric explains that Fortinbras and the English ambassadors have arrived. Hamlet announces that Fortinbras will be the next king of Denmark and dies.

Lines 326–353: Fortinbras asks what has happened, and Horatio promises to tell him. We learn that Rosencrantz and Guildenstern are dead. Fortinbras claims the Danish throne and orders that Hamlet be given a military funeral.

HAMLET IN PERFORMANCE: THE RSC AND BEYOND

The best way to understand a Shakespeare play is to see it or ideally to participate in it. By examining a range of productions, we may gain a sense of the extraordinary variety of approaches and interpretations that are possible—a variety that gives Shakespeare his unique capacity to be reinvented and made "our contemporary" four centuries after his death.

We begin with a brief overview of the play's theatrical and cinematic life, offering historical perspectives on how it has been performed. We then analyze in more detail a series of productions staged over the last half-century by the Royal Shakespeare Company. The sense of dialogue between productions that can only occur when a company is dedicated to the revival and investigation of the Shakespeare canon over a long period, together with the uniquely comprehensive archival resource of promptbooks, program notes, reviews and interviews held on behalf of the RSC at the Shakespeare Birthplace Trust in Stratford-upon-Avon, allows an "RSC stage history" to become a crucible in which the chemistry of the play can be explored.

Finally, we go to the horse's mouth. Modern theater is dominated by the figure of the director. He, or sometimes she (like musical conducting, theater directing remains a male-dominated profession), must hold together the whole play, whereas the actor must concentrate on his or her part. The director's viewpoint is therefore especially valuable. Shakespeare's plasticity is wonderfully revealed when we hear directors of highly successful productions answering the same questions in very different ways.

FOUR CENTURIES OF *HAMLET:* AN OVERVIEW

Hamlet is the best-known and most discussed of all Shakespeare's plays. It is also one of the most frequently performed. The many early references to it suggest that this has always been the case. There is then a remarkably full stage history which reveals a certain continuity and predictability by way of a perpetual focus on the figure of the prince himself, claims for the "naturalistic" quality of the actor's performance, a sense of the play's special capacity to catch the contemporary Zeitgeist, cutting and rearranging of the text, and the international dimension and appeal of the play. The legendary centrality of the prince—with nearly forty percent of the lines—has led to the focus on the performance of the leading actor in the main part, particularly in historical productions in which the cutting of the text increased the relative size of the role. Such a focus is problematic but inevitable and does have some value, as the modern critic Anthony Dawson recognizes:

> I am aware of perpetuating the discredited tradition of equating performance history with detailed accounts of how one or another famous actor played a single role. But one explanation is that the available source materials make such an emphasis almost unavoidable; moreover, leading actors express in heightened ways features of cultural style, and when they take on Hamlet they help to reveal an era's understanding of subjectivity.[1]

Thanks to an anonymous elegist writing on the death of Richard Burbage, the leading actor in Shakespeare's company, we know that Burbage played the part in the early seventeenth century:

> He's gone and with him what a world are dead!
> Which he reviv'd, to be revived so,
> No more young Hamlet, old Hieronymo
> Kind Lear, the grieved Moor, and more beside,
> That lived in him; have now forever died,
> Oft have I seen him, leap into the grave
> Smiting the person which he seem'd to have
> Of a sad lover with so true an eye
> That there I would have sworn, he meant to die;
> Oft have I seen him, play this part in jest,

So lively, that spectators, and the rest
Of his sad crew, whilst he but seem'd to bleed,
Amazed, thought even then he died indeed.[2]

Assuming that the lines describe the graveyard scene in Act 5
Scene 1 of *Hamlet*, we are also given some idea of how he played the
part. In general Burbage is praised for the realism of his performances. It is striking that all the great actors who followed in his
footsteps are similarly praised despite very different conceptions of
the part and performance styles. There is also a tendency for actors
themselves to trace a lineal descent for their performance, as though
perhaps this might validate or authenticate their interpretation. This
was certainly the case after the Restoration of the monarchy in
1660 when the part was played for Sir William Davenant's company
by Thomas Betterton. John Downes, company bookkeeper and
prompter, reports that

> *Hamlet* being Perform'd by Mr *Betterton*, Sir *William* (having
> seen Mr *Taylor* of the *Black-Fryars* Company Act it, who being
> Instructed by the Author Mr *Shaksepeur*) taught Mr *Betterton*
> in every Particle of it; which by his exact Performance of it,
> gain'd him Esteem and Reputation, Superlative to all other
> Plays . . . No more succeeding Tragedy for several Years got
> more reputation, or Money to the Company than this.[3]

In fact Joseph Taylor, who inherited Burbage's roles, joined the
King's Men at the Blackfriars three years after Shakespeare's death
so could not have been personally instructed by the author, but he
probably performed them in a similar way. Betterton played Hamlet
to great acclaim until he was seventy:

> had you been to-night at the play-house, you had seen the
> force of action in perfection: your admired Mr Betterton
> behaved himself so well, that though now about seventy, he
> acted youth; and by the prevalent power of proper manner,
> gesture, and voice, appeared through the whole drama a
> young man of great expectation, vivacity, and enterprise. The

soliloquy where he began the celebrated sentence of "To be or not to be?," the expostulation, where he explains with his mother in the closet, the noble ardour, after seeing his father's ghost; and his generous distress for the death of Ophelia, are each of them circumstances which dwell strongly upon the minds of his audience, and would certainly affect their behaviour on any parallel occasions in their own lives.[4]

The early eighteenth-century actor-manager Colley Cibber described Betterton's performance as restrained, "governed by decency, manly, but not braving; his voice never rising into that seeming outrage, or wild defiance of what he naturally revered."[5] The actor seems to have attended to Hamlet's advice to the players at the beginning of Act 3 Scene 2, although these lines were cut in the so-called "Players' Quarto" (1676) which was used, as were the Ambassadors, Polonius' talk with Reynaldo, his advice to his son, Laertes' advice to Ophelia, and most of Fortinbras. Many other speeches were thinned, including all the soliloquies apart from "To be, or not to be," which was presumably too well-known to be cut. *Hamlet*'s complicated textual history and length has led to a stage history characterized by cuts and exclusions designed to create a fast-paced script concentrating on narrative and action.

David Garrick, the outstanding eighteenth-century Hamlet, used a version of the same text for much of his theatrical career until 1772 when he decided to cut most of the fifth act and have Hamlet reappear after Ophelia's final exit, fight and forgive Laertes and kill Claudius. This drastic action had the positive effect of enabling much of the material from the first four acts to be restored, adding depth to the other characters and making Hamlet a more complex, ambiguous figure. Garrick's performance was noted for its liveliness and energy and was based on a conviction of Hamlet's deeply felt love for his dead father. In an age of feeling, "The basis of Hamlet's character seems to be an extreme sensibility of mind, apt to be strongly impressed by its situation, and overpowered by the feelings which that situation excites."[6] Walter Scott characterized Garrick's acting as "impetuous, sudden, striking, and versatile."[7] He was also known for carefully thought-out stage business, including a collapsing chair, a wig wired so that the hair stood on end and his famous "start" on first seeing the ghost. The German scientist and Anglophile Georg Lichtenberg described how

> His whole demeanour is so expressive of terror that it made my flesh creep even before he began to speak. The almost terror-struck silence of the audience, which preceded this appearance and filled one with a sense of insecurity, probably did much to enhance this effect. At last he speaks, not at the beginning, but at the end of a breath, with a trembling voice: "Angels and ministers of grace defend us!"[8]

The liveliness of Garrick's interpretation contrasted markedly with the late eighteenth-century actor John Philip Kemble's melancholy prince. The memoirist Mary Russell Mitford thought him "the only satisfactory Hamlet I ever saw—owing much to personal grace and beauty—something to a natural melancholy, or rather pensiveness of manner—much, of course, to consummate art."[9] The Regency star Edmund Kean, by contrast, was passionate and impetuous. At the end of Act 3 Scene 1, for example, according to the Scottish poet Theodore Martin, after screaming "get thee to a nunnery" at Ophelia, he was about to leave

> when he stops, turns round, and casting back the saddest, almost tearful look, stands lingering for some time, and then with a slow, almost gliding step, comes back, seizes Ophelia's hand, imprints a lingering kiss upon it with a deep-drawn sigh, and straightway dashes more impetuously than before out of the door, which he slams violently behind him.[10]

William Charles Macready's performance in the mid-nineteenth century was described as a "composite,"[11] combining "the classical dignity of John Kemble with the intense earnestness and colloquial familiarity of Edmund Kean."[12] Reviewers praised his naturalism and ability to suggest subtle, complex feelings, but in his diary Macready confesses how difficult he found it to achieve "the ease and dignified familiarity, the apparent levity of manner, with the deep purpose that lies beneath."[13] Edwin Booth, the great American actor, was praised for his portrait of a "reflective, sensitive, gentle, generous nature, tormented, borne down and made miserable by an occasion . . . to which it is not equal."[14] Booth softened and refined the role.

Accounts of Henry Irving's performance at the Lyceum are contradictory, although he was astonishingly successful; some critics faulted him for "the entire absence of tragic passion"[15] while others talked of his "real frenzy."[16] He is credited with introducing a "psychological Hamlet."[17] Eden Phillpotts later analyzed his performance in terms of the psychological connection between his intellectuality, insanity and failure to act.[18] Irving's chosen successor as Hamlet was Johnston Forbes-Robertson, whose performance likewise drew contradictory notices. George Bernard Shaw praised his verse-speaking for the way he "does not utter half a line; then stop to act; then go on with another half line . . . he plays as Shakespeare should be played, on the line and to the line, with the utterance and acting simultaneous, inseparable and in fact identical."[19] While all reviewers agreed on the delicacy of his performance, some found him "affable" and "light-hearted"; Shaw talked of "celestial gaiety"[20] while others mention his "gentle melancholy."[21] This production reintroduced Fortinbras in the last act after the character had been banished from the stage for over two hundred years, an innovation suggested by Shaw but regarded as anticlimactic by many at the time.

The matinee idol John Barrymore was praised by James Agate as "nearer to Shakespeare's whole creation than any other I have seen."[22] To John Gielgud he suggested "tenderness, remoteness, and neurosis,"[23] and he also impressed the young Laurence Olivier: "Everything about him was exciting. He was athletic, he had charisma, and to my young mind, he played the part to perfection."[24] Olivier was impressed also by the way in which Barrymore emphasized certain words in a line, although critics were less enthusiastic. Olivier drew a telling theatrical line directly back through Barrymore to Booth, from Booth to Kean and hence ultimately to Burbage.[25]

Evolving twentieth-century production styles were influenced by the attempts of the late-Victorian producer William Poel to re-create an authentically Elizabethan bare stage as opposed to a cluttered historical realism with elaborate scenery. There was also a trend toward ensemble-playing which meant that focus was no longer exclusively on the star. Interpretations, meanwhile, veered between exploration of the politics of the play and interest in sexuality in the light of Freud's theory of the family romance. Late twentieth and early twenty-first-century productions were often concerned with self-conscious dramatic devices (overhearings, the play-within-the-play) and references to play-acting, a phenomenon that became known as "meta-theatricality" (theater about theater). Performances of *Hamlet* frequently sought to interrogate their own meaning.

The play's contemporary significance was signaled in the 1925 Birmingham Repertory production which became known as "Hamlet in plus fours" on account of its modern-day set and dress. Postwar disillusionment infected Colin Keith-Johnston's "snarling prince."[26] Not all were convinced, but *The Sunday Times'* reviewer was one of many who responded to its modern treatment: "A certain matter-of-factness of diction, combined with the absence of gesture

3. Realistic historical staging, with elaborate sets and large casts of spear-carriers in attendance, characterized the play in the eighteenth, nineteenth and early twentieth centuries: this is the duel scene in the 1913 Forbes-Robertson production on the cavernous stage of London's Drury Lane Theatre.

and pose, do give a certain added humanity and life, even if sometimes at the expense of majesty."[27] Gielgud's judgment on the
production was "UNspeakable,"[28] but it influenced his own performance at the Old Vic in 1930; as one critic puts it, "Like Barrymore
with his veiled demonic streak and Keith-Johnston with his open
hostility, Gielgud brought out the darker side of Hamlet's nature."[29]
The unabridged text in the Gielgud production (conflated from the
Quarto and Folio versions of the play) included Hamlet's bawdy talk
to Ophelia and his mother, which hitherto had usually been cut. In
the course of his career, Gielgud played the part in six different productions in total and critics are divided in their judgment on each.
W. A. Darlington sums up his performances over fifteen years in
terms of a progression from "a sensitive youth, aghast at the wickedness of the world which he had just discovered, to a sophisticated
man to whom that wickedness is no surprise."[30] Gielgud's intellectu-
alism is often contrasted, somewhat crudely with Olivier's physical-
ity, but as Dawson points out, "Both were 'modern' though in
different ways."[31] Olivier's Hamlet is best known for the film version
of 1948; the stage version on which it was based a decade earlier
and directed by Tyrone Guthrie is regarded as "more forceful and
energetic and volatile."[32] Both stage and screen versions were
strongly influenced by Freud's "Oedipal" reading of the part of Hamlet, as well as by the Romantic image of the solitary, anguished intellectual: as the opening voice-over of the film put it, "This is the
tragedy of a man who could not make up his mind."

In recent years there have been many notable Hamlets: Paul
Scofield, Richard Burton, David Warner, Nicol Williamson, Michael
Pennington, Daniel Day-Lewis, Ian Charleson, Ben Kingsley,
Jonathan Pryce, Derek Jacobi, Mark Rylance, Kevin Kline, Kenneth
Branagh, Alex Jennings, Ralph Fiennes, Sam West, Simon Russell
Beale, Adrian Lester, Toby Stephens: the list goes on. Playgoers and
critics no longer look for a definitive *Hamlet* and all these productions
have been variously praised and appraised. Several had striking
innovations and experiments: Pryce, for instance, conjured up the
voice of the ghost from within Hamlet's own body, while Lester (in
Peter Brook's supremely lucid, heavily cut production of 2000 at the
Bouffes du Nord in Paris) played the "solid flesh" soliloquy at the very

beginning of the action, giving a rationale for a Hamlet that was more modern everyman, "intelligent, decisive, extremely hurt,"[33] than Renaissance prince. The radical spirit of the 1960s interrogated the play's status as cultural icon by deconstructing and reconstructing the text in Charles Marowitz's *Hamlet Collage* (1965) and Joseph Papp's American *Naked Hamlet* (1968). Tom Stoppard's *Rosencrantz and Guildenstern Are Dead* (1966) owes its inspiration to the same questioning spirit.

The historical focus on Hamlet tended to exclude the importance of other characters. There have, however, been notable Ophelias including Susannah Cibber playing opposite Garrick, Harriet Smithson with Kemble, Helena Faucit with Macready, Mrs. Charles Kean to her husband's prince and Kate Terry with Charles Albert Fechter. Kate's younger sister, Ellen Terry, playing opposite Irving, was much praised and led to the role enjoying greater prominence. The challenge for an actor has been in the title role, though, and there has been a tradition going back to Sarah Siddons in 1775 for women actors to take it on including Charlotte Cushman, Sarah Bernhardt in a notable 1899 production in Paris, Asta Nielsen (in the silent film of 1921), Eva Le Gallienne and more recently Judith Anderson, Diane Venora and Frances de la Tour. Bernhardt indeed argued that the role was more suitable for a mature woman than an immature man, since "The woman more readily looks the part, yet has the maturity of mind to grasp it."[34]

From an early date the play has had extraordinary international connections and appeal. One of the first recorded performances was in 1607 off the coast of Sierra Leone by sailors aboard a ship called the *Dragon* on the way to the East Indies. Troupes of visiting English actors performed throughout northern Europe in the sixteenth and seventeenth centuries: indeed, Shakespeare probably knew about the castle at Elsinore because two of his colleagues (Thomas Pope and Will Kempe) had played there in the 1580s. *Hamlet* was certainly seen in Germany not long after it was written.

In the eighteenth century it was the French Enlightenment sage Voltaire who shaped attitudes to Shakespeare in continental Europe. His view of *Hamlet* was that it was a great play, despite breaking neoclassical rules and patent "absurdités" such as the introduction of

4. Sarah Bernhardt as Hamlet. Of all Shakespeare's male tragic roles the one that has been played most often and most effectively by female actors: in his book *Women as Hamlet* (2007), the critic Tony Howard notes that Bernhardt was the first Hamlet on film and Eve Donne the first Hamlet on radio.

gravediggers in the last act.[35] German Romantics such as Goethe, Schiller and Schlegel claimed a special affinity with *Hamlet* and Schlegel and Ludwig Tieck (c.1795) produced a fine German translation. Successful French Hamlets have included François Joseph Talma and Charles Albert Fechter. In nineteenth-century Russia "Hamletism" was the term coined by Turgenev to describe the introspective political malaise of the ruling classes. Plays such as Chekhov's *Ivanov* (1887) and *The Seagull* (1896) provided explicit commentary on the character of Hamlet. In Eastern Europe in the twentieth century, productions of *Hamlet* were staged which obliquely critiqued oppressive and corrupt governments, notably Moscow's Taganka Theatre *Hamlet* directed by Yuri Lyubimov, which used a translation by Boris Pasternak and ran from 1971 to 1980, and a Romanian production with Ion Caramitru in the title role— this was recognizably a critique of the tyrannical regime of the Ceauşescus, who were evoked by Claudius and Gertrude. When the Ceauşescu regime was overthrown in 1989, Caramitru was recognized in the street by a general commanding a tank squadron. The actor was pulled up onto the tank and taken to the television station, where the battle for power was being fought. He was among the men who announced to the world that regime change had taken place. Hamlet had teamed up with Fortinbras to oversee the demise of Claudius and Gertrude.

Hamlet has been no less popular in the cinema than the theater. The first onscreen Hamlet was Sarah Bernhardt. Forbes-Robertson starred in a twenty-two-minute silent version in 1913 and the Danish silent film star Asta Nielsen played Hamlet in an astonishing 1921 version in which a female Hamlet has been brought up as male to provide an heir to the Danish throne. Laurence Olivier directed and starred in a brooding black-and-white version (1948), full of vertiginous long shots and use of voice-over for soliloquies. Richard Burton's 1964 stage production directed by Gielgud was filmed, as was Tony Richardson's 1967 Roundhouse production starring Nicol Williamson as a very modern Hamlet. Grigori Kozintsev's rigorous, intellectual 1964 black-and-white Russian version took as its theme "Denmark's a prison." This contrasted sharply with Franco Zeffirelli's 1990 version starring Mel Gibson and Glenn

Close set in medieval Denmark which eliminated politics altogether and focused on the play's family dynamics and made Hamlet into a version of the action hero. Kenneth Branagh, like Olivier, directed himself in the lead role: his sumptuous four-hour 1996 version was set in Regency costume and shot at Blenheim Palace with a star-studded cast. Using a conflated Quarto and Folio text, it maintains a balance between the private and the political. Fortinbras' great-coated army arrive in the last act to storm the palace in a scene recalling the storming of the Winter Palace in Sergei Eisenstein's *October* (1926). Michael Almereyda's *Hamlet* (2000) with Ethan Hawke as Hamlet updated the story to modern-day Manhattan where corrupt gray "suits" run the Denmark Corporation in a spiritual landscape of urban isolation and Hamlet's meditation on his own inadequacy as a man of violence is wittily delivered as he wanders the aisles of a Blockbuster video store, passing the section of movies marked "Action."*

AT THE RSC

Young Hamlet: Modernity and Politics

Hamlet is the best-known play in the history of the world, but no two productions are the same: at the level of text as well as interpretation and stage-business, every director will seek to remint the old familiar words and to make Shakespeare speak in answer to the pressure of new times.   (Jonathan Bate)[36]

The mutability of *Hamlet* is demonstrated by the wide variety of approaches which the Royal Shakespeare Company have taken in their dozen revivals of the play since the 1960s. Modern concerns regarding politics, psychology, religion, and the metatheatrical nature of the play have shaped themselves into productions that reflect the time in which they were produced. Whether with the judicious cutting of the lengthy text or with choices in setting, the difficulty in pinning down *Hamlet* is also its director's blessing—an

*See p. 235 for a discography of DVD versions.

opportunity to reflect a uniquely personal vision of the play, with an actor who will bring out the essential elements of that reading:

> Actor and audience alike have an oddly personal relationship with the part and the play. It seems to identify itself with the particular age and body of the time in which it is being played. Productions are often seen as pinpointing the nature and quality of the day's disaffected youth, though this quality can vary from gentle disappointed fatalism to angry violent nihilism without a word being altered.[37]

In 1965, Peter Hall's production had the youth of the day queuing round the block for tickets. Camping out in sleeping bags, they waited determinedly to have the chance of seeing the twenty-four-year-old David Warner speak for their generation. And speak he did: his soliloquies were addressed directly to the audience from the forefront of the stage in a naturalistic language, the text was cut to emphasize his loneliness and isolation,[38] and the aspect of the individual against officialdom was emphasized.

> Warner found his closest companions to be the theatre audience. . . . Peter Hall . . . began with his reaction to a particular political climate, as [Tony] Church[39] described it, "the corrupted end of a long conservative administration . . . sex scandals [Profumo[40]] and all that going on," the oppressiveness of which produced disaffection in the youth of Great Britain. On the surface, then, Hall wanted to make a production that was "relevant" and spoke to the audience of the sixties, a unique and eventful decade.[41]

On the "How all occasions do inform against me . . . " soliloquy, Warner himself commented that

> There was a lot going on then in the sixties, Vietnam and everything, and although this production was not commenting on that, I . . . was feeling something there about that particular situation, "The imminent death of twenty thousand

5. David Warner as Hamlet, wearing student scarf, japing with Rosencrantz (John Bell, left) and Guildenstern (James Laurenson) in Peter Hall's 1965 production.

men . . . Go to their graves. . . ." I grew to like this speech, and it began to mean more things as one just played with it.[42]

Peter Hall explained in a lecture that

> *Hamlet* is one of mankind's great images. It turns a new face to each century, even to each decade. It is a mirror which gives back the reflections of the age that is contemplating it. And the need to define these reflections produces, on average, a new appreciation of *Hamlet* every twelve days. . . . For our decade I think the play will be about the disillusionment which produces an apathy of the will so deep that commitment to politics, to religion or to life is impossible. For a man said to do nothing, Hamlet does a great deal. For a man said to refuse experience, he experiences a great deal. He is always on the brink of action, but something inside him, this disease of disillusionment, stops the final, committed action. . . . [Talking of the young intellectuals of his day, Hall felt]: There is a sense of what-the-hell-anyway, over us looms the Mushroom Cloud. And politics are a game and a lie, whether in our own country or in the East/West dialogue which goes on interminably without anything very real being said. This negative response is deep and appalling.[43]

The cold, self-perpetuating nature of the political machine was also prevalent in Steven Pimlott's 2001 production. Whereas in 1965 historical costumes were made with modern fabrics, loosely referencing the twentieth century, Pimlott went for a completely modern interpretation:

> Searchlights and swivelling surveillance cameras make spies of everyone in [a] windowless Elsinore. . . . In this contemporary court, the wily new king Claudius (Larry Lamb) is every inch the president. Made over by image consultants as used by Blair and Clinton, he always appears hand-in-hand with his smiling soignée First Lady, Gertrude, a gang of whooping, clapping yes-men, presswomen and suited, armed, security guards in their wake. This is a world we all recognize.[44]

The production started and ended with around twenty anonymous-looking sycophantic suited types, clapping Claudius and later his successor, Fortinbras. Despite the momentous events of the play the indifferent world of politics survived. Almost otherworldly and uncanny in their uniformity, they appeared as an unstoppable and timeless crowd, without any sense of loyalty, compassion, or understanding of humanity, homing in on Fortinbras with our hero's dead body still warm on stage.

The incapability of an individual and uncorrupted life in this bureaucratic world was emphasized in the setting. The designer Alison Chitty favored

> ... minimal furnishing, wide empty spaces, shades of bureaucratic grey, and you [got] a corresponding sense of watching the play under laboratory conditions. Pimlott is a believer in modern-dress Shakespeare, too, which on this occasion means jeans, leather jackets, name-tags, courtiers dressed like City traders ... [45]

David Warner and Sam West, respective Hamlets in 1965 and 2001, wore defining items of clothing which set them apart and marked them as part of contemporary rebellious and disaffected youth. Warner's long, red student scarf has remained an iconic theatrical image. Sam West first appeared in black jeans and a black "hoodie," a "hunched and hooded figure squatting with his back to the audience, snooping on the court."[46] As Rosencrantz and Guildenstern tried to find out his secrets, they plied him with a joint of marijuana.

> Pimlott's thoroughly modern production is set upon confounding traditional expectations and sometimes he manages to do so with a vengeance. The guards try to blast the Ghost away with machine-gun fire. A leather-jacketed Hamlet finishes off Polonius with a pistol rather than his knife. On the Prince's orders, Horatio videos the murderous Play scene, so that his close-ups of a twitchy Claudius and Gertrude loom large before us. And Ben Meyjes's splendid Laertes, possessed

by the furies, holds up the king with machine-gun fire and what suitably looks like an incipient Palace revolution.[47]

Moving away from politics, Matthew Warchus' quasi-cinematic production of 1997 completely cut out the Fortinbras subplot and focused on the families of the court.

Hamlet is a play absolutely saturated with the words "father," "mother," "sister," "brother," "son," "daughter," "uncle." . . . I cut about 35% of the text of the play in order to focus on the domestic story—on the two families who I imagine in this production live together with their staff in an isolated house.[48]

Warchus conflated the three existing versions of the play, reordering events and including rarely played scenes, such as Horatio's Q1 reassurance to Gertrude that her banished son is safe. The cuts were justified by the director in an interview with journalist Lyn Gardner in *The Guardian:*

"I know that by cutting the play you could diminish it, but by cutting a couple of courses from a banquet you can also make the flavours sharper and richer" . . . he knows that in excising the political dimension of the play, he risks turning it into a small domestic incident rather than a full-scale tragedy. "My hope is that when the story is told very vividly, very passionately, audiences will recognise it as a blueprint for what happens more widely. Shakespeare is so good at both macrocosm and microcosm. I feel that what I am doing is taking the play out of the hands of the academics and intellectuals, and bringing [it] back into the arena of relationships. More than any other play I have directed, I am doing this with my heart, not my head."[49]

Warchus succeeded in creating a Hamlet that was accessible and exciting, "about a wounded individual rather than the rank corruption within a tyranny."[50] Its modern setting led to many inventive touches: Hamlet taking Polaroids of Claudius at a wedding party which looked like "a gaudy purple disco,"[51] and later using them to show Gertrude the comparison with her dead husband; the audience unsure if Hamlet, carrying around a revolver in a brown paper bag, was going to use it on himself or others; Ophelia handing out pills instead of flowers.

There's a clarity and energy here that silences the usual anxieties about updating a classic from Elizabeth I to Elizabeth II. [Alex] Jennings hugs [Derbhla] Crotty, then pushes her away, stubs his cigarette out on the floor and tells her to get to a nunnery. There's a whole new spin to her saying he's blasted with "ecstasy."[52]

In 1980 director John Barton picked up on the many references in the play to role-playing and theatricality, making it the central metaphor for his production in collaboration with his cast and designer. Michael Pennington, who played Hamlet, explained how

the distinction between self-dramatization and real feeling, theatricality and life, runs right through the play, and was beginning to influence my reception of the text; and soon the theatrical world itself—hampers, cloaks and property swords—began to appear in rehearsal.[53]

Reviewing this production, the critic Irving Wardle pointed out that

Hamlet, everyone agrees, is Shakespeare's most obsessively theatrical work. This production puts that idea to the test of the basic scenic elements, ransacking the text for disguisings and routines, and always allowing the spectator a full view of the concrete instruments that create the sense of illusion. Where is Elsinore? It is a stage. Who is Hamlet? A man who may not be able to take action but who can always put on a show. What happens happens bang centre stage: otherwise characters retreat to the benches and philosophise across wide open space as if they had no part in the events.[54]

Another reviewer noted that

The style of the production is, in a sense, dictated by Ralph Koltai's design: a thrusting wooden platform over which five rehearsal lights hover and behind which are arrayed such necessary props as a thunder-sheet, a table for the swords, a huge dragged suit of armour, for people to hide behind.[55]

6. *Hamlet* is the most self-consciously theatrical of the tragedies: Hamlet himself is fascinated by actors and the idea of playing a part (does he *act* his madness?) and his deep concern with "acting" in relation to thinking and feeling introduces a play on the two senses of "to act." The presence of the players and the play-within-the-play is crucial to all this, but the highly rhetorical linguistic style of *The Murder of Gonzago* (otherwise known as *The Mousetrap*), together with the dumb show, require a different theatrical style from that of the main play. Masks were used in Buzz Goodbody's intimate 1975 production in the studio theater The Other Place.

Heaven or Hell: Hamlet and the Ghost

"Who's there?" *Hamlet* famously begins. The question, centred on the ambiguous figure of the Ghost, haunts the entire play.

(Stephen Greenblatt)[56]

As the catalyst for the play's action, the staging of the Ghost is key in indicating what type of production and what type of *Hamlet* the audience are about to see. However, one of the difficulties with staging *Hamlet* in the modern era is creating a Ghost that will have the terrifying and awe-inspiring impact that it had on audiences of previous centuries.

Many directors have eschewed any attempt to make the Ghost frightening, especially when the production has a modern setting. In Matthew Warchus' 1997 modern-dress production,

> As Hamlet, Alex Jennings appears centre stage, holding his father's ashes in an urn, while on the screen behind we see black and white footage of the father playing in the snow with his son. Over the speakers, we hear the words of the usurping king, Claudius: "Though yet of Hamlet our dear brother's death the memory be green . . ." In this strong personal production, which axes the public-political side, Hamlet's memory of his father, the motive for revenge, never loses its freshness. . . . Into [the] wedding celebrations, amid champagne, fireworks, balloons and bridesmaids, walks the ghost of Hamlet's father (Edward Petheridge) . . . [entering] in a smoking jacket, [he] speaks with quick authority, then drifts away.[57]

Steven Pimlott's 2001 production had an extremely animated and fast-moving Ghost. He clutched at the distraught Hamlet and held him in his arms when imparting his story of betrayal. When Hamlet went too far in berating his mother the Ghost strode purposefully into the room, rather than just appearing, and almost grabbed Hamlet, as if to say "That's enough!"

In 1965 David Warner played Hamlet as a man obsessed with his father, not only by the loss of him, but by his inability to match up to him in stature. In order to emphasize this the Ghost appeared as a tremendously tall figure. Roger Howells, the stage manager, explained that the device used to create this effect was like a "dalek." When staged in Stratford, two men, one standing on the ground and the other on the platform above him, maneuvered the Ghost from inside a "shell." The voice of Patrick Magee[58] was sound-recorded and then boomed over the speakers to create an otherworldly effect. Critic Anthony Dawson remarked that

> the sense of being outmanned was the dominant effect. The Ghost entered with raised arms through the doors at the back as the sentries and Prince huddled around the cannon downstage . . . on "sweep to my revenge," he swept, ironically, to the long arms of his father, to be cradled within them for the remainder of the scene. He seemed to be "looking for the comforts of the nursery" (*Times*, 20 Aug.), and it was clearly his father rather than his mother, here and throughout, that fired his imagination. But the gap between heroic parent and inadequate child was overtly underlined by the stage image, generated as it were by Hamlet's inner compulsions: the father huge and protective, the son comfortless and unfit. Even after the Ghost's departure under the stage, as he reeled about getting his friends to swear their secrecy, Hamlet kept falling on the ground as if attempting to return to his father's protective embrace. How could such a man effectively take on the polished King or his politic prime minister?[59]

David Warner explained how the powerful image of the Ghost's embrace gave the scene a feeling of "total love and belief in the father." Warner "reacted quite violently to the Ghost's request for revenge even to shouting 'WHAT!' (not in text) and then sobbing throughout the Ghost's long speech."[60]

> For the revenge [Hamlet] really wishes, and achieves, is on himself for not being the great Hamlet his father was. . . . As the hollow voice beneath the stage cries "Swear!," his son lov-

ingly measures his length on the ground, as if on a grave; but
the voice moves, he cannot cover it. Clutching violently at his
mother on her bed he looks up to find the huge presence of his
father towering between them.[61]

Obviously, Hamlet's sense of intense grief plays a large part in the
way he perceives the world. Grief can often bring with it an exaggeration of the senses, a cruel self-awareness and feelings of isolation.
As Stanley Wells points out, Shakespeare's central concern in writing Hamlet was "Reactions to death."[62] For Hamlet, actor Michael
Pennington believed,

> Grief seems to have sharpened his sense of falsehood in the
> world around him, but in other ways the immeasurable shock
> he has received has sent him to sleep. The torpor is deep and dis-
> turbing to watch, lifting in utterances—"My father, methinks
> I see my father"—which are more hallucinatory than senti-
> mental. Anybody familiar with bereavement can recognise the
> symptoms. In dramatic terms, until the news of the Ghost's
> appearance animates him, gives him something to believe in he
> is a dramatic hero of whom nothing much can be expected.[63]

In the production starring Pennington, the Ghost sat on a bench and
quietly told Hamlet what had happened. Director John Barton's
highlighting of theatricality also informed his Hamlet's reaction to
the Ghost:

> From Hamlet's viewpoint, perhaps even the Ghost is a Satanic
> actor, until the closet scene when Hamlet gently presses his
> mother's face round and, in a shared moment of stunned dis-
> belief, she too sees the Ghost.[64]

Hamlet's grief stems from an acute awareness of the importance,
the preciousness of human life. Anger at his mother's inability to see,
to be aware, of the truth of her situation, prompts one of the most
potent dramatic scenes ever written. In this production, Gertrude
not only saw into her own soul, but in witnessing the Ghost became

fully aware of what Hamlet saw and felt. The effect was so powerful that she fainted.

Michael Boyd's 2004 staging of the supernatural was striking and imaginative. The Ghost appeared with slow progression through the audience to the stage, skeleton-like with his mouth contorted into a silent scream. With its truly frightening visage, this nightmarish apparition was one of the few modern stagings of the Ghost to truly unsettle the audience:

> Instead of the usual stern but fatherly figure, in the "fair and warlike form" of his living self, old Hamlet here hauls himself into the play as a bowed, deathly-white, half-naked spook, with hollow red sockets for eyes, scraping his broadsword along the ground to nerve-shatteringly ominous effect. He hawks up his speeches in an agonised vomit of vengefulness. That he seems to hail from an alien belief system as well as from another world is entirely deliberate. . . . Boyd has been inspired by Stephen Greenblatt's recent book *Hamlet in Purgatory*, which highlights the tragedy's unsettling premise: "A young man from Wittenberg, with a distinctly Protestant temperament, is haunted by a distinctly Catholic ghost." Or, as the director puts it, "There has been a political and intellectual revolution, and then Hamlet re-encounters the past in the shape of his father's spirit and has to negotiate with it."[65]

If we were in any doubt that this Ghost had suffered the terrors of hell, we had none by the end of the scene when a trapdoor opened to reveal intense red light, the fires of Purgatory. The Ghost fell forward, face first, into the awaiting pit.

From the first appearance of the Ghost there is a sense of inevitability in Hamlet's fate. As he progresses through the play, he undergoes an acceptance of his own mortality. Hamlet's acceptance and "readiness" for death was something which the designer for Boyd's production, Tom Piper, built into the characters' costuming:

> Laertes changes from light, golden boy to black avenger. Hamlet begins as a black avenger and ends up in light grey, a sort of

Everyman colour, because on his return in Act 5, Hamlet becomes more accepting, more at peace in a sense. Grey tones also give a sense of being half in and half out of the world. It's as though, at the end, Hamlet is beginning to accept that he's about to join the world of the ash people—the gravedigger is also in grey.[66]

Greg Hicks, who played the startling Ghost, also played the Player King and the First Gravedigger: "It's a great treble because there are resonances of Hamlet's father in each one of the roles, especially the gravedigger."[67]

Michael Boyd's doubling of roles provided a sense of the dead being present among the living and looking after their loved ones in spirit:

When I asked her [Meg Fraser, who played Ophelia] to play the second gravedigger too it was because I thought there was something very moving in the fact that, in that benign scene, Hamlet was with people who loved him: his father and Ophelia.[68]

Meg Fraser commented on this comforting but macabre idea: "I also play the second gravedigger—Ophelia digs her own grave! . . . And now I wear the same make-up for both parts because it's about making connections rather than being naturalistic."[69]

The references to grief and death were markedly used in the set for the Adrian Noble production in 1992:

The unweeded garden of Elsinore exists downstage in Bob Crowley's design. The right arm of the subterranean ghost pushes through like the arm in John Boorman's *Deliverance*, and Ophelia plucks her flowers here shortly before the gravediggers prepare her tomb. If Denmark is a prison, it is also, finally, a graveyard. The stage is littered with pink garlands and funeral mounds.[70]

As indicated, the Ghost in this production emerged from a garden, which formed the front part of the stage, and was later used for Ophelia's madness scene and the burial.

What you are left with after Hamlet's return from England is a landscape of grief. By the end the whole stage is a huge grave-yard, not literally with tombstones, but just dead flowers everywhere.[71]

Love and Madness

Hamlet evokes the long-distance loneliness and isolation of three lost, young things—Hamlet, Laertes and Ophelia—caught up in a political and personal revenge that's the death of them.   (Nicholas de Jongh)[72]

The parallel stories of two families and how their children cope with the death of their fathers is central to the plot of *Hamlet*. Hamlet's dilemma after seeing the Ghost lies in the fact that he is too aware of the possible consequences of his actions. The intelligence of his imagination is such that he knows that the Ghost's request for revenge has two possible outcomes for him: death or madness. As hot-blooded avenger he will provoke the punishment of the state, whereas not to act—to withdraw—would only compound and mul-tiply his already unbearable grief and frustration to a state of mad-ness. Both of these options are against his nature and his sensibility. However, Shakespeare demonstrates their tragic consequences in the reactions of Polonius' children, Laertes and Ophelia.

Most actors, although they may reach a peak of frenzy, do not play Hamlet as genuinely mad. In Ron Daniels' 1989 production, however, the disintegrating mind of Hamlet was evidenced in Elsi-nore's state of collapse.

Set in what appears as an exclusive sanatorium with extensive views over the North Sea, Ron Daniels's production presents a group of cheerfully contented inmates who all fall victim to a killer disease. . . . Antony McDonald's vertiginously angled, hydraulically operated set suggests that Elsinore is sliding into the sea.

Its opening court scene presents an image of harmony and political health, with only Mark Rylance's spiritlessly dejected Hamlet signalling the plague that will strike them down.[73]

The large planes of flat, subdued color and sparse detail have a two-fold effect. They highlight the characters and, at the same time, emphasize their littleness against the massive ruins and the stormy sea.

> The heart of Denmark is rotten, and Daniels concentrates on that heart. Questions of legitimacy, kingship and ambition are treated in terms not of the State but of individual fate. Intrigue is social, courtly, politic, not broadly political. The huge windows open on the sea and the rabble is heard only as an electronic noise, as of sirens. Daniels seems to want to lift the court out of history, to a plane on which the psychological and metaphysical themes can be purely explored.[74]

Known as "the pyjama Hamlet," due to the fact that Mark Rylance wore pyjama bottoms from entering for the "To be, or not to be" soliloquy to his exile to England, Rylance's performance took Hamlet's loss of sanity to extreme and believable levels. When the production toured and did a special performance at Broadmoor, a hospital for the criminally insane, one inmate wrote to his local paper, explaining that Rylance "was able to capture every aspect of a person's slip into the world of psychopathic, manipulative paranoia . . . Many of us here in Broadmoor are able to understand Hamlet's disturbed state of mind because we have experienced such traumas."[75]

> In Ron Daniels's RSC production of *Hamlet*, the hero is . . . a Black Prince of pain and destruction. Antony McDonald's sets are an expressionistic clash between sloping floors and tilted walls, as if the court were in danger of imminent collapse . . . the threat comes from Hamlet. We first see Mark Rylance as a tense, pale, hunched figure tightly buttoned in a long, heavy overcoat. His eyes are glazed over with too much introspection. He is clearly on the brink of a crack-up, and his encounter with the Ghost topples him over. This Hamlet suffers from a combination of obsessional brooding and a retarded emotional maturity. In public, he acts up to his breakdown, until it takes over and he regresses to a difficult, irascible adolescence. . . . Daniels

and Rylance show Hamlet to be a moral vessel which is too weak to bear its just cause. When, at the end of a superb, harrowing bedroom scene, he kisses his mother on the mouth, it begins as a kiss of comfort and complicity and ends in a shocked recognition of fear and freedom. Of course, you lose the "romantic" Hamlet; but you gain in hard emotional authenticity. This is a deeply shocking production in the most crucial sense: it shocks you into the difficult recognition that necessary moral actions can be performed by people who do not carry the usual moral price tag. And so our sympathy and pity for Hamlet is hard-earned and therefore all the more real.[76]

Frances Barber as Ophelia in 1985 was universally praised for her extremely moving performance. She saw Ophelia as an extension of Hamlet's character, presenting

the female counterpart and counterpoint to him. She provides the feminine qualities lacking in his sensibilities. Shakespeare uses her innocence and naiveté to illustrate this imbalance and highlight its consequences; the destruction of a potent feminine force, caught up in a male-dominated power struggle. . . . I noticed Roger [Rees] as Hamlet became more lucid and reasonable as his obsessions took him over. He also used particular gestures each time he saw his father's ghost, and he was truly in danger of losing his mind. If I was to follow through my theme of Ophelia as a female counterpart to the Prince, it seemed interesting to incorporate some of Hamlet's gestures into the most inappropriate moments of her own madness, highlighting her then as his female counterpoint. Consequently one of Roger's most striking gestures was that of banging his chest violently after the ghost has appeared to him for the first time, as if his heart truly is breaking. . . . I decided to bang my chest and beat my heart as violently as I could at the most unexpected moment, during the sweetness of the song . . . people are "certified" if they are likely to do harm to others or to themselves. I wanted to suggest that whilst Hamlet is likely to do harm to others at his most revengeful, Ophelia is capable of doing herself great harm at her most tranquil. . . . When Laertes enters the scene, I clasped his face, echoing Roger in the nunnery scene, but in this case singing gently and weeping for the loss of everything good in her life—a direct contrast to Hamlet's spitting accusations. . . . Another gesture that occurred during one rehearsal was coincidentally an echo of the closet scene in which a distraught Gertrude clasps her son to her bosom and strokes his hair. Kenneth Branagh (Laertes) sank into my arms as Ophelia sings, while I stroked his hair, unaware at that point of the parallel mother/son image.[77]

Ophelia's loneliness and isolation are equal to, if not greater than, Hamlet's. The loss of Hamlet and the death of her father, the absence of Laertes, leave her no one to turn to in her distraction. Actresses in recent productions have often employed visual associations with Ophelia's loved ones in the madness scenes, indicating a lost mind helplessly turning to those she loves by assimilating their actions, keeping part of them alive and with her even though they are absent. In Meg Fraser's performance in 2005,

Ophelia mimics or echoes her father's gestures when she's mad, for example the authoritative clap. I came by it accidentally in rehearsal but I love the way it gives the audience such a shock! . . . Ophelia's wearing the same colour her dad wears—the Polonius family are in silvers.[78]

This idea was strongly adopted in 1992 when Joanne Pearce's Ophelia wore her dead father's clothes. Her innocence, isolation and vulnerability were highlighted by this effective piece of costuming:

The mad scene began with the shattered young woman shuffling along in her father's clothes, the shirt bloodstained and the shoes, clownlike, much too large.[79]

Many modern productions pick up on the fact that Hamlet and Ophelia are both condemned by paternal domination. Tony Church, who played Polonius twice, in 1965 and in 1980, commented:

The appalling news that Hamlet has apparently been driven mad by Ophelia's rejection leads Polonius in the text straight into the problem of reporting this event to the King; here we added the business of the father covering his poor frightened daughter with his robes of state, and leading her protectively from the stage. Later, in the mad scene, Ophelia appeared wearing her dead father's robe, and it was only after the first night that I remembered that Glenda Jackson, the Ophelia in 1965, had used the same business. This led me to reflect on the nature of parental oppression; Glenda's reasoning was based on the suffocation of her spirit by her father—that although he had frightened her, she could not escape him. My Polonius of 1980, it could be said, overpowered his daughter in the end by too much love.[80]

Elsinore, the heart of Denmark, is sterile and corrupt. There is a complete lack of responsibility from the older generation in this play, in caring for the fragility of their young. Despite the larger themes which the play deals with, these productions demonstrated that it is the emotional dependence and twisted parental relationships which give the play its emotional pull. Everything conspires to kill the young before they have a chance to grow. None survive the cruel parental world in which they live. Although Hamlet returns from England a changed man, he has been condemned from the moment his father utters his dreadful command. "Remember me": the words in their simplicity echo in the mind with each fresh death of the unprepared or tormented—those that perish before their time.

THE DIRECTOR'S CUT: MICHAEL BOYD, JOHN CAIRD, AND RON DANIELS

Ron Daniels, who was born in Brazil, was a founding member of the Teatro Oficina in São Paulo. In 1977 he was appointed Artistic Director of the Royal Shakespeare Company's Stratford-upon-Avon studio theater, The Other Place, and in 1980 he became an Associate Director of the RSC. In 1991 he became Associate Artistic Director of the American Repertory Theatre in Cambridge, Massachusetts. More recently he has worked out of New York as a freelance director. He has directed most of Shakespeare's major tragedies and history plays. He directed two RSC productions of *Hamlet:* with Roger Rees as the Prince in 1984 and with Mark Rylance in 1989; the interview concentrates principally on the latter, which became known as the "pyjama Hamlet," with Rylance's performance singled out for particular praise by the critics.

John Caird, born in 1948 in Canada to British parents, staged and directed more than twenty plays, both classic and contemporary, while he was an Associate Director at the Royal Shakespeare Company. He has subsequently directed many musicals, plays and operas, both in London (e.g. for the National Theatre and the Almeida) and internationally. Together with Trevor Nunn, he directed the celebrated production of Charles Dickens' *Nicholas Nickleby* for the RSC in 1980, as well as the internationally successful *Les Misérables* in 1985. His production of *Hamlet* in 2000, for the National Theatre in London on the proscenium-arch Lyttelton stage, featured Simon Russell Beale, one of the outstanding Hamlets of the modern age.

Michael Boyd, born in 1955, trained as a director at the Malaya Bronnaya Theatre in Moscow. He then worked at the Belgrade Theatre in Coventry and the Sheffield Crucible before founding his own company, the Tron in Glasgow. He became an Associate Director of the RSC in 1996, coming to prominence with his millennial staging of the three parts of *Henry VI* and *Richard III* in the company's "This England" cycle of history plays, which won him an Olivier award for Best Director. In 2003, he took over as Artistic Director, achieving a notable success in 2006–07 with his ambitious Complete Works Festival, whereby all Shakespeare's plays were staged in Stratford-upon-Avon over the course of a year, some by the RSC and others by visiting companies. His 2004 production of *Hamlet* starred Toby Stephens, son of the noted actors Robert Stephens and Dame Maggie Smith, as Hamlet.

Design choices seem crucial in establishing the atmosphere of the first act of *Hamlet*, with its movement between the guards outside on the platform, the formal exchanges at court, where

7. The domestic setting of Ron Daniels' 1989 *Hamlet:* Elsinore as a mansion instead of a castle.

Hamlet's black costume sets him so conspicuously apart, and the private conversations of Polonius and his children: what was the process whereby you arrived at a vision for the look and style of the opening scenes?

Daniels: Our basic approach was that this was to be a "domestic" Hamlet. My earlier [1984] production, with Roger Rees in the title role and with designs by Maria Bjornson, had been set somewhere in the vast expanses between heaven and earth—a "cosmic" and imposing Hamlet set literally among the clouds, some of which were painted on a vast transparent curtain above the stage and others on the huge ramp which finally parted to reveal Ophelia's grave beneath it. Though retaining a few of these elements [the encounter between Hamlet and the Ghost took place literally in the sky, on a platform suspended high above the stage], the 1989 production, designed by

Antony McDonald, was to be much more intimate, rooted in personal relationships, a tragedy set in the heart of a family as well as of a state: the action was to take place in a mansion, a home, really, perched on the edge of a cliff high above the turbulent sea.

Caird: My designer, Tim Hatley, and I didn't think of the opening scenes as a separate issue. We were more concerned with creating a performance space for the whole play. In *Hamlet* one needs a grave-yard, a battlement, a fencing ground, a cloister, and so on. I was also keen to give the whole play a suffocatingly religious setting.

In my production the two main design images were graveyard and travel, based on the "undiscovered country from whose bourn no traveller returns." There were stone flags on the floor, many of them engraved with the names of the dead, alcoves from which the ghostly characters of the play emerge as if to re-enact an old story, and a large pile of old and dusty luggage out of which all of the set-tings of the play could be made. The set was part cathedral, part cas-tle, part graveyard, part attic.

Boyd: We wanted a space which could create tension, allow eaves-dropping, open out as Claudius' grip on Hamlet and Denmark weak-ens, and generally encourage swift and fluid movement of scenes and actors. A rational, cold space for Claudius' "modern," "reform-ing" court. A black circular palisade, with no visible exits or entrances, the only visible way into the world from outside was from the audience, and was used exclusively by the Ghost and Players.

Hamlet's language is famously introspective and self-questioning, while King Claudius is very adept at controlling language for polit-ical ends: is this a contrast that you explored in your production?

Daniels: It seems to me that in Shakespeare, content perfectly defines the form. The words Shakespeare chooses to give Polonius and how he constructs his sentences are a precise indication of who Polonius is as a human being. Claudius' concerns are the affairs of estate—he is a man of action, a consummate political (and sexual) animal who, with the exception of his one moment of soul-searching (which he deals with with a good deal of brusque impatience), demonstrates little if any interest in the workings of his own heart. The language he uses perfectly reflects this "objective" posture, whereas Hamlet's "subjective" language reveals his continuing obsession with himself and with the struggles raging deep within him. What other character in Shakespeare agonizes about his own state of mind so relentlessly?

Caird: I'm not sure I agree with that statement. Hamlet is incredibly clever with language, both in his political and introspective utterances. He manipulates people every bit as successfully as Claudius does. You could say that he handles Polonius much better than Claudius, who seems at a loss for words in the face of Polonius' loquacity.

It's also not true to say that Claudius isn't introspective. One of the turning points of the plot is a profound introspection from Claudius. The scene in the chapel where he questions his actions and is in despair about the state of his soul is about as introspective as you can imagine anybody ever being. I think almost all characters in Shakespeare manipulate language, because they are Shakespeare's creatures; they do what Shakespeare himself does in creating them.

I think the more interesting question is *why* does Claudius try to manipulate Hamlet when he could quite easily kill him? He has killed Hamlet's father, he has made himself king, he has married Hamlet's mother . . . if he's such a brutal machiavellian politician, why doesn't he just kill Hamlet? The answer is that he kills his brother so that he can become him. It's an attempted act of transformation. That's why he tries genuinely, desperately, to persuade Hamlet that everything is the same as it used to be. His father may be dead but he has a new father now. It's Hamlet's incapacity to accept this new status quo that throws Claudius into confusion and ultimately forces him into the position of having Hamlet killed. But it takes more than half the play for Claudius to be forced to this point.

Boyd: We saw the play being driven by the possible actions of a usurped prince in a dangerous court, rather than by a "given" of Hamlet's state of mind. We chose to celebrate Hamlet's brilliant control of language under extreme pressure rather than relax into a "state" of introspection. This felt more active, true and exciting. That said, as the production matured, Toby [Stephens, playing Hamlet] was able to give more space to the lyrical wonder in Hamlet's thought, without losing the prevailing sense of danger.

The Ghost appears to come from Roman Catholic Purgatory, whereas young Hamlet is studying at Wittenberg, a university synonymous with Martin Luther and Protestantism: did the religious controversies of the age play any part in your production?

Daniels: These religious controversies are indeed fascinating but they are perhaps of more interest in the study than in the rehearsal room, where what matters is human behavior and motivation. What makes Hamlet, who perhaps understands that he is the protagonist of a revenger's tragedy, incapable of carrying out his obligation to revenge his father's death? What other imperative is short-circuiting his will to action? What is forcing him to deviate from the destiny imposed on him?

Caird: Religion had a great deal to do with my interpretation but not religious controversies. The main reason I set the play in a discernibly Renaissance period is that I don't think the play works if it's set in a post-Enlightenment world. The central characters are deeply concerned with the mortality of their souls. Without the religious and spiritual context in which Shakespeare was writing it's hard to make sense of the play philosophically and intellectually.

I don't think the difference between Protestantism and Catholicism is so crucial to the meaning of the play and Wittenberg itself is relatively unimportant. Ostensibly the company of players comes from Wittenberg, because one assumes that's where Hamlet and Horatio must have met them. But that would make Wittenberg a town with troupes of child-actors taking over from adult companies and we know that wasn't the case in Wittenberg. As always Shakespeare is using his own experiences and playing fast and loose with geography and chronology. Shakespeare's Wittenberg is more like Oxford than a Lutheran university, and when the Players arrive on the scene it suddenly becomes London.

Boyd: Shakespeare is clearly writing about the deep damage caused by the English Reformation, the suppression of the old Church, and the resulting schism in the country. Hamlet is of the new "Protes-

8. Greg Hicks: Michael Boyd's terrifying Ghost from Purgatory.

tant" generation, but is forced to learn that "there are more things in heaven and earth . . . than are dreamt of" in the reformed thinking of Wittenberg. The fact that "the time is out of joint" runs through the middle of *Hamlet* and all of Shakespeare's work.

Greg Hicks was truly supernatural—chalk white, nearly naked, agonized and burdened with a giant broadsword from a bygone heroic age, which he slowly dragged with painful Shinto precision across the metal grating on the floor. It was genuinely frightening and gave Toby Stephens a powerful problem to solve.

Was your Hamlet's "antic disposition" always a performance or were there moments when he veered into genuine madness?

Daniels: I don't think the "antic disposition" was ever a performance. Certainly, Hamlet out-clowns Polonius in the Fishmonger scene, giving the foolish old man a taste of his own foolishness, and Hamlet's fury and his pain in the nunnery scene are almost beyond his control. However, these are different responses, one humorous and the other unbearably violent, to specific instances within a larger continuum of despair, a despair that is utterly disabling.

9. Mark Rylance as Ron Daniels' pajama-wearing Hamlet, berating Gertrude (Clare Higgins) in the closet scene: she holds the pictures of the two brothers who became her two husbands.

For this production we used the Bad Quarto structure, in which the nunnery scene is placed well before the Fishmonger scene: the first time Hamlet appeared after the battlement sequence was when he came on stage, a forlorn, suicidal figure still dressed in his pajamas, to agonize over whether he should be or not be—a man in the throes of an unbearable inner crisis, genuinely "transformed" and very far from the "understanding of himself."

Caird: I see a lot of *Hamlets* where the actor plays the madness card in order to escape a proper investigation of the part. Of course it's exciting for an actor to walk onto the stage looking or acting completely nuts, but there's nothing in the language of the scenes to suggest madness at all. Hamlet doesn't say anything mad. I came to the view, after rehearsing it and extrapolating all the sense I could from what Hamlet says in each of his scenes, that Hamlet is the only sane person in the play. Almost everyone else is to some extent mad, with the obvious exception of Horatio. Polonius says and does mad things. Ophelia, Gertrude, Claudius, Laertes . . . they all find themselves in truly mad situations and react madly to them. What's amazing about Hamlet is that in the circumstances in which he finds himself, he doesn't go mad. Instead he gets saner and saner as the play continues. By the time he returns from England he's extraordinarily balanced and wise. He has moments of rashness and anger in the play, one of which results in the death of Polonius, but I can't think of a single thing he does in the play that would suggest for one moment that he's mad.

Boyd: Hamlet begins the play under great mental stress, but it is the world that is mad. He is in mourning and has been effectively usurped with the collusion of his mother, and yet is being forced to celebrate his mother's wedding to his usurper.

He is probably at his wildest with his dead father, Ophelia, and his mother, i.e. when he is most profoundly emotionally threatened, but he is not mad. As the victim of the mad time and the one born to set it right, he bears the imprint of the madness of the time. The antic disposition is a time-honored camouflage employed by Hieronimo (in *The Spanish Tragedy*) and Arbella Stuart (in her cousin Elizabeth I's court) to make themselves seem harmless to a watchful and oppressive state.

How did you deal with the brutality of Hamlet's behavior toward Ophelia in the "nunnery" and "country matters" exchanges?

Daniels: In the most brutal way possible. The scene became quite physically as well as verbally explosive. Much as Hamlet believes Gertrude has betrayed the memory of his father by posting "with such dexterity to incestuous sheets," he also believes Ophelia has betrayed him by obeying her father's orders that she "lock herself from his resort, admit no messengers, receive no token . . . "—and I've always been fascinated by Hamlet's strange encounter with her when he breaks into her chamber and falls "to such perusal of my face as he would draw it." What did Hamlet mean to convey by such a mysterious encounter—and what did Ophelia understand by it that caused her to be so terrified? Did he look into her soul and did he see her guilt at her act of betrayal?

"Frailty, thy name is woman." All women. Does this then not refer as much to Ophelia as to Gertrude? And what horror does this reveal, of Woman merely as the painted seductress, ambling and lisping and awakening dangerous and uncontrollable desires in all men that can only lead to murder and incest? Tormented and pathological reasoning, certainly, which can only lead to violent and irrational behavior.

Caird: I don't think he is being brutal, or certainly not intentionally. The character of Ophelia has to be seen in thematic terms. She's not a fully drawn character. She represents the possibility of a future life. She is the only nobly born woman in the play of childbearing age and therefore the only available person for Hamlet to marry and have children with. Hamlet's father was called Hamlet, and for all one knows his father was called Hamlet too. The state of Denmark is one in which kings called Hamlet get married and have boys called Hamlet, and so life continues. Claudius aborts this natural order.

The crucial line in the nunnery scene is "I say we will have no more marriages." It's a tragic utterance. It says "I cannot go on pretending with this woman that we're in love and that we're going to get married and have children and everything's going to be happy. It cannot be. The world is diseased, mad and dead. No more children must be born into it." "Get thee to a nunnery" means precisely that. It's nothing to do with a whorehouse, as some scholars have suggested. Whorehouses in Shakespeare are bawdy, complicated places, full of life. Look at *Measure for Measure* and the *Henry IV* plays. The Denmark of *Hamlet* is no place for a whorehouse. The nunnery here is the same place as the cold unproductive cloister with which Theseus threatens Hermia in the opening scene of *A Midsummer Night's Dream.*

It is germane that when Ophelia dies, Gertrude brings the news of her death. Gertrude is the other woman in the play; a woman who won't have any more children, and who has forgotten her duty to the child she already has. Ophelia is the woman who should one day have taken over the role of wife and mother from Gertrude as Hamlet should have become his father's successor. Gertrude says this very clearly at Ophelia's obsequies. She had believed that her son would marry Ophelia and life would thereby continue into the future, but by marrying Claudius and forgetting her love for her husband and son she has made a horrible miscalculation, albeit for very human reasons.

If Gertrude was present while Ophelia was drowning, why didn't she help her? If she is reporting what she was told by someone else, who then told her? And why doesn't Shakespeare use that character to report the news to us? Why didn't he use a shepherd or the Gentleman from Ophelia's madness scene? The reason is thematic. If Hamlet is not to marry Ophelia and have children with her, then everything Gertrude has lived for dies with Ophelia. Nothing that she's ever done has any future value. The death of Ophelia contains her own death and ultimately the death of her son. By making her the bearer of these tidings, Shakespeare gives the actress playing Gertrude a pivotal moment in the development of her role.

Boyd: Hamlet suspects that Ophelia is being abused and reduced to a political chess piece by her father (and therefore his master the king), but Ophelia is also clearly lying, and Hamlet cannot tell the degree to which she is compliant in an attempt to entrap him. Remember also that Hamlet is under observation in both the nunnery scene and the Players scene, and taking pains to appear mad.

How did you distinguish between the style of the play-within-the-play and that of the main drama?

Daniels: Clearly a style has to be found for the play-within-a-play which places it outside the boundaries of realistic action. Our solution was to perform it as a shadow play.

Caird: Hamlet's advice to the players is so specific and apt and modern—it's what any director of any age would want to say to his actors. To have the players in the play-within-the-play acting in a different style from the main protagonists you would have to have one or other of the casts ignoring Hamlet's, and therefore also Shakespeare's, instructions!

I used a staging trick. The play-within-the-play was performed at the very edge of the stage with Claudius, Gertrude, and Polonius watching from upstage. The two audiences—for *The Mousetrap* at Elsinore and for *Hamlet* at the National Theatre—became reflections of one another. By the device of building false prosceniums on either side of the stage, I created "wings." Hamlet stood in the wings reacting as a director or author would in the wings of an actual theater.

10. Toby Stephens and Meg Fraser as Hamlet and Ophelia in Michael Boyd's production.

The National Theatre audience could thereby watch Hamlet watching the play while he simultaneously observed the reactions of Claudius and Gertrude as they watched from their own auditorium. This solved the problem of Hamlet having to whisper things quietly enough for Claudius and Gertrude not to hear them, but loudly enough for Ophelia and the National Theatre audience to hear.

Boyd: Our players were brilliant, prone to coarseness, and seemingly harmless cousins of the mechanicals, but they were led by Greg Hicks, who carried with him the awful authority of the Ghost. Like the inhabitants of Purgatory, they had been driven out of town. Like Shakespeare's own companies at times, they were being used as a political weapon.

Some Hamlets don't kill Claudius while he is trying to pray after the play-scene because they really want to send him to hell rather than heaven, whereas other Hamlets seem to be looking for an excuse not to execute the action. How did you approach this key moment?

Caird: I think you have to take Hamlet at face value. In soliloquy Hamlet cannot lie to his audience. If the actor playing Hamlet is to have any moral authority he can't sometimes be telling the truth to the audience and sometimes not. Especially when in other soliloquies he debates the very nature of truth and reality.

I think the sight of Claudius praying sets up a moral perturbation in Hamlet that Shakespeare was fascinated by. Why else would he have created a scene in which Claudius prays? Much easier to have made Claudius an Iago, or a Richard III, a man incapable of remorse. In order to create added layers of moral complexity to the play, Shakespeare puts Claudius at the center of the drama for the first time. This creates sympathy for him. What would the audience think of their hero if he killed a man while he was praying? The debate in Hamlet's mind is echoed by a debate in the audience's mind.

Daniels: In performance terms, is it really possible to distinguish between these two approaches? And may not both approaches co-exist at one and the same moment?

It seems to me that one of Hamlet's most astonishing qualities is his rigorous and unwavering honesty. Hamlet never lies to himself or to us—the soliloquies are moments of utter truth-telling. There is absolutely no equivocation as he lays before us his most secret doubts and fears.

So—and though Hamlet is clearly not alone on stage, his speech is another soliloquy, another moment of truth-telling!—does it not follow that we should believe him when he tells us his reason for not cutting Claudius' throat?

What's more, Hamlet is on his way to Gertrude's chamber. His mother stays! Claudius, now guilty beyond doubt, will keep for a more propitious moment.

In both practical and psychological terms, the closet scene presents problems, since Hamlet can see and hear the Ghost, but Gertrude can't. How did you deal with this?

Caird: The closet scene gives you the opportunity to see Hamlet and his parents together as a family. Just before the Ghost's final exit I had him and Gertrude move so close to Hamlet that just for a moment he could touch both their faces at the same time. This moment returned him to his childhood. From then on, things become much clearer for him in the play. He has killed Polonius and is therefore no better than Claudius, the man he sought to kill. He starts to understand what his mother has done and the limits of her culpability. He forgives her.

Earlier in the play, other people have seen the Ghost, so you know he isn't a figment of Hamlet's imagination. But he isn't real to Gertrude, or doesn't appear to her. This is psychologically apt. She can't "see" her husband any longer. If she could still see him she wouldn't have married his brother. It is Hamlet's perception of his father that brings her to her senses. He reminds her of her former happiness and her love for her husband and son. This is the beginning of Gertrude's madness. She never recovers from this scene.

Daniels: In one sense this presents no problem at all: Hamlet sees the Ghost and Gertrude does not. Those are the givens of the scene. It is a convention that the audience, possibly more trusting than actors and directors, completely and unquestioningly accepts.

Clearly, whatever difficulty we have with the scene, it did not suit Shakespeare's design that Gertrude should see the Ghost—it would probably have taken the scene into a completely different direction were she to have done so.

Perhaps for our benefit, if we cannot accept Shakespeare at face value, we need to ask why is it that Gertrude does not see the now not so monstrous and rather piteous apparition—in night attire? Are only those characters who are guilt-free capable of seeing the Ghost? Is that explanation enough? Sufficient to lay that question to rest?

Did you discuss whether or not Gertrude is having an affair with Claudius before the murder of Old Hamlet? Or is that not a useful question for director and actors?

Caird: I don't think it's a useful question on its own. Better to link it with another. Does Gertrude know that Claudius has murdered her husband? There's no textual evidence to suggest that she does. At no point does Hamlet accuse her of being complicit. And at no point does she assert her innocence. It's not explored. The question could be rephrased. If Gertrude was having an affair with Claudius before he murdered his brother, is it more likely she was complicit in the murder? One would certainly think the more advanced the affair between Gertrude and Claudius, the more morally blind Gertrude must have been to what Claudius was up to. But Gertrude is to some extent the portrait of a morally blind person, so the question of complicity is an interesting one for the actress to consider. The actor playing Claudius also has a stake in the question. Has an affair with Gertrude propelled him to the murder of his brother?

It is difficult to imagine that Shakespeare intended Gertrude to be complicit in the murder. It would make everything she subsequently says to Hamlet impossibly hypocritical. It would also make Claudius and Gertrude into the Macbeths. Claudius is certainly a sketch for Macbeth, but the crucial difference between Gertrude and Lady Macbeth is complicity. Gertrude is far more interesting a character if her flaw is moral blindness rather than downright amorality.

Daniels: As useful as asking how many children does Lady Macbeth have? These are questions that fill in the psychological history of the characters and that create performance texture. Questions the actor will answer only for him- or herself in whatever way he or she finds most stimulating to the imagination. The answers will inevitably remain a secret since there is no textual evidence for them. They are the actors' private fantasies that the audience can never partake in, but these secrets will inform in subtle but important ways every moment of the characters' lives on stage.

What kind of man was the Old King when he lived? Was he always busy at the office (or off fighting wars) and did he neglect his wife? How unhappy was she and did she turn to Claudius for consolation? Is Gertrude now, on her wedding day, a happy and sexually satisfied woman? How close were Hamlet and his father who, truth be told, seems so forbidding and so aloof, an irascible and bitter old man? And how much time did Hamlet spend as a little boy, playing in his beautiful mother's closet? Do the memories of his innocence, of her motherly love—and of her subsequent betrayal—color the way he now enters the chamber? The way he speaks to her?

Certainly this is a story about kings and queens and princes and it may feel that questions like these tend to "suburbanize" the narrative.

And it may be that academics feel impatient if not infuriated by such banality. But beyond all the poetry, all the spiritual aspirations and deepest meanings of the plays, the personal relationships between fathers and mothers and their sons and daughters lie at the heart of most if not the entire canon. How many plays center around the death of a father (or the king, which of course is the same thing)? How many daughters disobey their fathers (or, like Ophelia, pay the price for their obedience)? How many sons struggle with the desire or the need to kill their fathers? Bringing these relationships to life in the most intimate and truest way possible is the task that befalls the director and the actors—and if in doing so the questions asked and strategies adopted (along with a most rigorous analysis of the text, of course) may appear at first to reduce the scope and magnitude of the narratives, these are the very strategies that bring heartfelt immediacy and credibility to the plays and make them leap off the page and pulsate with life.

In many readings, Hamlet seems to have undergone a huge change during the fourth-act rest when he is away at sea: was it like that in yours?

Daniels: Yes, the change is indeed huge. It is as if for Hamlet the agonizing inner struggle is over. His thoughts have indeed become bloody—he may not have actually wielded the knife, but he has sent his old friends Rosencrantz and Guildenstern to their death and they are not near his conscience. There is a curious serenity about him. The landscape of death is now awesomely familiar to him (no accident that at this moment he encounters Yorick once again) and he is not so much resigned as ready to face his own.

Caird: Yes, I think it has to be. The temperature of his language is so different from earlier in the play. It's to do with what happens to his mind immediately after he kills Polonius. He's such a deeply moral creature that once he has murdered someone he forfeits the right to his moral superiority over his uncle and his mother. He cannot thereafter decide how his own story should be resolved.

This is a philosophical discovery, and the metaphor for his subsequent mental development is a voyage. As in *Pericles, The Tempest,* and *Twelfth Night*, a journey by sea is an escape into a different world, a different way of life, or way of thought. Discovering that Ophelia has died unhinges him for a moment, but it does so only temporarily. In the very next scene he has recovered his equilibrium and seems quite sanguine when Horatio faces him with the possibility of his own death.

> There's a special providence in the fall of a sparrow. If it be now, 'tis not to come: if it be not to come, it will be now: if it be not now, yet it will come: the readiness is all. Since no man has aught of what he leaves, what is't to leave betimes? Let be.

The "Let be" is not in the folio, but Simon Russell Beale and I both thought it indispensable. It is the perfect spiritual punctuation for that speech and it must, surely, be by Shakespeare's hand. No other writer could have been at the same time so bold and so succinct.

Boyd: By the time of his return to Denmark, Hamlet has pondered on the resolute leadership of Fortinbras, killed two men, and arrived at a readiness to die. All of which seems to have stilled his bad dreams, and none of which bodes well for Claudius.

The exchange of rapiers in the duel is sometimes played as a matter of chance, sometimes with Hamlet knowing exactly what he is doing: how did your production handle it?

Daniels: My sense is that Hamlet perceives very quickly what is happening in the course of the duel. He is no longer an innocent in the face of worldly treachery and he can now give as good as he gets.

Caird: Hamlet can't know what's going on when the duel is happening. The text is very clear. As Laertes is dying, he tells Hamlet what he's done and he speaks with what seems like genuine remorse.

LAERTES   The treacherous instrument is in thy hand,
Unbated and envenomed. The foul practice
Hath turned itself on me: lo, here I lie,

> Never to rise again. Thy mother's poisoned.
> I can no more. The king, the king's to blame.
> HAMLET   The point envenomed too!

Shakespeare wouldn't have had Hamlet speaking that line if he already knew the point was envenomed.

Boyd: Once Hamlet knows for certain that the duel is a plot to murder him, there is nothing to stop him killing Laertes. Indeed, he'll probably have to if he's going to kill the king.

The play exists in three early texts of greatly differing lengths, suggesting that it evolved in performance in Shakespeare's lifetime and that cuts were applied at various times. In cutting your text to a manageable length, did you have a set of principles or was it more a case of following your directorial instincts?

Daniels: Common sense, I suppose. A desire to keep the action immediate and exciting, to make sure the text was clear and accessible. And understandable.

Caird: A bit of both. There are obvious economies to be made whatever text you use. You don't need the play-within-the-play and the dumb show. One or other suffices. Playing them both means Claudius has to be peculiarly blind or arbitrarily distracted while watching the dumb show. Hamlet asking for his own lines to be inserted in *The Murder of Gonzago* must have been added by Shakespeare for performances where the subsequent soliloquy—"O, what a rogue and peasant slave am I!"—was to be cut. If you include both, the former lines disable the climax in the latter—where Hamlet says "About my brain" and goes on to invent the idea of using the play as a means of discerning Claudius' guilt.

But the largest cuts I made were inspired by a clear principle. I took the view that Shakespeare's play is at heart a domestic and philosophical drama, not a history play. In many of the productions of *Hamlet* that I've seen, the scenes that seemed to be more like history play than domestic tragedy were always the dull points in the evening, where you could feel the audience switching off; the plot involving Cornelius, Voltemand, Fortinbras, and the Ambassadors; the mention of Norway or Poland seeming to distract the audience from the metaphorical power of the world that is Denmark. I started to feel as I studied the text leading up to rehearsals that there was a case for saying that the more political scenes may have been later additions, though certainly not by another hand. It is not too fanciful to think that Shakespeare may have been warned, or warned himself, that the language with which Hamlet describes the world was apparently so dangerously irreligious, even amoral in its tone, that his audience, and more importantly his noble sponsors, would find it impossible to accept, that it would behoove him to set it in a more political framework and especially to give some hope for the future at the end of the play.

In any event it seemed to me that Fortinbras has absolutely no moral right to say what has been written for him. We don't know him, we don't care about him, and yet he's given a moral authority at the end of the play, an authority he hasn't earned and that seems to be written without any irony. He isn't like Malcolm at the end of *Macbeth*, who has lived through the terrible events of the play and, cleansed by his experience, has every right to the crown. So I cut Fortinbras and all that goes with him, ending the play with Horatio's lines:

> Now cracks a noble heart. Goodnight sweet prince,
> And flights of angels sing thee to thy rest!

What more apposite words could there be to end a play about mortality, nobility, philosophy, and the meaning of earthly existence?

By the same token, I felt I couldn't do better than begin and end the play on the relationship between Hamlet and Horatio. At the start of the play I had Horatio arriving on the scene as if returning to it after a long absence. The other characters were enshrined in their tombs, all long dead. Horatio's memory of the events of the play brought them back to life. At the end of the play while Hamlet lies dying Horatio threatens to kill himself, but Hamlet stops him. If Horatio dies, who will tell Hamlet's story? Horatio is the only living witness. We may even ask another question: who other than Horatio could have told Shakespeare the story? It is diverting to imagine a silent final scene to *Hamlet* that we, the surviving inhabitants of Elsinore, watch at a distance from the battlements. Horatio is leaving the castle to return to Wittenberg and falls in with the company of Players, starting on their long trip back to London. We see him deep in conversation with the First Player who listens intently. The story is being told for the first time. It has started on its own long circular journey. From Hamlet to Horatio, from Horatio to the Player, from the Player to the page, from the page to the stage. Horatio has survived for the same reason that Kent and Edgar survive at the end of *Lear*, to "speak what we feel, not what we ought to say."

Boyd: We exploited the brevity and directness of the First Quarto, which feels like a cut playing script and propels the action forward, particularly after the death of Polonius; but the suppleness, subtlety, and elegance of thought in the Folio reeks of the integrity of original authorship, and so we allowed its style to predominate.

I flirted until late in rehearsal with transposing "To Be" as a "suicide bomber" speech immediately before "Lights, lights, lights!," with the whole court frozen as Hamlet advanced slowly on Claudius, surrounded by Switzers. It worked as a thrilling dramatization of the difficulty of direct action, but it pushed the speech's vulnerability out the door, and so we restored it to the moment before Hamlet meets Ophelia.

REFERENCES

1. Anthony B. Dawson, *Shakespeare in Performance: Hamlet* (1995), p. 25.
2. Printed by J. P. Collier, *Annals of the Stage*, 1831, Vol. 1, in Gamini Salgado, *Eyewitnesses of Shakespeare: First Hand Accounts of Performances 1590–1890* (1975), pp. 38–9.
3. John Downes, *Roscius Anglicanus* (1708, repr. 1969), p. 21.
4. Richard Steele, in an originally unsigned review of *Hamlet* in *The Tatler, with Notes and a General Index: Complete in One Volume* (1835), p. 154.
5. Colley Cibber, *An Apology for the Life of Mr Colley Cibber* (repr. 1889), p. 61.

6. Henry Mackenzie, *The Mirror* (Edinburgh), No. 99, 17 April 1780.

7. Walter Scott, "Life of John Philip Kemble," *Quarterly Review*, 34 (1826), p. 214.

8. Georg Lichtenberg, *Lichtenberg's Visits to England*, translated and annotated by Margaret L. Mare and W. H. Quarrell (1969), p. 10.

9. Mary Russell Mitford, *The Life of Mary Russell Mitford* (1870), Vol. 2, p. 336.

10. Theodore Martin, "An Eye-Witness of John Kemble," *Nineteenth Century* (1880), p. 292.

11. Robert Hapgood, *Shakespeare in Production: Hamlet* (1999), p. 27.

12. James Henry Hackett, *Notes and Comments upon Certain Plays and Actors of Shakespeare* (early nineteenth century, printed 1968), p. 140.

13. William Charles Macready, *The Diaries of William Charles Macready 1833–1851*, ed. William Toynbee (1912), p. 242.

14. *New York Herald*, 28 November 1864.

15. J. Ranken Towse, "Henry Irving," *Century Magazine*, 27 March 1884, p. 666.

16. Charles Edward Russell, *Julia Marlowe* (1926), p. 39.

17. *Academy*, 18 September 1897.

18. Eden Phillpotts, "Irving as Hamlet," in *We Saw Him Act* (1939), p. 122.

19. George Bernard Shaw, *Shaw on Shakespeare*, ed. Edwin Wilson (1969), p. 91.

20. Shaw, *Shaw on Shakespeare*, p. 87.

21. *Daily News*, 13 September 1897.

22. James Agate, *Brief Chronicles* (1943), p. 247.

23. John Gielgud, *Notes from the Gods* (1994), p. 98.

24. Laurence Olivier, *On Acting* (1986), pp. 60–1.

25. Olivier, *On Acting*, p. 62.

26. Ivor Brown, quoted in Claire Cochrane, *Shakespeare and the Birmingham Repertory Theatre 1913–29* (1993), p. 119.

27. *Sunday Times*, 30 August 1925.

28. Gielgud, *Notes from the Gods*, p. 102.

29. Hapgood, *Shakespeare in Production*, p. 65.

30. Quoted in Richard Findlater, *The Player Kings* (1921), p. 201.

31. Dawson, *Shakespeare in Performance*, p. 116.

32. Hapgood, *Shakespeare in Production*, p. 69.

33. Andy Lavender, *Hamlet in Pieces: Shakespeare Reworked by Peter Brook, Robert Lepage, Robert Wilson* (2001), p. 232.

34. Sarah Bernhardt, *Harper's Bazaar*, 15 December 1900, quoted in Hapgood, *Shakespeare in Production*, p. 47.

35. Voltaire, "Essai sur la poésie épique" 1733, *Oeuvres Complètes* (1877–83) Vol. 8, pp. 317–18.

36. Jonathan Bate, "Which Hamlet?," note in *Hamlet*, RSC Programme, 2004.

37. Philip Franks, "Hamlet," in Russell Jackson and Robert Smallwood, eds. *Players of Shakespeare 3* (1993).

38. Seventy-five lines of Horatio's were cut.

39. Tony Church played Polonius in this production.

40. A political and intelligence scandal in the early 1960s which captured the attention of the British public and helped to discredit and topple the Conservative government of Harold Macmillan. Secretary of State for War John Profumo had an extramarital affair with showgirl Christine Keeler, who was also sleeping with a Russian spy.

41. Mary Z. Maher, *Modern Hamlets and Their Soliloquies* (2003), p. 177.

42. Maher, *Modern Hamlets*, p. 179.

43. Peter Hall, "Hamlet," in *Theatre at Work: Playwrights and Productions in the Modern British Theatre*, ed. Charles Marowitz and Simon Trussler (1967).

44. Georgina Brown, *Mail on Sunday*, 6 May 2001.

45. John Gross, *Sunday Telegraph*, 6 May 2001.

46. Susannah Clapp, *Observer*, 6 May 2001.

47. Nicholas de Jongh, *Evening Standard*, 3 May 2001.

48. Matthew Warchus, *Hamlet and The Spanish Tragedy*, RSC Education Pack (1997).

49. Lyn Gardner, interview with Matthew Warchus, *Guardian*, "Ban the Bard," 8 May 1997.

50. Michael Billington, *Guardian*, 10 May 1997.

51. Andrew Billen, *Observer*, 11 May 1997.

52. Robert Butler, *Independent*, 11 May 1997.

53. Michael Pennington, "Hamlet," in *Players of Shakespeare*, ed. Philip Brockbank (1985).

54. Irving Wardle, *The Times*, 3 July 1980.

55. Michael Billington, *Guardian*, 3 July 1980.

56. Greenblatt, "Who's There?," note in *Hamlet*, RSC Programme, 2004.

57. Robert Butler, *Independent*, 11 May 1997.

58. Patrick Magee was predominantly a classical stage actor, but his distinctive and impressively eerie voice got him many parts in films playing sinister villains for the horror studios of the 1960s and '70s, including Hammer, Amacus, and the films of Roger Corman.

59. Dawson, *Shakespeare in Performance*, p. 69.

60. Maher, *Modern Hamlets*, p. 166.

61. Ronald Bryden, *New Statesman,* 27 August 1965.
62. Stanley Wells, *Shakespeare: A Dramatic Life* (1994), p. 236.
63. Pennington, in Brockbank, *Players of Shakespeare,* p. 177.
64. Irving Wardle, *The Times,* 3 July 1980.
65. Paul Taylor, *Independent,* 29 July 2004.
66. *Hamlet,* RSC Online Playguide, 2005.
67. Greg Hicks, *Hamlet,* RSC Online Playguide, 2005.
68. Michael Boyd, *Hamlet,* RSC Online Playguide, 2005.
69. Meg Fraser, *Hamlet,* RSC Online Playguide, 2005.
70. Michael Coveney, *Observer,* 20 December 1992.
71. Bob Crowley, designer, in interview with Andy Lavender, *The Times,* 16 December 1992.
72. Nicholas de Jongh, *Evening Standard,* 3 May 2001.
73. Irving Wardle, *The Times,* 27 April 1989.
74. Michael Schmidt, *Daily Telegraph,* 28 April 1989.
75. *Guardian,* 28 December 1989.
76. John Peter, *Sunday Times,* 30 April 1989.
77. Frances Barber, "Ophelia in *Hamlet,*" in *Players of Shakespeare 2,* ed. Russell Jackson and Robert Smallwood (1988), p. 94.
78. Meg Fraser, *Hamlet,* RSC Online Playguide, 2005.
79. Dawson, *Shakespeare in Performance,* p. 65.
80. Tony Church, "Polonius in *Hamlet,*" in Brockbank, *Players of Shakespeare.*

SHAKESPEARE'S CAREER
IN THE THEATER

BEGINNINGS

William Shakespeare was an extraordinarily intelligent man who was born and died in an ordinary market town in the English Midlands. He lived an uneventful life in an eventful age. Born in April 1564, he was the eldest son of John Shakespeare, a glove-maker who was prominent on the town council until he fell into financial difficulties. Young William was educated at the local grammar in Stratford-upon-Avon, Warwickshire, where he gained a thorough grounding in the Latin language, the art of rhetoric, and classical poetry. He married Ann Hathaway and had three children (Susanna, then the twins Hamnet and Judith) before his twenty-first birthday: an exceptionally young age for the period. We do not know how he supported his family in the mid-1580s.

Like many clever country boys, he moved to the city in order to make his way in the world. Like many creative people, he found a career in the entertainment business. Public playhouses and professional full-time acting companies reliant on the market for their income were born in Shakespeare's childhood. When he arrived in London as a man, sometime in the late 1580s, a new phenomenon was in the making: the actor who is so successful that he becomes a "star." The word did not exist in its modern sense, but the pattern is recognizable: audiences went to the theater not so much to see a particular show as to witness the comedian Richard Tarlton or the dramatic actor Edward Alleyn.

Shakespeare was an actor before he was a writer. It appears not to have been long before he realized that he was never going to grow into a great comedian like Tarlton or a great tragedian like Alleyn. Instead, he found a role within his company as the man who patched up old plays, breathing new life, new dramatic twists, into tired repertory pieces. He paid close attention to the work of the university-educated dramatists who were writing history plays and tragedies for the public stage in a style more ambitious, sweeping, and poetically grand than anything which had been seen before. But he may also have noted that what his friend and rival Ben Jonson would call "Marlowe's mighty line" sometimes faltered in the mode of comedy. Going to university, as Christopher Marlowe did, was all well and good for honing the arts of rhetorical elaboration and classical allusion, but it could lead to a loss of the common touch. To stay close to a large segment of the potential audience for public theater, it was necessary to write for clowns as well as kings and to intersperse the flights of poetry with the humor of the tavern, the privy, and the brothel: Shakespeare was the first to establish himself early in his career as an equal master of tragedy, comedy, and history. He realized that theater could be the medium to make the national past available to a wider audience than the elite who could afford to read large history books: his signature early works include not only the classical tragedy *Titus Andronicus* but also the sequence of English historical plays on the Wars of the Roses.

He also invented a new role for himself, that of in-house company dramatist. Where his peers and predecessors had to sell their plays to the theater managers on a poorly paid piecework basis, Shakespeare took a percentage of the box-office income. The Lord Chamberlain's Men constituted themselves in 1594 as a joint stock company, with the profits being distributed among the core actors who had invested as sharers. Shakespeare acted himself—he appears in the cast lists of some of Ben Jonson's plays as well as the list of actors' names at the beginning of his own collected works—but his principal duty was to write two or three plays a year for the company. By holding shares, he was effectively earning himself a royalty on his work, something no author had ever done before in England. When the Lord Chamberlain's Men collected their fee for performance at court in the Christmas season of 1594, three of them went along to the Treasurer of the Chamber: not just Richard Burbage the tragedian and Will Kempe the clown, but also Shakespeare the scriptwriter. That was something new.

The next four years were the golden period in Shakespeare's career, though overshadowed by the death of his only son, Hamnet, aged eleven, in 1596. In his early thirties and in full command of both his poetic and his theatrical medium, he perfected his art of comedy, while also developing his tragic and historical writing in new ways. In 1598, Francis Meres, a Cambridge University graduate with his finger on the pulse of the London literary world, praised Shakespeare for his excellence across the genres:

> As Plautus and Seneca are accounted the best for comedy and tragedy among the Latins, so Shakespeare among the English is the most excellent in both kinds for the stage; for comedy, witness his *Gentlemen of Verona*, his *Errors*, his *Love Labours Lost*, his *Love Labours Won*, his *Midsummer Night Dream* and his *Merchant of Venice*: for tragedy his *Richard the 2*, *Richard the 3*, *Henry the 4*, *King John*, *Titus Andronicus* and his *Romeo and Juliet*.

For Meres, as for the many writers who praised the "honey-flowing vein" of *Venus and Adonis* and *Lucrece*, narrative poems written when the theaters were closed due to plague in 1593–94, Shakespeare was marked above all by his linguistic skill, by the gift of turning elegant poetic phrases.

PLAYHOUSES

Elizabethan playhouses were "thrust" or "one-room" theaters. To understand Shakespeare's original theatrical life, we have to forget about the indoor theater of later times, with its proscenium arch and curtain that would be opened at the beginning and closed at the end of each act. In the proscenium arch theater, stage and auditorium are effectively two separate rooms: the audience looks from one world into another as if through the imaginary "fourth wall" framed by the proscenium. The picture-frame stage, together with the elaborate scenic effects and backdrops beyond it, created the illusion of a self-contained world—especially once nineteenth-century developments in the control of artificial lighting meant that the auditorium could be darkened and the spectators made to focus on the lighted stage. Shakespeare, by contrast, wrote for a bare platform stage with a standing audience gathered around it in a courtyard in full daylight. The audience were always conscious of themselves and their fellow spectators, and they shared the same "room" as the actors. A sense of immediate presence and the creation of rapport with the audience were all-important. The actor could not afford to imagine he was in a closed world, with silent witnesses dutifully observing him from the darkness.

Shakespeare's theatrical career began at the Rose Theatre in Southwark. The stage was wide and shallow, trapezoid in shape, like a lozenge. This design had a great deal of potential for the theatrical equivalent of cinematic split-screen effects, whereby one group of characters would enter at the door at one end of the tiring-house wall at the back of the stage and another group through the door at the other end, thus creating two rival tableaux. Many of the battle-heavy and faction-filled plays that premiered at the Rose have scenes of just this sort.

At the rear of the Rose stage, there were three capacious exits, each over ten feet wide. Unfortunately, the very limited excavation of a fragmentary portion of the original Globe site, also in 1989, revealed nothing about the stage. The first Globe was built in 1599 with proportions similar to those of another theater, the Fortune, albeit that the former was polygonal and looked circular, whereas the latter was rectangular. The building contract for the Fortune survives and allows us to infer that the stage of the Globe was probably substantially wider than it was deep (perhaps forty-three feet wide and twenty-seven feet deep). It may well have been tapered at the front, like that of the Rose.

The capacity of the Globe was said to have been enormous, perhaps in excess of three thousand. It has been conjectured that about eight hundred people may have stood in the yard, with two thousand or more in the three layers of covered galleries. The other "public" playhouses were also of large capacity, whereas the indoor Blackfriars theater that Shakespeare's company began using in 1608—the former refectory of a monastery—had overall internal dimensions of a mere forty-six by sixty feet. It would have made for a much more intimate theatrical experience and held a much smaller capacity, probably of about six hundred people. Since they paid at least sixpence a head, the Blackfriars attracted a more select or "private" audience. The atmosphere would have been closer to that of an indoor performance before the court in the Whitehall Palace or at Richmond. That Shakespeare always wrote for indoor production at court as well as outdoor performance in the public theater should make us cautious about inferring, as some scholars have, that the opportunity provided by the intimacy of the Blackfriars led to a significant change toward a "chamber" style in his last plays—which, besides, were performed at both the Globe and the Blackfriars. After the occupation of the Blackfriars a five-act structure seems to have become more important to Shakespeare. That was because of artificial lighting: there were musical interludes between the acts, while the candles were trimmed and replaced. Again, though, something similar must have been necessary for indoor court performances throughout his career.

Front of house there were the "gatherers" who collected the money from audience members: a penny to stand in the open-air yard, another penny for a place in the covered galleries, sixpence for the prominent "lord's rooms" to the side of the stage. In the indoor "private" theaters, gallants from the audience who fancied making themselves part of the spectacle sat on stools on the edge of the stage itself. Scholars debate as to how widespread this practice was in the public theaters such as the Globe. Once the audience were in place and the money counted, the gatherers were available to be extras on stage. That is one reason why battles and crowd scenes often come later rather than early in Shakespeare's plays. There was no formal prohibition upon performance by women, and there certainly were women among the gatherers, so it is not beyond the bounds of possibility that female crowd members were played by females.

The play began at two o'clock in the afternoon and the theater had to be cleared by five. After the main show, there would be a jig—which consisted not only of dancing, but also of knockabout comedy (it is the origin of the farcical "afterpiece" in the eighteenth-century theater). So the time available for a Shakespeare play was about two and a half hours, somewhere between the "two hours' traffic" mentioned in the prologue to *Romeo and Juliet* and the "three hours' spectacle" referred to in the preface to the 1647 Folio of Beaumont and Fletcher's plays. The prologue to a play by Thomas Middleton refers to a thousand lines as "one hour's words," so the likelihood is that about 2,500, or a maximum of 3,000 lines made up the performed text. This is indeed the length of most of Shakespeare's comedies, whereas many of his tragedies and histories are much longer, raising the possibility that he wrote full scripts, possibly with eventual publication in mind, in the full knowledge that the stage version would be heavily cut. The short Quarto texts published in his lifetime—they used to be called "Bad" Quartos—provide fascinating evidence as to the kind of cutting that probably took place. So, for instance, the First Quarto of *Hamlet* neatly merges two occasions when Hamlet is overheard, the "fishmonger" and the "nunnery" scenes.

The social composition of the audience was mixed. The poet Sir John Davies wrote of "A thousand townsmen, gentlemen and whores, / Porters and servingmen" who would "together throng" at the public playhouses. Though moralists associated female play-going with adultery and the sex trade, many perfectly respectable citizens' wives were regular attendees. Some, no doubt, resembled the modern groupie: a story attested in two different sources has one citizen's wife making a post-show assignation with Richard Burbage and ending up in bed with Shakespeare—supposedly eliciting from the latter the quip that William the Conqueror was before Richard III. Defenders of theater liked to say that by witnessing the comeuppance of villains on the stage, audience members would repent of their own wrongdoings, but the reality is that most people went to the theater then, as they do now, for entertainment more than moral edification. Besides, it would be foolish to suppose that audiences behaved in a homogeneous way: a pamphlet of the 1630s tells of how two men went to see *Pericles* and one of them laughed while the other wept. Bishop John Hall complained that people went to church for the same reasons that they went to the theater: "for company, for custom, for recreation . . . to feed his eyes or his ears . . . or perhaps for sleep."

Men-about-town and clever young lawyers went to be seen as much as to see. In the modern popular imagination, shaped not least by *Shakespeare in Love* and the opening sequence of Laurence Olivier's *Henry V* film, the penny-paying groundlings stand in the yard hurling abuse or encouragement and hazelnuts or orange peel at the actors, while the sophisticates in the covered galleries appreciate Shakespeare's soaring poetry. The reality was probably the other way around. A "groundling" was a kind of fish, so the nickname suggests the penny audience standing below the level of the stage and gazing in silent openmouthed wonder at the spectacle unfolding above them. The more difficult audience members, who kept up a running commentary of clever remarks on the performance and who occasionally got into quarrels with players, were the gallants. Like Hollywood movies in modern times, Elizabethan and Jacobean plays exercised a powerful influence on the fashion and behavior of the young. John Marston mocks the lawyers who would open their lips, perhaps to court a girl, and out would "flow / Naught but pure Juliet and Romeo."

THE ENSEMBLE AT WORK

In the absence of typewriters and photocopying machines, reading aloud would have been the means by which the company got to know a new play. The tradition of the playwright reading his complete script to the assembled company endured for generations. A copy would then have been taken to the Master of the Revels for licensing. The theater book-holder or prompter would then have copied the parts for distribution to the actors. A partbook consisted of the character's lines, with each speech preceded by the last three or four words of the speech before, the so-called cue. These would have been taken away and studied or "conned." During this period of learning the parts, an actor might have had some one-to-one instruction, perhaps from the dramatist, perhaps from a senior actor who had played the same part before, and, in the case of an apprentice, from his master. A high percentage of Desdemona's lines occur in dialogue with Othello, of Lady Macbeth's with Macbeth, Cleopatra's with Antony, and Volumnia's with Coriolanus. The roles would almost certainly have been taken by the apprentice of the lead actor, usually Burbage, who delivers the majority of the cues. Given that apprentices lodged with their masters, there would have been ample opportunity for personal instruction, which may be what made it possible for young men to play such demanding parts.

11. Hypothetical reconstruction of the interior of an Elizabethan playhouse during a performance.

After the parts were learned, there may have been no more than a single rehearsal before the first performance. With six different plays to be put on every week, there was no time for more. Actors, then, would go into a show with a very limited sense of the whole. The notion of a collective rehearsal process that is itself a process of discovery for the actors is wholly modern and would have been incomprehensible to Shakespeare and his original ensemble. Given the number of parts an actor had to hold in his memory, the forgetting of lines was probably more frequent than in the modern theater. The book-holder was on hand to prompt.

Backstage personnel included the property man, the tire-man who oversaw the costumes, call-boys, attendants, and the musicians, who might play at various times from the main stage, the rooms above and within the tiring-house. Scriptwriters sometimes made a nuisance of themselves backstage. There was often tension between the acting companies and the freelance playwrights from whom they purchased scripts: it was a smart move on the part of

Shakespeare and the Lord Chamberlain's Men to bring the writing process in-house.

Scenery was limited, though sometimes set-pieces were brought on (a bank of flowers, a bed, the mouth of hell). The trapdoor from below, the gallery stage above, and the curtained discovery-space at the back allowed for an array of special effects: the rising of ghosts and apparitions, the descent of gods, dialogue between a character at a window and another at ground level, the revelation of a statue or a pair of lovers playing at chess. Ingenious use could be made of props, as with the ass's head in *A Midsummer Night's Dream*. In a theater that does not clutter the stage with the material paraphernalia of everyday life, those objects that are deployed may take on powerful symbolic weight, as when Shylock bears his weighing scales in one hand and knife in the other, thus becoming a parody of the figure of Justice who traditionally bears a sword and a balance. Among the more significant items in the property cupboard of Shakespeare's company, there would have been a throne (the "chair of state"), joint stools, books, bottles, coins, purses, letters (which are brought on stage, read, or referred to on about eighty occasions in the complete works), maps, gloves, a set of stocks (in which Kent is put in *King Lear*), rings, rapiers, daggers, broadswords, staves, pistols, masks and vizards, heads and skulls, torches and tapers and lanterns which served to signal night scenes on the daylit stage, a buck's head, an ass's head, animal costumes. Live animals also put in appearances, most notably the dog Crab in *The Two Gentlemen of Verona* and possibly a young polar bear in *The Winter's Tale*.

The costumes were the most important visual dimension of the play. Playwrights were paid between £2 and £6 per script, whereas Alleyn was not averse to paying £20 for "a black velvet cloak with sleeves embroidered all with silver and gold." No matter the period of the play, actors always wore contemporary costume. The excitement for the audience came not from any impression of historical accuracy, but from the richness of the attire and perhaps the transgressive thrill of the knowledge that here were commoners like themselves strutting in the costumes of courtiers in effective defiance of the strict sumptuary laws whereby in real life people had to wear the clothes that befitted their social station.

To an even greater degree than props, costumes could carry symbolic importance. Racial characteristics could be suggested: a breastplate and helmet for a Roman soldier, a turban for a Turk, long robes for exotic characters such as Moors, a gabardine for a Jew. The figure of Time, as in *The Winter's Tale*, would be equipped with hourglass, scythe, and wings; Rumour, who speaks the prologue of *2 Henry IV*, wore a costume adorned with a thousand tongues. The wardrobe in the tiring-house of the Globe would have contained much of the same stock as that of rival manager Philip Henslowe at the Rose: green gowns for outlaws and foresters, black for melancholy men such as Jaques and people in mourning such as the Countess in *All's Well That Ends Well* (at the beginning of *Hamlet*, the prince is still in mourning black when everyone else is in festive garb for the wedding of the new king), a gown and hood for a friar (or a feigned friar like the duke in *Measure for Measure*), blue coats and tawny to distinguish the followers of rival factions, a leather apron and ruler for a carpenter (as in the opening scene of *Julius Caesar*—and in *A Midsummer Night's Dream*, where this is the only sign that Peter Quince is a carpenter), a cockle hat with staff and a pair of sandals for a pilgrim or palmer (the disguise assumed by Helen in *All's Well*), bodices and kirtles with farthingales beneath for the boys who are to be dressed as girls. A gender switch such as that of Rosalind or Jessica seems to have taken between fifty and eighty lines of dialogue—Viola does not resume her "maiden weeds," but remains in her boy's costume to the end of *Twelfth Night* because a change would have slowed down the action at just the moment it was speeding to a climax. Henslowe's inventory also included "a robe for to go invisible": Oberon, Puck, and Ariel must have had something similar.

As the costumes appealed to the eyes, so there was music for the ears. Comedies included many songs. Desdemona's willow song, perhaps a late addition to the text, is a rare and thus exceptionally poignant example from tragedy. Trumpets and tuckets sounded for ceremonial entrances, drums denoted an army on the march. Background music could create atmosphere, as at the beginning of *Twelfth Night*, during the lovers' dialogue near the end of *The Merchant of Venice*, when the statue seemingly comes to life in *The Winter's Tale*, and for the revival of Pericles and of Lear (in the Quarto text, but not the Folio). The haunting sound of the hautboy suggested a realm beyond the human, as when the god Hercules is imagined deserting Mark Antony. Dances symbolized the harmony of the end of a comedy—though in Shakespeare's world of mingled joy and sorrow, someone is usually left out of the circle.

The most important resource was, of course, the actors themselves. They needed many skills: in the words of one contemporary commentator, "dancing, activity, music, song, elocution, ability of body, memory, skill of weapon, pregnancy of wit." Their bodies were as significant as their voices. Hamlet tells the player to "suit the action to the word, the word to the action": moments of strong emotion, known as "passions," relied on a repertoire of dramatic gestures as well as a modulation of the voice. When Titus Andronicus has had his hand chopped off, he asks "How can I grace my talk, / Wanting a hand to give it action?" A pen portrait of "The Character of an Excellent Actor" by the dramatist John Webster is almost certainly based on his impression of Shakespeare's leading man, Richard Burbage: "By a full and significant action of body, he charms our attention: sit in a full theatre, and you will think you see so many lines drawn from the circumference of so many ears, whiles the actor is the centre. . . ."

Though Burbage was admired above all others, praise was also heaped upon the apprentice players whose alto voices fitted them for the parts of women. A spectator at Oxford in 1610 records how the audience were reduced to tears by the pathos of Desdemona's death. The puritans who fumed about the biblical prohibition upon cross-dressing and the encouragement to sodomy constituted by the sight of an adult male kissing a teenage boy on stage were a small minority. Little is known, however, about the characteristics of the leading apprentices in Shakespeare's company. It may perhaps be inferred that one was a lot taller than the other, since Shakespeare often wrote for a pair of female friends, one tall and fair, the other short and dark (Helena and Hermia, Rosalind and Celia, Beatrice and Hero).

We know little about Shakespeare's own acting roles—an early allusion indicates that he often took royal parts, and a venerable tradition gives him old Adam in *As You Like It* and the ghost of old King

Hamlet. Save for Burbage's lead roles and the generic part of the clown, all such castings are mere speculation. We do not even know for sure whether the original Falstaff was Will Kempe or another actor who specialized in comic roles, Thomas Pope.

Kempe left the company in early 1599. Tradition has it that he fell out with Shakespeare over the matter of excessive improvisation. He was replaced by Robert Armin, who was less of a clown and more of a cerebral wit: this explains the difference between such parts as Lancelet Gobbo and Dogberry, which were written for Kempe, and the more verbally sophisticated Feste and Lear's Fool, which were written for Armin.

One thing that is clear from surviving "plots" or storyboards of plays from the period is that a degree of doubling was necessary. *2 Henry VI* has over sixty speaking parts, but more than half of the characters only appear in a single scene and most scenes have only six to eight speakers. At a stretch, the play could be performed by thirteen actors. When Thomas Platter saw *Julius Caesar* at the Globe in 1599, he noted that there were about fifteen. Why doesn't Paris go to the Capulet ball in *Romeo and Juliet?* Perhaps because he was doubled with Mercutio, who does. In *The Winter's Tale*, Mamillius might have come back as Perdita and Antigonus been doubled by Camillo, making the partnership with Paulina at the end a very neat touch. Titania and Oberon are often played by the same pair as Hippolyta and Theseus, suggesting a symbolic matching of the rulers of the worlds of night and day, but it is questionable whether there would have been time for the necessary costume changes. As so often, one is left in a realm of tantalizing speculation.

THE KING'S MAN

The new king, James I, who had held the Scottish throne as James VI since he had been an infant, immediately took the Lord Chamberlain's Men under his direct patronage. Henceforth they would be the King's Men, and for the rest of Shakespeare's career they were favored with far more court performances than any of their rivals. There even seem to have been rumors early in the reign that Shakespeare and Burbage were being considered for knighthoods, an unprecedented honor for mere actors—and one that in the event was not accorded to a member of the profession for nearly three hundred years, when the title was bestowed upon Henry Irving, the leading Shakespearean actor of Queen Victoria's reign.

Shakespeare's productivity rate slowed in the Jacobean years, not because of age or some personal trauma, but because there were frequent outbreaks of plague, causing the theaters to be closed for long periods. The King's Men were forced to spend many months on the road. Between November 1603 and 1608, they were to be found at various towns in the south and Midlands, though Shakespeare probably did not tour with them by this time. He had bought a large house back home in Stratford and was accumulating other property. He may indeed have stopped acting soon after the new king took the throne. With the London theaters closed so much of the time and a large repertoire on the stocks, Shakespeare seems to have focused his energies on writing a few long and complex tragedies that could have been played on demand at court: *Othello, King Lear, Antony and Cleopatra, Coriolanus,* and *Cymbeline* are among his longest and poetically grandest plays. *Macbeth* only survives in a shorter text, which shows signs of adaptation after Shakespeare's death. The bitterly satirical *Timon of Athens,* apparently a collaboration with Thomas Middleton that may have failed on the stage, also belongs to this period. In comedy, too, he wrote longer and morally darker works than in the Elizabethan period, pushing at the very bounds of the form in *Measure for Measure* and *All's Well That Ends Well.*

From 1608 onward, when the King's Men began occupying the indoor Blackfriars playhouse (as a winter house, meaning that they only used the outdoor Globe in summer?), Shakespeare turned to a more romantic style. His company had a great success with a revived and altered version of an old pastoral play called *Mucedorus.* It even featured a bear. The younger dramatist John Fletcher, meanwhile, sometimes working in collaboration with Francis Beaumont, was pioneering a new style of tragicomedy, a mix of romance and royalism laced with intrigue and pastoral excursions. Shakespeare experimented with this idiom in *Cymbeline* and it was presumably with his blessing that Fletcher eventually took over as the King's Men's company dramatist. The two writers apparently collaborated on three plays in the years 1612–14: a lost romance called *Cardenio* (based on the love-madness of a character in Cervantes' *Don Quixote*), *Henry VIII* (originally staged with the title "All Is True"), and *The Two Noble Kinsmen*, a dramatization of Chaucer's "Knight's Tale." These were written after Shakespeare's two final solo-authored plays, *The Winter's Tale*, a self-consciously old-fashioned work dramatizing the pastoral romance of his old enemy Robert Greene, and *The Tempest*, which at one and the same time drew together multiple theatrical traditions, diverse reading, and contemporary interest in the fate of a ship that had been wrecked on the way to the New World.

The collaborations with Fletcher suggest that Shakespeare's career ended with a slow fade rather than the sudden retirement supposed by the nineteenth-century Romantic critics who read Prospero's epilogue to *The Tempest* as Shakespeare's personal farewell to his art. In the last few years of his life Shakespeare certainly spent more of his time in Stratford-upon-Avon, where he became further involved in property dealing and litigation. But his London life also continued. In 1613 he made his first major London property purchase: a freehold house in the Blackfriars district, close to his company's indoor theater. *The Two Noble Kinsmen* may have been written as late as 1614, and Shakespeare was in London on business a little over a year before he died of an unknown cause at home in Stratford-upon-Avon in 1616, probably on his fifty-second birthday.

About half the sum of his works were published in his lifetime, in texts of variable quality. A few years after his death, his fellow actors began putting together an authorized edition of his complete *Comedies, Histories and Tragedies*. It appeared in 1623, in large "Folio" format. This collection of thirty-six plays gave Shakespeare his immortality. In the words of his fellow dramatist Ben Jonson, who contributed two poems of praise at the start of the Folio, the body of his work made him "a monument without a tomb":

And art alive still while thy book doth live
And we have wits to read and praise to give . . .
He was not of an age, but for all time!

SHAKESPEARE'S WORKS: A CHRONOLOGY

1589–91	*? Arden of Faversham* (possible part authorship)
1589–92	*The Taming of the Shrew*
1589–92	*? Edward the Third* (possible part authorship)
1591	*The Second Part of Henry the Sixth*, originally called *The First Part of the Contention Betwixt the Two Famous Houses of York and Lancaster* (element of co-authorship possible)
1591	*The Third Part of Henry the Sixth*, originally called *The True Tragedy of Richard Duke of York* (element of co-authorship probable)
1591–92	*The Two Gentlemen of Verona*
1591–92; perhaps revised 1594	*The Lamentable Tragedy of Titus Andronicus* (probably co-written with, or revising an earlier version by, George Peele)
1592	*The First Part of Henry the Sixth*, probably with Thomas Nashe and others
1592/94	*King Richard the Third*
1593	*Venus and Adonis* (poem)
1593–94	*The Rape of Lucrece* (poem)
1593–1608	*Sonnets* (154 poems, published 1609 with *A Lover's Complaint*, a poem of disputed authorship)
1592–94 or 1600–03	*Sir Thomas More* (a single scene for a play originally by Anthony Munday, with other revisions by Henry Chettle, Thomas Dekker, and Thomas Heywood)
1594	*The Comedy of Errors*

1595	*Love's Labour's Lost*
1595–97	*Love's Labour's Won* (a lost play, unless the original title for another comedy)
1595–96	*A Midsummer Night's Dream*
1595–96	*The Tragedy of Romeo and Juliet*
1595–96	*King Richard the Second*
1595–97	*The Life and Death of King John* (possibly earlier)
1596–97	*The Merchant of Venice*
1596–97	*The First Part of Henry the Fourth*
1597–98	*The Second Part of Henry the Fourth*
1598	*Much Ado About Nothing*
1598–99	*The Passionate Pilgrim* (20 poems, some not by Shakespeare)
1599	*The Life of Henry the Fifth*
1599	"To the Queen" (epilogue for a court performance)
1599	*As You Like It*
1599	*The Tragedy of Julius Caesar*
1600–01	*The Tragedy of Hamlet, Prince of Denmark* (perhaps revising an earlier version)
1600–01	*The Merry Wives of Windsor* (perhaps revising version of 1597–99)
1601	"Let the Bird of Loudest Lay" (poem, known since 1807 as "The Phoenix and Turtle"[turtle-dove])
1601	*Twelfth Night, or What You Will*
1601–02	*The Tragedy of Troilus and Cressida*
1604	*The Tragedy of Othello, the Moor of Venice*
1604	*Measure for Measure*
1605	*All's Well That Ends Well*
1605	*The Life of Timon of Athens*, with Thomas Middleton
1605–06	*The Tragedy of King Lear*

1605–08	? contribution to *The Four Plays in One* (lost, except for *A Yorkshire Tragedy*, mostly by Thomas Middleton)
1606	*The Tragedy of Macbeth* (surviving text has additional scenes by Thomas Middleton)
1606–07	*The Tragedy of Antony and Cleopatra*
1608	*The Tragedy of Coriolanus*
1608	*Pericles, Prince of Tyre*, with George Wilkins
1610	*The Tragedy of Cymbeline*
1611	*The Winter's Tale*
1611	*The Tempest*
1612–13	*Cardenio*, with John Fletcher (survives only in later adaptation called *Double Falsehood* by Lewis Theobald)
1613	*Henry VIII (All Is True)*, with John Fletcher
1613–14	*The Two Noble Kinsmen*, with John Fletcher

FURTHER READING AND VIEWING

CRITICAL APPROACHES

Adelman, Janet, *Suffocating Mothers: Fantasies of Maternal Origin in Shakespeare's Plays, Hamlet to The Tempest* (1992). Psychoanalytical approach.

Bradley, A. C., *Shakespearean Tragedy* (1904). Immensely influential.

Colie, Rosalie L., *Shakespeare's Living Art* (1974). Excellent on the idea of melancholy.

Frye, Roland Mushat, *The Renaissance Hamlet: Issues and Responses 1600* (1984). Invaluable historical placing.

Granville-Barker, Harley, *Hamlet* in his *Prefaces to Shakespeare* Vol. 1 (1946). Very satisfying reading by a great man of the theater.

Greenblatt, Stephen, *Hamlet in Purgatory* (2001). Powerful reading of context of religious controversy.

Jones, Ernest, *Hamlet and Oedipus* (1949). Extended Freudian reading.

Knight, G. Wilson, "The Embassy of Death" in his *The Wheel of Fire* (1930, repr. 2001). Very strong on imagery.

Mercer, Peter, *Hamlet and the Acting of Revenge* (1987). Worth comparing with Prosser.

O'Toole, Fintan, *Shakespeare Is Hard, but So Is Life* (2002), originally published as *No More Heroes* (1995). Highly sensible introductory account, with strong emphasis on politics; dispels the myth of the "tragic flaw."

Prosser, Eleanor, *Hamlet and Revenge* (1967). Worth comparing with Mercer.

Rosenberg, Marvin, *The Masks of Hamlet* (1992). Scene-by-scene account, using actors' and directors' interpretations down the ages.

Wilson, J. Dover, *What Happens in Hamlet* (1935). Thorough investigation of key problems.

THE PLAY IN PERFORMANCE

Brooke, Michael, "*Hamlet* on Screen," www.screenonline.org.uk/tv/id/566312/index.html. Valuable overview. Registered schools, colleges, universities, and libraries have access to video clips, including extracts from the 1913 silent version, Olivier's 1948 film, and the 1964 production at Elsinore.

Dawson, Anthony B., *Hamlet*, Shakespeare in Performance (1996). Excellent roundup.

Hapgood, Robert ed., *Hamlet, Prince of Denmark*, Shakespeare in Production (1999). Good accounts of wide range of productions.

Howard, Tony, *Women as Hamlet: Performance and Interpretation in Theatre, Film and Fiction* (2007). Fascinating, and of even further-reaching interest than its title suggests.

Lavender, Andy, *Hamlet in Pieces: Shakespeare Reworked by Peter Brook, Robert Lepage, Robert Wilson* (2001). Lively accounts of experimental versions.

Maher, Mary Z., *Modern Hamlets and Their Soliloquies* (2003). Based on interviews with actors, including David Warner, Ben Kingsley, Kevin Kline.

Players of Shakespeare 1, 2, 3 (1985–93). Each of these three volumes includes excellent interviews with actors who have played major roles in *Hamlet*.

Royal Shakespeare Company, "Exploring Shakespeare: Hamlet," www.rsc.org.uk/learning/hamletandmacbeth/keyidea/hamletkeyidea.htm. Rehearsal footage, actor and director interviews, commentary on Michael Boyd's 2004 production.

For a more detailed Shakespeare bibliography and selections from a wide range of critical accounts of the play, with linking commentary, visit the edition website, www.therscshakespeare.com.

AVAILABLE ON DVD

Hamlet, directed by Hay Plumb (1913, DVD 2004). The longest Shakespeare film from the age of silent film.

Hamlet, directed by Laurence Olivier (1948). Highly influential.

Hamlet, directed by Grigori Kozintsev (1964). Powerful Russian version.

Richard Burton's Hamlet, directed by Bill Colleran (1964). Film of American stage production.

Hamlet at Elsinore, directed by Philip Saville (1964). Film of BBC television production that played at Elsinore; not currently available, but extracts may be seen via screenonline website (see above).

Hamlet, directed by Tony Richardson (1969). Film of London Roundhouse stage production starring Nicol Williamson.

Hamlet, BBC Television Shakespeare, directed by Rodney Bennett (1980). Starring Derek Jacobi.

Hamlet, directed by Franco Zeffirelli (1990). Starring Mel Gibson.

Hamlet, directed by Kenneth Branagh (1996). Uncut text.

Hamlet, directed by Michael Almereyda (2000). Underrated version transposed to contemporary New York.

The Tragedy of Hamlet, directed by Peter Brook (BBC4 television, tx. 6 March 2002, DVD 2006). Starring Adrian Lester; superbly lucid version, in heavily cut text, with a documentary "Brook by Brook."

ACKNOWLEDGMENTS AND PICTURE CREDITS

Preparation of "*Hamlet* in Performance" was assisted by a generous grant from the CAPITAL Centre (Creativity and Performance in Teaching and Learning) of the University of Warwick for research in the RSC archive at the Shakespeare Birthplace Trust. The Arts and Humanities Research Council (AHRC) funded a term's research leave that enabled Jonathan Bate to work on "The Director's Cut."

Picture research by Helen Robson and Jan Sewell. Grateful acknowledgment is made to the Shakespeare Birthplace Trust for assistance with picture research and reproduction fees.

Images of RSC productions are supplied by the Shakespeare Centre Library and Archive, Stratford-upon-Avon. This library, maintained by the Shakespeare Birthplace Trust, holds the most important collection of Shakespeare material in the UK, including the Royal Shakespeare Company's official archives. It is open to the public free of charge.

For more information see www.shakespeare.org.uk.

1. "Rapier and Dagger" in private collection © Bardbiz Limited
2. "They change rapiers" in private collection © Bardbiz Limited
3. London's Drury Lane Theatre, Forbes Robertson (1913). Reproduced by permission of the Shakespeare Birthplace Trust
4. Sarah Bernhardt (1899). Reproduced by permission of the Shakespeare Birthplace Trust
5. Directed by Peter Brook (1965). Reg Wilson © Royal Shakespeare Company
6. Directed by Buzz Goodbody (1975). Joe Cocks Studio Collection © Shakespeare Birthplace Trust
7. Directed by Ron Daniels (1989). Joe Cocks Studio Collection © Shakespeare Birthplace Trust